Early Recollections

Early Recollections

Interpretative Method and Application

Harold H. Mosak and Roger Di Pietro

Routledge
Taylor & Francis Group
New York   London

Published in 2006 by
Routledge
Taylor & Francis Group
270 Madison Avenue
New York, NY 10016

Published in Great Britain by
Routledge
Taylor & Francis Group
2 Park Square
Milton Park, Abingdon
Oxon OX14 4RN

Printed in the United States of America on acid-free paper
10 9 8 7 6 5 4 3 2 1

International Standard Book Number-10: 0-415-95287-5 (Hardcover)
International Standard Book Number-13: 978-0-415-95287-3 (Hardcover)
Library of Congress Card Number 2005028586

Library of Congress Cataloging-in-Publication Data

Mosak, Harold H.
  Early recollections : interpretative method and application / by Harold H. Mosak, Roger Di Pietro.
    p. cm.
  Includes bibliographical references and index.
  ISBN 0-415-95287-5 (hb : alk. paper)
  1. Early memories. 2. Recollection (Psychology) I. Di Pietro, Roger. II. Croake, James W. III. Title.

BF378.E17M67 2005
155.4'1312--dc22

2005028586

Taylor & Francis Group
is the Academic Division of Informa plc.

Visit the Taylor & Francis Web site at
http://www.taylorandfrancis.com

and the Routledge Web site at
http://www.routledge-ny.com

In recollection of my parents, Nathan and Lena Mosak.
—Harold H. Mosak, Ph.D.

The only reason why I can see this far is because I stood
on the shoulders of my parents, Arnold and Dolores.
—Roger Di Pietro, Psy.D.

Contents

Preface

When Freud wrote *The Question of Lay Analysis*, he adopted a non-traditional style. Instead of writing a traditional professional text, he addressed the reader directly, using the subtitle "Conversations with an Impartial Reader." We have made the decision in writing this book to follow Freud's lead, to address the reader directly, and make the writing "personal."

While the reader may be "impartial," we are obviously not. Both of the authors have been trained in the Adlerian tradition, and our own interpretations are grounded in Adlerian theory and practice. However, early recollections can be used by a wide spectrum of non-Adlerian clinicians, counselors, coaches, and psychohistorians, whatever psychological orientation they may espouse. Chapter 19, for example, illustrates a Freudian interpretation of a set of early recollections. We have in addition included descriptions of other forms of administration than ours as well as other methods of interpretation. Our intention is not to "sell" the Adlerian methods but rather to acquaint the reader with the wide applicability and utility of this earliest projective technique.

As Bauman (2003) pointed out in *The Chronicle of Higher Education*, it is difficult to write a book that will appeal to both faculty and students. Consequently we have asked both students and colleagues to offer their comments and suggestions of this book in draft form. We are most grateful to Dave Baker M.A., Dr. Rose Boldt, Joel Bornstein M.A., Albert E. Kircher M.A., and Elizabeth Traina for their assistance. Whatever its merits, the book is a better book for their critiques.

The recollections provided in this book are truncated, fabricated, or altered in some form to present a concise example and to protect patient identities. While many changes were made to the recollections, the themes of the original recollections have been retained through the use of symbolically parallel and factually equivalent material.

So, "impartial readers," let's start our conversation.

Harold H. Mosak, Ph.D.
Roger Di Pietro, Psy.D.

Introduction

Half a lifetime ago, I was lucky enough to have been taught by four remarkable men: Carl Rogers, my teacher at the University of Chicago; Jacob L. Moreno, under whom I studied at his institute in Beacon, New York; and Rudolf Dreikurs and Harold Mosak, both of whom taught me at the Alfred Adler Institute (now called the Adler School of Professional Psychology) in Chicago. All four of these men knew of my relationships with the others, and each in his own (usually subtle) way tried to influence me. My final decision was to become an Adlerian. However, I continued to be much impressed with Rogers's nondirective method, which I had used for more than 10 years in my work as a clinical psychologist, and with Moreno's work in psychodrama.

At the time that Rogers and Moreno were influencing my clinical work, I had two encounters with the Adlerian system that left me unimpressed; these came nine years apart, the first about 1935 while I was working at the Rikers Island Penitentiary in New York City and the second in 1944 while I was working in Auburn, New York. My next encounter also came nine years later, in 1953, but was far more positive: Rudolf Dreikurs heard me give a speech in Chicago on Immediate Therapy and soon afterward offered me a scholarship at the Alfred Adler Institute where I took courses with him and Harold Mosak.

During my previous 15 years in prison work — as a clinical trainee at Rikers Island, a psychologist at Auburn Prison and Elmira Reformatory, the chief psychologist at San Quentin, and finally the supervising psychologist for the Department of Correction of Wisconsin — my constant concern (and this is true for all psychologists and psychiatrists in prisons) was diagnosis, not treatment! I had to make all kinds of judgments, such as what kind of vocational training should be done, who was ready for parole, and, while at San Quentin, the highly unpleasant task of deciding whether men who were awaiting execution were mentally stable enough to be killed. No one could escape me in this task. I found that every one of these men awaiting execution, perhaps about two dozen, was sane enough to be murdered by the state.

In making diagnoses, psychologists and psychiatrists have several ways of arriving at decisions. The most often used method is the interview, usually with additional information from others; in prison situations, these others may include aides, nurses, guards, and other professionals. Another method is the study of prior records: in some institutions, including prisons, some individuals have had frequent prior evaluations. All individuals have personality diagnoses. Another method is to depend in part or entirely on a paper and pencil test such as the Minnesota Multiphasic Personality Inventory (MMPI). Yet another method is to depend primarily on what are known as projective tests.

A projective test is a somewhat unstructured or loose procedure in which a skilled psycho-analyst observes how someone placed in an ambiguous situation operates, and from that the diagnostician-analyst comes to various conclusions. You, the reader, have been a psycho-analyst in this sense, and you also have been psycho-analyzed many times in your life. Every time you meet a new person, you are a psycho-analyst: You watch that person and listen to him or her and come to some kind of conclusion about the person — whether you like him or her, whether you want further contact, how intelligent that person appears to be, how stable a personality, and so on. You usually do all this in a matter of seconds, and most likely you are right, just as most of the people who size you up are most likely right about you. We humans are amateur diagnosticians of everyone we meet — classmates, teachers, doctors, dentists, and so on.

However, when it comes to making official diagnoses that will go on a person's permanent record, or evaluations for vocational purposes that will determine the direction of a person's life, or clinical decisions at the beginning of personal psychotherapy, one must have a good understanding of human psychology and pathology, an awareness of the many categories of mental and emotional disorders, and the skills to understand a person in depth. Some of the objective kinds of evaluations are of little use in making decisions of such importance. I would not trust the findings of the MMPI, for example, for one minute, because the replies of anyone who wants to make a false good impression cannot be trusted, even if they do not appear to have been faked according to that inventory's "Lie Scale."

Of the many projective tests, the best known are the Rorschach Inkblot Test and the Thematic Apperception Test (TAT). Clients taking the Rorschach test look at 10 ink blots and indicate what they see. Clients taking the TAT look at certain drawings and make up a story about each drawing that has a past, present, and a future. Each, evaluated by a trained and skilled person, provides some information to the psychoanalyst. Not everyone who is trained is a good diagnostician, and there is really no objective way to determine anyone's ability. Whether a professional is "good" is determined by the judgments of other psycho-diagnosticians.

Carl G. Jung (pronounced *yoong,* not *jung*) developed one of the earliest projective techniques, the Word Association Test. His system used a standard set of words, and the client was to reply as soon as possible with an associated word. Example: Mother — Father, with Mother, the first word, called a *stimulus,* and Father the *response.* So a primary factor to be studied in the test is what the replies are to various stimuli. A second factor would be the length of time it took to reply. A third factor would be the affective responses: the tone of voice in the replies, the expression on the client's face, and so on.

However, in my judgment the method of early recollections (ER), a procedure that Ruth Munroe called the first of the projective techniques, is by far the best. It has two immediate advantages. First, in contrast to the other projective techniques mentioned — Rorschach, TAT, and the Word Association Test — no test materials are required; anyone at any time could use this test. Second, ERs permit the evaluation of the client's status at the time of testing and, much more important, reveal personal dynamics, where one has been, where one is, and where one is going. All other projective tests do not have this built in; they tend to be static, telling where one is now, but nothing or very little about the past or intended future. You will soon see some examples of this so that in reading this book you will already have a sense of each of these three assessment methods.

Early recollections are evoked in a simple manner. You say the following to a client: "I want to ask you to tell me a memory from your childhood (prior to your 10th birthday)." You watch carefully the response of the person, who may close his eyes or lean back or examine you or say, "Would you mind repeating that?" or "I can't think of any" even before he starts searching for early memories. But most will think a bit and you will either get a very short one such as (these are real replies):

> I must have been either one year old or a bit older. I was standing in my crib and I was holding on to the side rail, and I remember hearing two people talking, and I am not sure who they were.

Or you may get a much longer one:

> I was seated on a railroad car seat, and my mother was to my left and my father to my right. I could look out the window and could see the telephone poles whizzing by from behind me and then going before me, so I know I was seated with my back to the front of the train, and I also knew that my parents wanted to keep me there between them. Bored by inactivity, I began to squirm down the seat carefully not to attract their attention, and soon I was on my knees and I started crawling forward. I remember the strong smell of dust as I inched along, careful not to touch anyone's legs, and finally I was blocked, could go no further. I must have gone through a dozen or so seats. Now I was at a wall. Near me I saw a very attractive object. It was made of shiny brass, an oil can, the kind you turn upside down and let oil come out a long tube. I picked it up and saw a man's shoes and carefully I started to spill oil on his shoes. He yelled, looked down, started to shout, and another man in uniform went down on the floor, pulled me out with me trying to hold on to something, and then he picked me up and asked who I belong to. I saw my father stand up, and the conductor brought me to him, and I knew I would be beaten.

Now, what would you make of these? Write down what you think these ERs mean about these two men, both in their forties. How would you describe them, keeping in mind that your task is to describe them right now in terms of their personalities at the present time, based on their retelling of their earliest memories?

By the way, while an Adlerian therapist would analyze each memory separately, a professional using ER would want at least four, better eight, memories to get a more complete picture. Let me give you an example: A librarian came to see me, and during the diagnostic period of the Adlerian procedure, as devised by Rudolf Dreikurs, he gave me 10 memories. I recall the first one:

> I am standing in a playpen, and I am looking at a door. Something looked interesting.

In his 10 recollections, there was no mention of any other person. It turned out that he had no friends. His reasons for coming to therapy were he felt he was going nowhere, he had no interests, and he kept thinking about suicide. As a result of therapy he decided to come out of his very dark closet, make friends, and, with the help of role-playing, first with me and later with two of his work associates, he began to gain confidence. He no longer lowered his eyes when he passed someone. Rather, he looked the person right in the eyes and smiled.

The important thing about ERs in this case was that I was able to get a fairly complete understanding of this man before he finally told me about his loneliness and avoidance of people. And if after reading the ER and the paragraph after it, you more or less came to the same conclusion, you have talent for this kind of detective work.

Detective work?

Psychotherapy differs from counseling. A counselor is an expert on some aspect of life. That is, if you need a direct answer to a particular problem, a counselor can tell you exactly what to do. You do it, and the problem is solved. When I worked as a family counselor, I knew, usually as soon as I heard the problems reported by parents, what the solution to the problem was. Parents who had tried for years, for example, to get their children to keep their rooms clean or to stop wetting the bed were soon given an exact solution for their problems, one that worked 100% of the time when they followed the directions explicitly. So, keep this in mind: A counselor already knows exactly what you must do to solve your problem.

Therapy is different from counseling in that counseling is always tried first, and when clients don't follow your advice, you must investigate their resistance therapeutically. Why clients don't follow your advice has to do more with life style issues than anything else. For example, if a couple come in for counseling to reduce their frequent fighting, you could give them solutions on how not to fight (that would be counseling). But if they continue fighting, there are underlying psychological reasons for their arguments, such as how they perceive the ways men and women should interact, or that each believes he or she knows the right way of doing something whereas the spouse does not. The presence of psychological reasons indicates a need for therapy, not counseling.

A psychotherapist offers knowledge of people, always based on some theory — the theory of the therapist, and/or the theory of another person such as Sigmund Freud, Albert Ellis, or Carl Rogers, who have quite different basic concepts and different methodologies. The therapist consequently is a facilitator, a behind-the-curtain voice asking questions of various kinds, mostly of the Socratic type, to help the client gain insight into what is bothering him or her and to gain the determination to change perceptions of self, others, and the world.

Early recollections are unparalleled in helping the therapist to get in line with the truth. The example of the librarian who had no one in his early memories would arouse a therapist's suspicion that the client's problem is social. Without ERs, the therapist might have to wait patiently until something in this area came up, respecting the client's privilege to open up only after he is sure of his therapist.

Memories are pure gold for those who know how to interpret them. Right now, most of the people who know about ERs are Adlerians, but ERs really belong to the world. The purpose of this book is not only to give additional help to those who already know and use ERs but, more important, to spread to all psychotherapists knowledge about a technique that everyone should know and use in the same sense that they use interviews, listening techniques, role-playing, and so forth.

Memories are mostly symbolic, and they carry important messages to the client, who naturally cannot understand their meanings, and to the therapist who has learned to make sense out of them.

Ask yourself this question: Why would a 50-year-old man remember first that one day he was on the floor of the kitchen with his two sisters and that he knew something was going on in the bathroom, where his parents were at the time? Why would someone remember being on a boat looking desperately for her father? Why would someone remember other children tying him to a tree? Why would a woman remember her father smiling? Why would a man remember being on the roof with his mother and several other women and looking down to see his father? Why would another man remember his father hoisting him onto his shoulders, enabling him to see Charles Lindbergh as he passed by in the back of an open automobile?

Every one of these ERs had a special meaning that no one can understand just by reading them. The key to understanding depends on knowing something of Adlerian theory on decoding the meaning of ERs.

A big problem of psychotherapy nowadays has to do with economics: therapists are pushed to do high-quality therapy in a short time. Very few people can afford to pay for traditional couch-type psychoanalysis, which calls for three to five sessions a week, sometimes for months or years. The quality of therapy does depend to some extent on time, but I have found, having treated both a man and a woman for more than 10 years, that if there is not improvement early on, therapy can become interminable. Early recollections provide an effective and efficient assessment. They speed up psychotherapy. A therapist's procedure and a therapist's bag of tricks are important, and from my point of view, one of the most important of the tricks is the ability to use ERs properly. At this point you should have an overall preliminary understanding of the topic.

Allow me to tell you a bit about Dr. Harold Mosak. First, he has extensive clinical experience; no other Adlerian, with the possible exception of the late Dr. Kurt Adler, the son of Alfred Adler, has to my knowledge seen more patients than Mosak. Second, he has the gift of humor and can see the funny side of everything as well as the negative side; one might expect him to write a book about humor, and indeed he has (Mosak, 1987). Third, he has a solid knowledge of diagnostic categories and an ability to detect which are meaningful and which are not, a necessary skill for any diagnostician who is to make judgments. Finally, he has something that in Yiddish is known as *sechel*, meaning wisdom-judgment-savvy-understanding-wit-common sense-clarity and so on; Harold Mosak has *sechel* to an extreme.

He was my first teacher in Adlerian psychology, and I was privileged to work with him for about 10 years in the Alfred Adler Institute as well as to hear him speak at a number of professional meetings, often on the value of ERs. No one knows the value of ERs to the degree that he does, and reluctantly, I believe his understanding beats my own!

Raymond J. Corsini, Ph.D.

1

What Are Early Recollections and What Can We Learn From Them?

Early recollections (ERs) are stories of events that a person *says* occurred before he or she was 10 years of age. Everyone has ERs, and people often use them to illustrate a particular point, express an emotion, explain their behavior, or just reminisce. These stories frequently begin with "I remember this one time when . . ." or "I remember during my fifth birthday party . . . " or some other account of a specific event that they recall from their youth.

Early recollections are different from reports, which people often confuse with ERs. Reports are generalizations such as "My father and I used to go fishing almost every Sunday" or "As a kid, I went to the movies all the time." While reports may be useful in understanding the person, they are not relevant to the focus of this book. Early recollections are *specific* incidents that clients tell us, and they are very useful in understanding the people telling them. In this book we will present the idea that ERs are a series of small mysteries that, once solved, can be woven together to produce a detailed tapestry of how a person perceives the world, others, and himself or herself. As you will see, ERs are filled with symbols and metaphors that, correctly interpreted, describe fundamental aspects of individuals.

Why before 10? That is the age at which people develop the ability to record actions and perceptions in chronological order. Before the age of

1

10, most people do not have continuous memory. That is, they cannot remember the sequence of events properly. Therefore, when adults reflect back on events that occurred prior to the development of continuous memory they patch up, alter, or in some way corrupt the "true" event by projecting material onto it. Memories function in an interesting way. People recall events, but not as clearly as a photograph. Adults shade, highlight, and fill in some aspects of those things they remember from their youth. To keep the story coherent, they have to fill in the missing parts of the story that their memories cannot furnish. They are not conscious of the information that they use to "patch up" (or in "psychologese," "confabulate") the story. And that is perhaps the most interesting and most revealing part of the ER. Because people cannot remember all parts of the recollection, they tend to attach or project certain details or feelings or concepts onto the recollection to make it coherent. In addition, those things that people choose to remember, or not remember, about the event add meaning to the recollection. Those additions or subtractions and the selection of events that are remembered provide clinical data that can be used to understand people.

The information gathered from ERs reflects a person's current view of others, the world, and himself or herself. Our stance is that ERs do not explain a person's childhood, nor are they meant to elicit causal explanations. That is, ERs do not suggest that because something happened in childhood, an individual must act in a particular way. We accept each person's ability to choose his or her actions and reactions.

Early recollections give us an idea about an individual's current perceptions. It is important to understand that the content of the remembrance is a projection; therefore, it makes no difference if the recollection is real or imagined. Whatever is told is clinically useful because the material comes from the client. That is, the stories told of events are projected through the film of the client's personality.

Think of the actual event as the white light from a film projector bulb. Just as the light from a projector takes on the hues of celluloid, stories cannot emerge from within a person without being colored by how that person views the world. For example, if people are depressed, they may darken the actual event by focusing on the negative. On the other hand, if people are anxious, they may choose to see the event, and life, as dangerous and threatening. It does not matter what the event was, or if it happened at all, because the themes of those ERs that are presented can be interpreted. People choose not only *what* to remember but *how* to remember it!

Two examples that demonstrate that ERs don't have to have actually occurred or happened as remembered can be seen in the following recollections.

The first is a birth memory:

> I remember being born. I was in my mother's womb. It was moist and warm. Suddenly I was being wrenched free. Two hands were grabbing me. That's all I remember.

The second is a prenatal memory from someone diagnosed with schizophrenia:

> This was before I was born. I was in my mother's belly. There was a fire in the apartment building across the street. My mother walked over to the window and watched. Firemen were climbing a ladder. There were a lot of people on the street. It was exciting!

Early recollections can be used as a projective assessment because people project their beliefs onto these memories. That is exactly what makes ERs so powerful in understanding people. Festinger (1957) demonstrated that people have a low tolerance for cognitive dissonance. That is, they have a difficult time holding two opposing ideas in their minds. They do as they think, and they think as they do. In other words, people hold onto, and express, stories that are in agreement with how they perceive the world. It is for this reason that incidents are remembered and retold in accord with individual self-perceptions and world views. Therefore, once we have the client's ERs, we have many of the clues to unravel the mystery of the person.

Choice and Life Style

Everyone has a personality. Some you like. Others you butt heads with. Loosely, personality is how people see the world. For example, if they seem overly suspicious of others, people call them "paranoid." If people operate with disregard for others in aggressive or destructive ways, they are called "antisocial." Personality and action are intertwined. How one chooses to act influences how one thinks. Conversely, how a person thinks affects how a person acts. But there is another element to personality: choice. It is how one chooses to think and act that redefines his or her personality, which we will discuss here as one's life style — the terms are interchangeable.

This book is fundamentally based on the contributions of Alfred Adler. We choose to define personality in Adlerian terms as one's style of life. Specifically, life style can be understood as the individual's attitudinal set, that is, the person's collection of convictions about life. These convictions guide how people perceive the world and how they choose to belong in the world. The life style has four components: the self-concept, self-ideal, *Weltbild*, and ethical convictions.

The self-concept consists of people's views of themselves, in terms of what they are and are not. People may say, for example, "I'm charitable" or "I'm not a mean person." The self-ideal (a term Adler coined in the early 20th century) can be understood as what people believe they should be or should accomplish in order to have a place in the world, to be significant. For example, "I should do better." The *Weltbild* (we retain Adler's term) represents people's "picture of the world." It is how people perceive every-thing external to themselves. This is how people view life and others. In other words, the Weltbild can be considered the set of beliefs a person has of everything external to himself or herself, including what the person believes others and the world expects of him or her. They maybe different than the convictions the person has about the self. It also includes concep-tions of and attitude towards others. This includes the division along gen-der lines, such as "Men are callous," and "Women are bad drivers." Ethical convictions are exactly what you think they are. They are an individual's moral standards, not necessarily society's, and prescribe appropriate con-duct, such as "Honesty is the best policy."

Currently, there is a mistaken thought epidemic. Much of the way people describe themselves or others mistakenly implies a genetic destiny. Too frequently, people claim that their anger or depression or whatever emotion they're feeling is inherent in their genes. They consequently look to medicine as the solution. However, can life style be found in DNA? No. Though emotions do spring from within people, they are not genetic. There are no sadness, or happiness, or depression, or envy, or anger chro-mosomes. Nevertheless, we are bombarded with individuals who shirk the responsibility of daily living, and particularly their misdeeds, and place it on something other than their own free choice.

What is a common excuse for those who refuse to take responsibility for their actions? (Hint: Think legal defense.) What line of thinking might be more appropriate for 18th-century mechanistic understanding than the complexities of the human brain, the world's most sophisticated 3-pound analog computer?

That line of thinking is causal.

People may be reluctant to take responsibility for their actions and blame a mental condition or a predisposing illness or situation. This is especially true if there is a possibility of punishment. (Think about how some people blame their childhoods or economic problems when faced with a lawsuit.) Many people believe that if X happened, then Y must happen. They try to negate the power of individual choice. We see it regu-larly when people make excuses for their behavior and do not want to take personal responsibility. One excuse we have heard is "I came from an abusive home, and that is why I beat my wife." People who think this way are missing an important fact: Not everyone who grows up in an abusive home develops into a spouse abuser. Others might say, "I've seen enough of that. It was terrible, and I will never become abusive." As long as people have free choice, causality will not work as an excuse. Consequently, the power of choice is important in determining life style and can easily disprove the claimed validity for causal events. So even though people may have had certain things role-modeled for them while they were growing up, they are not compelled to repeat them. In other words, people choose what they allow to influence them in order to achieve a particular goal. For example, if someone wants to cheat on their diet, they can blame the food advertisers for putting out such persuasive advertisements, friends who tempt them to eat something they shouldn't, bakeries that direct such sweet smelling aroma into the air, a sale that was about to end, co-workers who bring in sweets and then "just leave them there until somebody eats them," the view that "life is too short, so why not live it up," or adopt whatever rationale is necessary in order to get what they want.

What else is related to a person's thoughts and behavior? Each person must ask himself or herself, How did I choose to react to previous events, and, more important, how did I perceive those experiences? People act and understand based on their perceptions. For human beings, perception is reality. Perceptions of others and of the world guide the individual to act in certain ways. How one perceives leads to real consequences.

Each person develops through childhood and into adulthood encountering innumerable experiences. People learn (or do not learn — human beings have the ability to choose, consciously or unconsciously) from these events a great number of things, such as what is important in life, what is to be avoided, how to interact with others, how they see themselves and the world around them. It is how a person chooses to interpret and act, as well as react, to situations that influences the development of that person's personality. It is what the individual has learned from the environment, plus the individual's interpretation of that environment, that shapes a person. Simply put, there are no strands of personality DNA in human genes. How each person chooses to perceive and incorporate those events shapes that person's life style. Consequently, that person's personality guides perception and behavior to reach whatever goals he or she chooses in life.

One learns who one is, what is important in life, and how to succeed at it through interpreting these events. These interpretations forge individual character. These interpretations are as varied as individuals are, and they explain the variability of human behavior. Just as people see things differently, they act differently in regard to these events. For example, when two hijacked passenger jets flew into the World Trade Center, some people left the towers as fast as they could by stairwell. Others helped those who were hurt leave the building. Some chose to stay with people who could not leave the building. Others jumped to their deaths. Some individuals decided to remain inside a burning and crumbling building, while others chose to rush into those burning buildings and save as many people as possible before the towers collapsed. Each of these people had a different perspective and a different goal. Their personalities, or life styles, guided how they perceived and interpreted the event and how they chose to react to it.

Early recollections hold valuable information for those who are able to determine their true meaning. Early recollections hold the key to understanding how individuals choose to see themselves and the world and what they value in life. Choice is the fulcrum that changes the balance of the individual. Choosing what to focus on determines an individual's emotions and actions. Early recollections help us to determine what is important to a client. Early recollections, once told, tell on a person. They provide evidence of a person's priorities, goals, and methods in achieving goals. They are the solvable mysteries of who one is, where one stands, and where one is heading.

Life Style Projected Into ERs

Take a moment and close your eyes and think of, actually be able to visualize, an event in your life that occurred before you were 10 years of age. Please take your time.

Got one?

OK. That event you have recalled makes a statement of who you are and what you believe. Welcome, you have just entered the world of projective testing. The event you remembered is most likely not accurate and has been filtered through your personality or, as we refer to it, life style. Whatever event you recalled, temporally large or small makes no difference, tells much about you.

How, you may ask, does some random memory have the power to indicate to others how you see the world and act within it? It's rather simple, really.

Early recollections are stories of events that may, or may not, have occurred. Memories are very flexible and are not always reliable or accurate. Have you ever forgotten where you put your keys? Can you remember all of your first-grade classmates' first *and* last names? You probably could in first grade!

Having unreliable and inaccurate memories can be advantageous. For example, people can remember events in such a way that stops them from doing something that could hurt them or that gives them confidence to do a project. If you recall an event from your past where you scarred your chin by going over a jump on your bicycle, you are more likely to refrain from similar dangerous behavior when that memory comes to mind. Or you may remember how you spelled the word "buzzard" right in a spelling bee in third grade and are then instilled with confidence to move forward on some measure of your abilities, such as a licensing exam.

People may also forget those things that do not help them or that contradict their self-perceptions. Here are some examples: Depressed people may not remember when they conquered previous challenges. Paranoid individuals may not remember events in which their trust in others paid off. Athletes who are participating in an event may not recall previous losses because it contradicts their goal of winning.

In regard to ERs, blind spots in memory allow people to fill in the details or make up the memories completely. Now think about the event we just asked you to recall. We suspect that the event you remember is different from the actual event to some degree because it got filtered through your life style.

For example, if you thought of an occasion at which other people were present and ask them what happened at that event, you may receive several different answers. They may not recall the incident, as it may not be relevant to them. They may recall it as you did, or more likely, give a completely different interpretation of the event. Try it the next time you talk with your siblings or friends; you'll see. So how can two people who were at the same event at the same time come up with two different interpretations?

Here's a real-life example. A brother and a sister gave their ERs, one after the other. Each gave an ER about a school dance. The brother said that he and his sister walked two miles across some fields to reach a Friday night dance at their school. When they arrived at the dance, the door was closed. And though he could hear that something was going on, they could not get in. He was frustrated. His sister told a similar story of walking two miles across a field to reach the dance, but she remembers going into the dance and having a good time.

So who was right?

Frankly, it doesn't matter. It is the themes and the metaphors contained in the ERs that are important in understanding individuals.

Why metaphors? Before humans develop language abilities, most of their learning is visual and symbolic. Symbols used during childhood (a stove symbolizes something hot, and brussels sprouts mean "yucky") are a simpler cousin of the metaphor. Human beings start off life under-standing things symbolically and later on add the ability to think meta-phorically. They continue to use symbols and metaphors for the rest of their lives. Metaphors are seen not only in ERs but also in great works of literature, film, and art. Almost all, if not all, ERs have at least one meta-phor, and it is our duty to identify and interpret those metaphors.

We will interpret this one recollection as an example. You cannot gener-alize from a sample of one, and must get several recollections to make a coherent and more accurate interpretation (Ansbacher, 1953; Mosak, 1958; Purcell, 1952). Nevertheless, we will use this sample to demonstrate how ERs provide evidence of personality and perception. Though both siblings may see it as difficult to join others socially, clearly this one recol-lection shows that the brother is pessimistic and feels that he is shut out from social events. However, the sister feels that although it may be diffi-cult to join with others, it is worth the hike because after the journey the good times roll.

So how can two people see the same event so differently?

Simple. They either saw it differently at the time of the event, or are recalling it in their own way. And though either may insist on a different version, they'll never know which is factual because people remember things in ways that are shaped by differences in their life styles. Besides, it does not matter who was factually correct as this is a projective test, and whatever is given is a projection of current functioning. This example clearly shows how people may see the same event very differently.

The Function of Memory

As George Santayana (1924) once wrote, "Those who cannot remember the past are condemned to repeat it." You may be asking, "So what does that have to do with me?" Well, memories chronicle, in their own way, your history and try to predict the future. You try to repeat previous successes and avoid repeating earlier failures. You learn from events and keep these events in memory to guide you in life. They tell you what is important, what to do, what not to do, and so on. However, you retain only those memories that paint a coherent picture, and you forget or mod-ify the rest to fit your view of the world and others. Memory is a matter of construction rather than reconstruction (Bartlett, 1932).

Memories are adaptive; they help people to survive. And as beings who, for the most part, value self-preservation, people tend to keep these mem-ories within reach for when they are needed. You may be asking yourself, "Isn't it self-defeating to have somewhat unreliable memories help us survive?" The clearest answer to that is "yes and no."

"Yes," because people frequently forget important things. They forget their keys, medication, important dates, facts, and so on. That is the self-defeating part. The "no" comes from the fact that people tend to forget things that are not in accord with their goals. (Think of Festinger's 1957 contribution about cognitive dissonance discussed earlier.) When people are trying to succeed, they don't think about their failures; they forget most of the really dumb things they did in childhood and particularly adolescence, and this forgetting helps them to survive by not encumbering them with the inherent incompatibilities, inconsistencies, and contradictions that exist in life. Though it might be nice to remember everything, think of forgetting things that are not relevant as allowing you to think more efficiently. (Besides, if you could remember *everything*, there would be no game shows. Everyone would remember the answers!)

What memories are recalled, or how they are recalled, is often influenced by the need to make decisions. For example, let's say you are buying a vehicle and are in the decision-making process between a truck and a sedan. You may recall that time your parents hauled those 4-by-8-foot sheets of plywood in the family station wagon so they could build you a fort in the backyard, and how happy you were. Do you think that your decision is tilting toward a bigger vehicle? Probably. Why else would you select that memory? You could have just as easily remembered a time when the station wagon looked embarrassing.

Early recollections as discussed in this book should be viewed as little mysteries that, once solved, illuminate the foundation of who a person is and how that person sees others, the world, and his or her place in it.

Don't believe it?

Here is your chance to give interpretation a try. The following is a recollection from a woman. Read it and figure out how she sees and reacts to others.

> I was in first grade. The boy sitting in front of me had diarrhea. It ran down his leg and gushed onto the carpet. There was so much of it. I was really disgusted. I almost vomited. It was intolerable! I ran away from him as fast as I could!

Before we give you the answer, think about what is being said in this ER. Once you get past the gross visualization of the event, think about the message being conveyed. Early recollections speak in metaphor. What metaphor is this woman using to express her perceptions?

Again, take your time. Look at the information given. If you were a newspaper reporter, what might be the headline of this story? If someone relates this recollection in a therapy session or at a party or over the phone, what are they unconsciously trying to convey? How does this seemingly random story tell you how this woman sees other people? How about if we tell you that she does not trust men? Does that assist in the interpretation? It is a story so grossly simple that you might miss the meaning it has for this person.

Ready for the interpretation?

Here you have a woman who perceives men as "full of shit" and runs away from them as fast as she can.

Makes sense now, doesn't it? It makes clear this woman's view of men and how she is to act with them in the future. It does not make any difference if the event occurred or didn't; it is a projection of her personality. The event is being filtered through current understanding and indicates how the person now thinks and feels. It is important to remember that ERs are about now, not then.

ERs as a Projective Technique

For our purpose perhaps it is easier to conceptualize memory as being comprised of systems. There are two memory systems that you need to understand in your comprehension of how and why using ERs is a useful projective technique. These are the episodic memory and semantic memory systems. The first holds specific memories of events that happened previously. The second is much more of a general knowledge database. The difference is that, say, between the remembrance of seeing a particular Ferrari (episodic memory), and the ability to think of sports cars in general (semantic memory). (For more information, see Tulving, 1972, 1983).

In reviewing Tulving's work, W. C. Gordon (1989) wrote that these systems, though distinctive, influence each other such that a person's later experiences change episodic memory.

Gordon continues:

> Virtually all theories of memory processing make the assumption that encoding takes place while memories are in short-term storage or while they are being actively processed. In addition, most such models assume that when a memory is retrieved from permanent storage, that memory or some copy of it re-enters awareness or the short-term memory store. When we combine these assumptions, we are faced with a particular implication. Once a memory has been retrieved, that memory may be susceptible to being re-encoded in short-term storage. In other words, one might predict that a memory that has been retrieved is capable of being altered or modified in some way. This hypothesis

raises an interesting possibility. It may be that retrieval is more than simply a process by which we activate and use stored memories. Retrieval may also be a process by which we are able to update or re-code memories that have long been in storage. (pp. 278–279)

In short, an individual's current mind-set influences his or her memories of specific events. Therefore, ERs are not immune from recent situations, but are in fact corrupted by current perspectives. As a result, the gathering of ERs can be used as a projective technique.

Practicality of Using ERs

The use of ERs as a projective technique has been demonstrated as a reliable and valid measure (see Chapter 17) for the functional assessment of individuals. Functional assessments do not label people, but they do describe their functioning, which can be more clinically useful.

The American Psychiatric Association publishes various editions of the *Diagnostic and Statistical Manual of Mental Disorders,* often referred to by those in the field as DSM. The DSM is the standard used for diagnosing people in North America. The purpose of the DSM is to assist clinicians in clarifying diagnoses; in other words, it classifies and labels mental disorders.

For a diagnosis to be made, a patient has to manifest a minimum number of symptoms that have been linked to a particular illness. For example, for an individual to be diagnosed as having a major depressive episode, five or more of nine possible symptoms have to be present. It's like having a dinner in a Chinese restaurant, where you are able to choose certain appetizers, soups, side dishes, main dishes, and desserts that constitute a meal. This "Chinese menu" approach has some flaws.

First, it is up to the clinician to properly identify those symptoms.

Second, the variability in many diagnoses allows for some overlap of symptoms among diagnoses. Having clinicians choose x number of symptoms out of y number of possible symptoms for a diagnosis has an inherent amount of inconsistency. Several people may be diagnosed with the same disorder, yet have many different symptoms and presentations. There are no clear boundaries on many diagnoses, with several of them clustering together because of the overlap. For example, can you see how diagnoses of antisocial, borderline, histrionic, and narcissistic personality disorders have common characteristics (otherwise known as Cluster B)? No category is a discrete entity separate from other categories.

Third, though the American Psychiatric Association (2000) has warned clinicians to refrain from a mechanical application of diagnoses by a symptom checklist, the opportunity exists for clinicians to categorize individuals. This is especially true for some novice clinicians who are eager to diagnose at the drop of a hat. Eavesdrop on an undergrad psychology students' lunch, and you just may hear many diagnoses bandied about, with just about everyone being branded with a disorder of some kind.

Anyone can meet some criteria of some diagnosis in the DSM. For example, an antisocial personality disorder diagnosis has six criteria, only three of which need to be met for a diagnosis. Most people may be able to pick out at least one or two criteria in themselves or others and then erroneously make a diagnosis for that category. And when people do not fit a particular diagnosis, some students and perhaps some clinicians erroneously append the "not otherwise specified" (NOS) label on a diagnosis (e.g., delirium NOS, alcohol-related disorder NOS). Translation: "We thought it was close to the diagnosis for a particular disorder, even if it didn't meet the criteria." So people can have diagnoses "in the ballpark," if you will. We believe that the blurring of lines among diagnoses and extending their range increases the probability of diagnostic inclusion, categorization, and labeling.

Fourth, the DSM provides nomenclature diagnoses. These do not tell you much about clients, other than their label in a category. You do not know what criteria were met for that label, and consequently you may not have an accurate representation of that person's thoughts and actions. For example, if someone tells you that a client has been diagnosed as having an antisocial personality disorder, you don't know which three (or more) of the six symptoms the person has.

Fifth, related to the previous point, the DSM focuses solely on pathology and does not describe the positive features of the person. It has clinicians looking for the negative in a person, without consideration of the positive and adaptive features of a disorder.

Though ERs cannot be used to formulate nomenclature (DSM) diagnoses, they are very useful for functional assessment. That is, ERs may not be able to differentiate between a psychotic and neurotic depression, but they can be used to diagnose how people who are depressed see themselves, others, and the world around them. They can also illuminate how, to use Adler's (1956) term, such people "arrange" their depression, and what they think they must do in order to have a place in the world. Once you have that information, you can understand people's coping mechanisms, work goals, social interaction, intimate relational behavior, and movement toward those goals. All are extremely important, perhaps more so than a diagnostic label. There is a difference between saying that a car is a blue Ford (a description), and saying that same car has great acceleration off the line but shimmies at speeds greater than 45 mph (a functional assessment). Which is better, a descriptive diagnosis that tells you what it is or a functional assessment that tells you what it does?

Adler (1956) favored the latter and referred to his system as a psychology of use rather than a psychology of possession. We prefer the concept of psychology of use because we believe it is more practical. For example, a person may have an IQ of 200, but if he or she does nothing with that intelligence, what good is it to have such a high IQ? (Think of it similar to having a Ferrari and only keeping it in the garage! You possess the Ferrari, but you don't use it.)

Consider what is needed for assessing somebody. First, you must remember that clinicians, partly through preference and partly because of managed care, no longer have 20 years to do therapy with patients. So you need a quick assessment. We are in the age of fast food, "bullet trains," instant communication, books like *The One-Minute Manager* (Blanchard & Johnson, 1983), and hypersonic flight. People, especially patients, have a greed for speed, provided it comes with accuracy. People want to be treated quickly and accurately whether in the emergency room or the therapist's office.

Take a moment to think of all the psychological assessment devices that meet the following criteria:

1. A test that offers quick administration, interpretation, and feedback.
2. A test that is inexpensive. Managed care often refuses to pay for something as routine as a Rorschach or TAT administration. So what can you use that costs almost nothing?
3. A test that is easy for the subject to comprehend. What assessment tool is easy to administer and understand?
4. A test that can be used to focus on current understanding and functioning without triggering people who are sensitive to intrusive measurement devices.
5. A test that avoids labeling, charting, or otherwise depersonalizing people through categorization.
6. A test that does not rely on psychological jargon.
7. A test that can be replicated 100 years in the future as easily as it was 100 years ago. That is, what test can be given the same way year after year without recertification or retraining of its administrators?
8. A test that does not need to be renewed every few years and does not require a scoring manual or scoring devices.
9. A test that clinicians of almost all theoretical orientations can use.
10. A test that is culturally fair and not dependent upon culturally biased questions and interpretations.

Now take a moment and list the assessments that meet all of those criteria.

When used properly, ERs meet all of those criteria.

Perhaps now you can see the importance and practicality of using ERs in assessment and therapy. Early recollections are inexpensive to gather. They can be collected and easily interpreted in minutes by a *well-trained* professional. Perhaps that is why there has been a recent increase in the literature on the use of ERs.

What's the catch?

First, this is something that should be done only by a trained professional. Second, it should not be used for "parlor analysis." Don't analyze your friends or relatives at a party.

This book presents the use of ERs as a projective technique that can be used to understand people. It is useful for psychologists, counselors, analysts, teachers, sociologists, human resource directors, or anyone who is interested in human behavior. Our reliance in the interpretation of ERs is on Adlerian theory, but it can be easily used with other orientations (Mosak, 1958). This theoretical underpinning deals with the here and now. When people come in for counseling, they do so to address a current problem, specifically how their personalities, or life styles, and coping mechanisms do not meet the demands of the world. In other words, they see the world and others in a certain way, but their perspective and behavior are causing friction with others or are not allowing them to reach their goals.

Adlerian Theory

Alfred Adler, a contemporary of Freud, believed that ERs revealed people's views of themselves, others, and the world around them and prepared them for their futures. Adler believed that only the manifest content of those recalled events is interpreted. (Freud believed that what was *not* presented in memories, the latent content, was more important.) In other words, Adler focused on what was actually stated by the person.

People act in accordance with their ERs, and one of the ways a therapist can judge if a client is making progress in therapy is by a change in his or her ERs (see Dreikurs, 1954; Eckstein, 1976; Mosak, 1958). A change will occur in the ER that shifts the meaning of the recollection and indicates the person's new perspective of the world. Here is a real-life example of an ER that a man gave at the beginning of therapy:

> Six years old. My sister and I are coming home from school. My [older] sister is supposed to look after me. When school let out,

we got on the bus to go home. We are going through downtown on our way home. My sister leaps up and says, "I have to do some shopping. Go home by yourself." I am getting anxious as I see the bus pass my corner, and I have not gotten off. I thought that busses only go in one direction and that I would end up going to the end of the earth. I don't have any memory of what happened after that.

Toward the end of his therapy, he gave the same ER but with an interesting change:

The bus went past my corner, and I went to the bus driver and told him that I needed to get off at the next block. I got off and walked the block back home.

It is interesting to note that prior to therapy, his recollection indicates that he needs a woman to take care of him, but that women are unpredictable and abandon him, and if he is left to his own devices, it will end in catastrophe. However, in the second recollection he takes care of himself, and no catastrophe occurs.

Adler (1931/1958) chose the subjective phenomenological approach. He advocated that "we must see with his [the client's] eyes and listen with his ears" (p. 72). The starting point is to put oneself in the shoes of the person giving the ER, or as Carl Rogers (1951) wrote, "It is the counselor's function to assume, in so far as he is able, the internal frame of reference of the client, to perceive the world as the client sees it, to perceive the client himself as he is seen by himself, to lay aside all perceptions from the external frame of reference while doing so, and to communicate something of this empathic understanding to the client" (p. 29).

Given that we will be using Adlerian theory as foundation and background for assessing and understanding ERs, it will be helpful for you to know some of the terms this theory uses. As we mentioned previously, the term life style is a synonym for personality. Adlerian theory, because it is a field theory (that is, people are seen in relation to their perceived environment), incorporates the concept of "life tasks." These life tasks can be divided into Adler's (1956, 1978) three tasks — the Work Task, the Social Task, the Sexual Task — and Dreikurs's and Mosak's (1967) tasks, the Self Task and the Spiritual Task. There is also the "Parenting and Family Task." These tasks may, in part or in full, be represented in clients' ERs. These areas of functioning are usually assessed in a good initial interview and throughout treatment. We have chosen to understand these important areas of functioning in terms of the Adlerian concept of tasks because it is easy to remember and understand and avoids the cumbersome "psychologese" that is often seen in textbooks. Why make it more difficult and abstract than it needs to be?

The Work Task represents a cooperative duty as people live dependently with others (e.g., someone plants the wheat, another makes the flour, another brings the flour to the baker who bakes the bread, and so forth). The Work Task is the way in which a person contributes to the common welfare. The Work Task can be broken into at least six subtasks. Vocational choice is what one chooses to do when one grows up. As you can imagine, life style is a major guide in choosing a profession or trade. Vocational preparation refers to the training received (e.g., dental or medical school, cosmetology training, plumber apprenticeship). People do things, such as get an education or training, which help them reach their goals. Vocational satisfaction is another subtask. Satisfaction is a measure of how much a person likes his or her job. The more closely one's work reflects one's goals and life style, the more satisfaction that work offers. Those who truly enjoy their jobs are often heard to say, "I'd do this job for nothing." Leadership is yet another subtask. Leadership is the level of comfort with leading or following. Leisure is the subtask that includes those areas of life that are not work related (e.g., hobbies, retirement, vacations). The last subtask is socio-vocational issues, in other words, how a person deals with coworkers and the public. This can also be seen in childhood school relationships. We have all seen children who are graded as "Not being able to work and play well with others."

The Social Task refers to how people adapt themselves to others and interact with them. It is the relationship between the "I" and the "you" (Buber, 1958). This task is subdivided into the belonging and transactional subtasks. Belonging is how a person chooses to belong. Is the person helpless, or dependent, or energetic, or belligerent, or whiny? What kind of behaviors does the person feel are necessary to gain the feeling that he or she belongs? Toward what kinds of groups does this person gravitate to achieve a feeling of belonging? The transactional subtask is how the individual interacts with others — whether the person sees himself or herself as OK or not OK (inferiority feeling) (Harris, 1999).

The Sexual Task has four subtasks. First is the sexual sole definition. In other words, what does it mean to be a man or woman? It is as much a social role as a biological role because people act in a social world. Sex role identification is how people identify with their perception of what is a man, a woman, a "real" man, or a "real" woman. Parents, movies, television, and culture can influence a person's understanding of what is masculine and feminine. Sexual development is the subtask defined by how people reach sexual developmental milestones and their reactions to them. The remaining subtask, sexual behavior, is everything related to sex. This includes, but is not limited to, sexual feelings, what is appropriate and inappropriate sexual behavior, who one should date and marry, and so on, although we need to remember that marriage is broader than sexual behavior (Dreikurs & Mosak, 1966). Marriage is a unique social relationship that should go much further than, and not be measured only by, sexual intimacy. There is the social relationship — a friendship, if you will. There is the financial relationship: who works where, how is money spent, and so on. There is the agreement as to who does what household chores, as well as all of the other areas in which two married persons have to operate.

The Self Task (Dreikurs & Mosak, 1967) refers to the conclusion people arrive at about themselves. It is how the "I" relates to "me" or "myself" (Dreikurs & Mosak, 1967). It is the conclusion that people come to about themselves as the "I" observes the "Me." The result may influence overall functioning. What might you put in the blank in the sentence "I _____ me"?

The Self Task is divided into several main subtasks. The first is survival, which includes biological, psychological, and social survival. This refers to our clients' health, self-esteem, and belonging. Second is body image. How do people perceive their own bodies? Is the body that exists similar to the person's perception of it? Does the client like his or her body? When the answer is false, you find people who have eating disorders or go through many plastic surgeries or behave in similar ways. You can see how perception changes behavior. Third is opinion, or how people think of themselves. Statements such as "I like myself" or "I hate myself" fall under this category. William James proposed that the self is subject plus object. Heidbreder (1933) elaborates on James's conception of the many "perceived selves that live in the actual world" (p. 177). For example, there are the selves that one person may have (family self, work self, spiritual self, etc.). Each self is represented differently in different contexts. The "I" and "me or myself" stand in relation to each other.

Last is evaluation, self-evaluation, which is divided along the lines of the "good me," the "bad me," and the "not me" (Sullivan, 1953). These three options represent a child's reception with warmth and compassion or with discouragement or with no feedback from the caretakers, respectively.

The Spiritual Task relates to how people give meaning to life: their relationship, if any, with God (what they do about religion) and their relationship to the universe (how they view life and death). The Parenting and Family Task involves how individuals perceive and interact with their families.

Again, these tasks are presented in a way that should make apparent sense. Though the tasks will not be further elaborated in the rest of the text, we briefly present them as areas of clinical interest that may appear in ERs. One of the many benefits of using Adlerian theory as a base of understanding is that it enables the use of commonsense terms that people can easily remember and comprehend. For example, the term Work Task appears to almost define itself upon first reading. One of the many goals of this book is to provide a text that is easy and (we hope) fun to read. We designed this book to be enjoyable to read and one that provides easy-to-understand, yet very useful, illustrations. To that end, throughout this book are examples of real-life ERs in truncated form. We have shortened some examples so that we can focus on what is being taught in that particular section.

This book presents many examples of ERs with guided interpretation of them to give you ample opportunity to become familiar with some of the processes involved. Though you will be given numerous chances to review and interpret ERs, that does not mean that you will be qualified to interpret them on your own, any more than reading about surgery will make you qualified to perform surgery. This book combines theory with guided practice and occasional quizzes, and we believe it is the best way to present the concept of ERs as a projective technique.

Early recollections may provide clues as to how people define and move in relation to these life tasks. In keeping with the idea of field theory, that is, people in relation to their perceived environment, it is important to understand how their life styles guide their thoughts, feelings, and behavior.

If you have to figure out people, what do you need to know?

You need to find out how they see themselves, others, and the world, and you need to know their ethical convictions. Remember that perceptions, thoughts, and actions are all in accord and do not contradict each other except on the surface. Early recollections provide information on perceptions, and from that we can predict thoughts and actions.

Is there a need to understand the perception of others? Yes, because people act in relation to others. Would you need to find out people's goals in life and what they are striving toward? Of course! Is the perception of the world important in understanding how the person acts in relation to it? Yes. If some people think, "the world is cruel," might they not act in a certain way toward it? Do you think it's important to know people's ethics? How might two people act differently if a prime ethical conviction for one is "Honesty is the best policy," and for the other, "Lie through your teeth and hide your sins"? All of these areas are very useful in comprehending how people think and act. Furthermore, all of these are represented in the life style convictions that are hidden in ERs.

Each person is a mystery, and as Corsini indicates in the introduction, we play the role of detectives. Early recollections are an extremely useful tool in deciphering people's secret code of metaphors, symbols, and themes. They show how people drive themselves, what they're driving toward, where they hit some bumps in the road and how they react to those bumps. It is people's life styles that allow them to live productively and adaptively, or live a life of friction, defeat, and loss.

Ask yourself one question before continuing. Can you think of any interpersonal problem that is *not* related to a person's personality?

Summary

Early recollections are memories of specific incidents that people tell us and are useful in understanding them. Early recollections must occur prior to the client's 10th birthday because that is the approximate length of the temporal window of human development before people have the ability to record actions and perceptions in chronological order. To keep the memory coherent, people fill in the missing parts of the story that their memories cannot furnish. They project their life style onto these ERs (the terms "life style" and "personality" are interchangeable). Choice is important in how people react. Life styles guide how they make choices. Therefore, perception leads to real consequences.

Memories are flexible and serve human purposes. What memories are recalled, or how they are recalled, is often influenced by an individual's need to make decisions. Therefore, ERs are relevant to current functioning. Though ERs cannot be used to formulate nomenclature (DSM) diagnoses, they are very useful for functional assessment.

Alfred Adler believed that ERs revealed people's view of themselves, others, and the world around them and prepared them for their future. People act in accordance with their life styles, and one of the ways a therapist can judge whether clients are making progress in therapy is by a change in their ERs. Adlerian theory incorporates the concept of "life tasks." These life tasks can be divided into the Self Task, the Work Task, the Social Task, the Sexual Task, the Parenting and Family Task, and the Spiritual Task. Early recollections may provide clues as to how people define and move in relation to these life tasks.

2

Test Administration

Early recollections are quick and easy to gather, and, for people with training, easy to interpret. This Chapter explains how to elicit ERs and how to avoid some of the possible pitfalls in doing it. Before we go further, we should first review Alfred Adler's understanding of the usefulness of ERs in assessment.

Adler (1937) stated that a person's ERs

> are found always to have a bearing on the central interests of that person's life. Early recollections give us hints and clues which are most valuable to follow when attempting the task of finding the direction of a person's striving. They are most helpful in revealing what one regards as values to be aimed for and what one senses as dangers to be avoided. They help us to see the kind of world which a particular person feels he is living in, and the ways he really found of meeting that world. They illuminate the origins of the style of life. The basic attitudes which have guided an individual throughout his life and which prevail, likewise, in his present situation, are reflected in those fragments which he has selected to epitomize his feeling about life, and to cherish in his memory as reminders. He has preserved these as his early recollections. (p. 287)

Therefore, it is important to remember that those ERs that people choose to communicate reflect their current view of life and thus can be used as a projective assessment to assist in understanding their life styles. You can assess ERs of clients as young as adolescents or as old as they come (no upper age limit).

The Administration Procedure

1. As elaborated in Shulman and Mosak (1988), ERs can be gathered in the following manner:

   "Go as far back as you can in childhood. When you go back, what early memory comes to your mind?" Another way to ask for early recollections is to say, "Think back, as far back as you can. What is the first incident you can remember from your life? Something about which you can say, 'One day I remember . . . '" (p. 111).

   You want to make sure that it is an event that clients can visualize. Remember to gather memories of events that clients believe to have occurred prior to their 10th birthday. (The memory of any event of any length is sufficient, as long as it is one *specific* incident.)

2. After you have recorded the ER verbatim you need to ask the person the following question if it has not already appeared in the ER: "What is the most vivid part of the recollection?" We ask for the most vivid part of the recollection because it helps the clinician to understand the essence of the recollection. It directs our attention to what the client believes is the central part. Perhaps more important, it may prevent us from placing emphasis on what *we* think is the most important part and subsequently misinterpreting the recollection. For example, suppose you receive an ER such as this one:

   My brother and I were getting our bicycles from the garage, and the other kids from the neighborhood were in the driveway waiting for us. My brother got his bicycle first and I was behind him as we walked out of the garage. I saw a neighborhood kid throw a baseball at another kid who wasn't looking, and he got hit in the head. My brother put down his bike to see if the kid was OK, and I just stood there watching.

   There are several different phrases that clinicians may *think* are the most important, but we are not certain unless we ask the client.

Reread the recollection and imagine that with each reading a different sentence or phrase is the gist of the memory. How does the differing emphasis put a different spin on the entire ER? For example, you may think that the client is in the shadow of his brother, or that he thinks people should wait for him, or that he sees the world as a dangerous place, or that he or his brother puts more emphasis on the safety of others than on his own safety. These are all present in the recollection. However, the client's answer to "What is the most vivid part of the recollection?" tells us what *the client* thinks is the most important part of the ER.

3. If clients have not already described their feeling during the course of the ER, we inquire, "What was your feeling at the time?" The information we get may give us additional detail about the person. For example, people who tend to seek excitement may recall more intense feelings than would those who tend to avoid their feelings. Similar to the question about the most vivid part, asking for the feeling may help the clinician understand the client better through the feeling the latter assigns to the memory. It greatly reduces the possibility that the clinician will project an emotion onto the memory, and it gives a better understanding of the purpose of the behavior.

For example, if a client gives you the following ER, what can you make out of the emotional content?

> I was about 8 when my brother took my toy, I don't remember which one, and then I pushed him down hard, and I got my toy back.

There are several possible feelings that could be involved. Please, take a moment and guess what the client felt in the recollection.

You are about to demonstrate to yourself the importance of getting the feeling of the recollection from the client. There are many possible choices, and each one carries a different meaning. How might you interpret the ER if the client's feeling was: agitated? alive? angry? aroused? ashamed? capable? caring? competitive? courageous? cowardly? degraded? disgusted? emasculated? effective? empty? elated? enraged? evil? exhilarated? frightened? glorious? horrified? invincible? impulsive? inadequate? inferior? superior? insecure? insignificant? intimidated? powerful? powerless? provoked? regretful? sabotaged? sad? self-confident? successful? vicious? victimized? Or no feeling at all? Or two feelings (e.g., angry then guilty, or wimpy and then powerful)?

Sometimes people may give feelings to different parts of the ER. For example, suppose a client gave the following recollection:

> I remember pushing my cousin down on the ground and running to my father. I felt invincible.

You might be inclined to interpret this ER differently than you would if the client gave you the same recollection but with two emotions:

> I remember pushing my cousin down on the ground and running to my father. I felt invincible and then terribly regretful.

Clearly, each one conveys different information about the client. As a matter of fact, go through those feelings listed and think how each one might change your conception of the client's self-image, perception of others, worldview, his place in the world, and his ethical convictions?

4. After obtaining the recollection, the client's age at the time, his or her feeling at the time, and the most vivid part of that memory, you can continue on to the next memory or investigate the memory you have just received. If there is something you want to clarify or if there is a question you have about the recollection, ask it. Otherwise, move on to the next recollection. Questions such as "What is your next memory?" or "What memory comes to your mind next?" are useful.

5. Accept ERs in any order. They do not have to be given in chronological order. Remember, ERs are those instances that are believed to have occurred *prior* to 10 years of age.

6. Usually, when you find repeating themes, you probably have received enough ERs. In our experience, clients usually give three to eight ERs.

7. If the person does not give you any ERs, or perhaps one, this may be a sign of resistance, personal anxiety or test anxiety, or the failure to understand the instructions. If so, you may elicit ERs in regard to particular events. Examples include: "What happened on your first day of school?" "Can you tell me about one of your birthdays?" "Do you ever recall being elated? Powerless? Enraged?" "Can you tell me about the day your sister (or brother) was born?"

Remember that the more you prime clients for eliciting ERs, the less weight the recollections carry in the interpretation of their life styles.

8. If the client gives only reports, see if you can persuade him or her to transform the report into an ER. Again, reports are generalized summaries of multiple events, such as "Every Sunday we went to the park," or "I went to the movies all the time when I was younger." You may explore the report for recollections by inquiring, "Do you remember one time this occurred?" Frequently the client may do this spontaneously.

9. If you cannot determine whether clients are giving ERs or reports, ask them to close their eyes and visualize what they are remembering (Shulman & Mosak, 1988). If they can do so, giving details, it is an ER. If not, it is very likely a report.

10. Do not accept family stories, photographs, and childhood dreams as ERs. However, a single recollection of a dream (e.g., "one night I dreamt") is an ER because it is a recollection of a singular event. Recurrent dreams (e.g., "I used to dream of tigers chasing me") are considered reports because they are not singular events. Early recollections of watching a television show or some similar event do count as ERs as the client is recollecting an event from childhood. Television shows and the like have themes and metaphors, and can be one specific event that the client can project onto or recollect because the event mirrors the client's life style.

11. Very long recollections are acceptable and can be interpreted in a way of describing a movie to someone. Surely you have described a movie to a friend, coworker, or family member. How did you do it? Most likely you described the characters, the plot, the setting, and the theme along with any other pertinent details. Do the same when interpreting lengthy ERs.

12. When you have completed gathering the ERs, you may review them with the person to give them a chance to elaborate or amend them. The information you have gathered, including the most vivid part of the recollection and the associated feeling of the recollection, will be used in the interpretation.

You now have a better understanding of how to elicit ERs and the importance of their components. If you are not an experienced interpreter, ERs *must be* interpreted with supervision from a clinician who is well versed in the interpretation process.

Though eliciting ERs is straightforward and efficient, there are some possible pitfalls that you need to know about. We'll discuss those challenges in the next section.

Challenges of Eliciting ERs

To most clients, the request for early memories is very clear. The recollections' apparent innocuousness does not raise the suspicion or anxiety of the majority of clients. They are usually quite willing to give us ERs because they see the task as something they can readily do, and the task lacks the mystery often associated with other projective material (e.g., the Rorschach Inkblot Test and dream interpretation). However, there are a number of problem areas that can challenge the process of gathering ERs.

Possible Problem #1

What might be some general problems connected with eliciting ERs? As no assessment is suitable for all people or populations, we can safely say that ERs cannot be elicited from everyone.

Think about all of the psychological conditions that may affect success here. For example, the brain-injured and those with other organic brain syndromes may not be able to accomplish it. Lashever (1990) was able to get valid ERs from people within the 40–54 IQ range. However, she found that the ratio of valid ERs to number of participants diminished as the IQ range decreased. All participants with an IQ of 80 to 100 were able to give valid ERs; 42 out of 52 (80%) with an IQ of 55 to 69 were able to give valid ERs; and only 11 out of 26 (42%) with an IQ between 40 to 54 were able to give valid ERs.

We cannot ask for memories from those who do not have the ability to communicate memories to us. Those with schizophrenia may be attending to their delusions and hallucinations rather than to our test no matter how interesting we think it is. Those with depression may be too apathetic or feel too hopeless to participate. (Would you want to take a test on a pre-coffee Monday morning? Think how difficult it would be for those who are depressed.) Some may feel as though this is just another test that may not change anything in their lives. Furthermore, it may increase their depression if they perceive themselves as so inferior that they need to be psychologically tested or view themselves as failures because they can't come up with ERs.

For those who are in a manic state, their racing thoughts may prevent the production of recollections. Those clients with paranoid delusions may in their suspiciousness think we are working against them and refuse to give ERs. These, and many other conditions, should be considered prior to trying to elicit ERs.

What might be another group that may not be suitable to give ERs? What do you think about asking children for ERs?

Though some subscribing to the Adlerian school of thought, such as Hedvig (1965), collect ERs from prepubescent children, others agree with Dreikurs that children's ERs are simply their contemporaneous recollections. Makes sense, doesn't it? It's kind of like asking them what happened last Thursday. That would make it much less of a projective test and more of a memory test.

Possible Problem #2

Some people for whom the task is suitable nevertheless "cannot" give ERs. You may be saying, "I am giving this test to clients who I'm sure are quite capable of giving me ERs, but they aren't. Why not?"

There are several possible reasons for this behavior.

1. Perhaps the reason lies with you. Are you giving them clear instructions? Sometimes people think they should give only the *earliest* possible memories, so they try to remember everything from immediately after their birth, and obviously cannot. Others may provide only memories of general events (reports). Some clients may give you recollections from their adolescence, which is too late for our purposes. Try repeating your directions or rewording them. It may help to have clients explain the directions back to you. This may solve the difficulty and help you elicit ERs.

2. Are your clients apprehensive or guarded? Some people are suspicious of everything and everyone, and others are merely cautious about testing. How might you feel if you were not familiar with psychological assessment, and someone whom you may barely know urged you to undergo a psychological evaluation? Often clients are apprehensive and may see the ER collection as an examination that can be passed or failed.

   Face validity is the degree that a procedure appears to measure what it is reported to measure. If clients are taking a test with low face validity (e.g., ERs or the Rorschach Inkblot Test), then they may be cautious for fear of failing and perhaps being labeled. When clients are administered the Rorschach Inkblot Test, for example, they cannot deduce the purpose of the test because it is so vague in comparison to direct questions. When individuals cannot figure out what is going on, they often act conservatively and guardedly. They may worry about inadvertently giving you information that they would prefer not become public. Their reservation about participating is their way of keeping themselves psychologically, or socially, or financially, or occupationally safe.

Some people do not offer ERs because they do not know if the results carry some external repercussions. Some clients may ask, "Will they find out I'm a loon?" Other clients think about consequences in other areas of functioning, such as social, work, and financial matters. They may ask, "Will I lose my pension?" or "Will you put me in an insane asylum?" or "Will this get me forced out of my job?" or "Will this ruin my 'guilty by reason of insanity' plea?" You need to attend to these concerns prior to requesting ERs.

What stimulus value do you provide for the client? Are you a unique stimulus that has some meaning for the client? Some clients find it easier to give their ERs to women, others to men. Some prefer giving their recollections to older clinicians, and some may favor younger ones. It may be easier to communicate ERs to one examiner rather than to another. Look at each client individually and examine what, if any, role you play for the client.

3. Some people who are quite able to give a number of ERs simply don't want to be part of the process. They may have been referred, pressured to seek help, or sentenced. For example, if a woman asks her husband to go to you for couple's counseling, and he is really not interested in therapy but shows up at the sessions to give the impression of dedication, he may not be eager to give you any ERs. Attention to the client's motivation prior to soliciting ERs is a must. You may place mild pressure upon individuals who do not offer any ERs. For example, in such a situation, Schneider (Mosak & Schneider, 1979) demonstrates on tape how he merely sits back after the person states that he cannot remember anything. It is as if Schneider is counting on the individual to produce ERs nevertheless. Clients often feel the pressure of (awkward) silence during sessions and may say something to you to avoid the quiet. This form of mild pressure is often successful.

Usually after people produce one ER, they associate to other memories. However, there are those who give only one or two and then quit. It is hazardous for us to attempt to formulate an understanding of life style on the basis of a single ER (Ansbacher, 1953; Mosak, 1958; Purcell, 1952). (Just as it would be difficult to comprehend Shakespeare's *Hamlet* from one scene.) Therefore, we suggest that you encourage people to take their time and search their memories.

If this procedure does not prove fruitful, you may prompt with very general questions: "Do you remember any holidays, birthday parties, trips?" When people still do not produce an ER, you can use more specific questioning that includes specific cues; such as "Tell me an event from the first day in school" or "Tell me about something that happened the day your sibling was born." However, the more specific your prompting, the less weight you should give to the ER because the ERs were not spontaneously offered.

This prompting method is similar to "testing the limits" associated with the Klopfer administration of the Rorschach test (Klopfer & Davidson, 1962). The person giving the directions to the Rorschach deliberately introduces concepts not formed by the participant when he or she shows no reaction to some of the significant stimuli in the blots. The purpose of testing the limits is to determine if a participant is able to see specific types of concepts, but it is given in a circumstance in which the client's production is impoverished. The obtained information generally is not used for scoring because the unstructured nature of the Rorschach has been altered.

Some clinicians have suggested that if one cannot elicit ERs, the clients should asked to fabricate some ERs (see Chapter 23). The assumption is that these made-up ERs are the equivalent of actual ERs. We don't encourage this procedure. Making up recollections is predicated on a false assumption: that all projective techniques are equivalent. Certainly not the same information is obtained from the TAT as from the Rorschach, even though both are projective tests. Similarly it cannot be assumed that true ERs and made-up ERs are equivalent.

You may be saying, "Hey, didn't you tell us that it does not make any difference if the recollections are true or not?" True and true. But a fabricated memory is very different from an erroneous memory. Both are false, but the client uses one to get through life; the other recollection is not a recollection at all and may not be relevant to the client's perception of the world. Barker and Bitter (1992) found little relation between made-up memories and ERs in regard to social interest. They found that made-up memories had higher social interest than what was projected in ERs, and the authors warn against substituting made-up memories for ERs.

4. Some people cannot produce any memories of events that occurred prior to their 10th birthday. They obviously struggle to fulfill the instructions, but are unable to recall anything before the age of 10. Commonly, these people had a traumatic experience at an early age, and they cannot remember any incidents before that age. For example, a client could not give an early recollection prior to age 14. Upon being questioned he revealed that he was incarcerated in a concentration camp at that age. In such circumstances we treat these late recollections as early recollections.

Alternatively, a major shift in family position during childhood (e.g., the death of a sibling) may inhibit the person from recalling events prior to the significant event. If this is the situation, it is possible, as Dreikurs (personal communication, 1951) indicated, that you may not be able to elicit an ER prior to that event. The earliest recollection may, for example, occur at age 11. However, in each case, the traumatic event must be established rather than assumed. The usual practice in this fairly uncommon situation is to accept these later recollections as ERs although there is no evidence for the validity of this practice.

When a later-aged recollection is given first, one attempts to move the person being assessed back to an earlier age. Sometimes during this process, the person remembers an earlier incident.

Possible Problem #3

A very different problem in gathering ERs is receiving an excess of them. Some people exhibit almost total recall and will offer you an unlimited number of ERs. This may be seen when working with a manic client. The usual practice is to restrict them to eight, which is the number of available spaces on the Life Style Inventory (Mosak & Shulman, 1988). That number will generally contain all of the information you need for an interpretation. If you cannot adequately summarize with eight ERs, then you may need to seek additional supervision, as eight recollections should be adequate. In addition, time considerations, which often translate into financial considerations, argue against collecting more ERs.

Possible Problem #4

Some clients may give only reports despite your instruction. If repetition or clarification of the instructions doesn't succeed in producing ERs, make another attempt to have the client convert those reports into recollections. Suppose a client told you, "I used to go to the movies every Saturday when I was a kid." You might then focus the client by saying, "For our purposes today I'm interested in single incidents, something to which you can say 'One day I remember . . . '" or "Please tell me about one of those times that you went to the movies."

Possible Problem #5

Sometimes it is not possible to distinguish between a report and an ER. Here the phrasing is important, "We would" or "I used to" are always indicative of a report. Some clients cannot tell whether the memory is their own or whether they've heard the story many times or seen a photograph. In these instances, ask your clients to close their eyes and attempt to visualize the incident as if they were watching it on a movie screen. If they can visualize it, then you should treat the information as an ER. If they cannot visualize the recollection, treat it as a report. Furthermore, you, as the clinician, must be able to visualize the ER in order to make it interpretable. If you cannot visualize the ER, then it is probably not a valid ER. Visualization of ERs helps the client focus on the event, and helps the clinician interpret the event. Not being able to visualize recollections is a problem when eliciting ERs from groups of people in a group setting. That's one reason we advise against working with groups, even though others have done it (e.g., Waldfogel, 1948).

Some clients may not be able to describe to you what their feelings were at the time of the event. Others can give a general narrative of the recollected event but cannot give details. You should make additional attempts to elicit these; sometimes you will be successful, sometimes not. We will discuss the meaning of such omissions in Chapter 8.

We hope that this section clarifies some possible pitfalls that you need to be aware of and attend to. We have provided some solutions to these problems and trust that you will augment your understanding as you explore new resolutions to these and other challenges. The information provided should assist you not only in eliciting ERs but also in interpreting them, as some responses should provide insight into the client. The Chapters that follow illustrate different types of interpretation that can be used with ERs. Each Chapter details a different method of understanding.

So if you are ready, let's act like investigative reporters and proceed to look into the first interpretation Chapter of many. It's called the Headline Method.

Summary

Early recollections that people choose to communicate are related to their current view of life and thus can be used as a projective assessment to assist in understanding their life styles. The ERs test can be used with clients ranging from adolescents to the oldest individuals (no upper age limit).

We ask for the most vivid part of the recollection because it helps the clinician to understand the essence of the recollection. Similarly, asking what the client felt at the time of the event may help the clinician understand the client better.

Except for experienced interpreters, ERs *must be* interpreted with supervision from a clinician who is well versed in the interpretation process.

There are a number of psychological conditions that affect success at gathering ERs (including, but not limited to, brain injury, organic brain syndromes, and severe depression). Other hurdles include vague directions, lack of interest on the part of the client, guardedness, or external ramifications for the client.

Queries about specific events, such as the first day of school, birthday parties, and so on may help the client focus on memories, but those recollections are not given as much weight clinically because the client didn't volunteer them. Too many recollections may also pose a problem for interpretation. Limit the number of ERs to eight because that should be a sufficient number to provide the information you need.

3

The Headline Method

Though many Adlerians and others have written about ERs, none has explicitly described a holistic method for interpretation. Students, especially those trained in the reductionistic forms of psychological interpretation, express frustration in their attempts to analyze ERs holistically. Mosak (Shulman & Mosak, 1988) devised the Headline Method to clarify the teaching of holistic interpretation. What we present in this Chapter is an opportunity to act as if we were newspaper reporters coming up with concise headlines of ERs. These "headlines" are quick and easy holistic interpretations.

Adler (1956) saw the ER as "The Story of My Life." If ERs were treated as if they were news stories, what headlines could we write that would give the essence of the story? What we choose to write will help uncover the central theme, the movement, of the ER.

Occasionally two themes may appear in a news story, and the headline may be written as a headline with a subhead (in journalistic terms, a "deck"). Two newspapers publishing the same story may have different headlines. One headline may be better than another for reasons to be discussed below, but both may be correct. The difference lies in the slant or focus or emphasis given to the headline. Since ERs are multifaceted (Mosak, Schneider, & Mosak, 1980; Plewa, 1935), it is evident that different interpretations may also give rise to headlines, each with a different slant, yet each correct.

We present the Headline Method first so as to start off simply. As we continue through the Chapters, we will introduce more complex methods of interpretation. So if you are ready, let's step into the role of a news reporter.

First, we need to brief you on what should be included in the construction of accurate headlines. Arth, Ashmore and Floyd (1997), in their journalism handbook, offer several guidelines for writing good headlines. Among these are:

1. Use active voice
2. Use present tense
3. Use short, pithy words
4. Avoid "to be" verbs
6. Be specific
7. Be accurate
15. Avoid contrived headlines (pp. 97–99)

We encourage you to use these guidelines when you use the Headline Method to summarize ERs. The action must be specific, rather than general. The use of a verb in the headline is very relevant as Adlerians look to describe clients' movement. You can see how writing headlines can concisely present the information given in ERs. Though not all of the above guidelines translate well into the Headline Method, you will see their importance and influence on the process.

Headlines of ERs

Here we present a sample of some ERs and possible headlines. But we are not going to make it too easy for you. First we'll present the recollection, and then ask you what you might write for a headline. Ready?

This first ER example comes from a man reflecting on an event.

> I always wanted a bicycle [That part is a report]. It was Christmas day. I remember it was very early in the morning and I ran down the hallway into the living room. As I made a right turn into the living room I saw a bright red Schwinn bicycle in front of the Christmas tree. I wanted it so much. I was in seventh heaven!

What might you write for a headline? Look at the major theme of the ER and add a dash of emotion, while keeping it true to the event.

Here's a tip. What are some of the keywords? Look at "wanted" and "seventh heaven" and come up with a basic theme.

Ready for some possible headlines?

- Boy gets heart's desire. Excited.
- Others fill child's longtime wish.
- Child exhilarated after wants fulfilled.

When you look at the headlines, you realize that they cover the basic theme of the ER. Furthermore, if this theme begins to repeat in the ERs, you can take a guess at what type of person holds these kinds of memories. Again, it is important to remember that you cannot understand a person's life style from just one ER (Ansbacher, 1953; Mosak, 1958; Purcell, 1952). Therefore, we must abide by that rule and hold off until later in this Chapter to look at a series of ERs to come to a proper interpretation.

Ready for another example?

Imagine being a reporter and listening to this woman's ER:

I missed a hurdle in our school's Olympics and came in second. I was frustrated because I was a better runner than the girl who won.

Most vivid: "Irritation as the other girl crossed the finish line ahead of me."

It is now up to you to create a headline. What are you going to write? Here are some key questions to ask yourself:

- What are the important things to look at to convey information to the reader quickly and effectively?
- What is the theme of this ER?
- What is this woman trying to tell us about herself?

Here are some things to investigate:

- Does this woman think it's OK to be in second place?
- Does she think life is fair?
- Is her true superiority acknowledged?

Take a moment and write down a headline. Review the recollection to see if it supports thatheadline. If it does, then you probably have a newspaper-worthy headline. Congratulations!

Some possible headlines:

- Girl believes first is the only place.
- Sometimes being better isn't recognized.

- Girl frustrated by slipup.
- Child upset for not being recognized as better runner.
- Girl's mistake puts her behind.
- Small error frustrates better runner.
- Girl misses out on first place.
- Superior girl frustrated after missing first place.
- Girl suffers from own mistake.

Here are some questions for you in regard to this ER:

- Can you see how these headlines apply to the recollection and what they may say about this woman now?
- Of all of the events this woman could have told us, why did she remember this event?
- How might this, along with other recollections, tell us how this woman sees herself, others, and the world?

Imagine what a series of ERs might tell about this person. Are you ready for the next challenge? We are promoting you from news reporter to investigative reporter. We have assembled a series of one person's ERs that we want you to read and come up with possible headlines for. View each of these headlines as a clue. When you have finished reading the ERs, piece the clues (headlines) together and come up with a conclusion about this woman.

ER 1. Age: 4

It was wintertime during a very heavy snowstorm. My dad and I were shoveling the driveway, and we heard a creak and then a huge crack as the roof of the garage collapsed under the weight of the snow. I was covered in snow and parts of the garage roof. I couldn't breathe. My dad picked me up and lifted me out of snow. He carried me to grandparents' house next door. They were happy to find out I was all right. Mother was inside the house, she was afraid of snowstorms.

Most vivid: "My father picking me up out of the snow."

Again, ask yourself what the main theme is. What are some possible headlines that are supported by the recollection? Ask yourself the following:

- What is happening here?
- What is each person doing?
- How can the gist of the recollection be worded?

If you are ready for some answers, here are some possible headlines. You can skip them if you think you know already or just want to challenge yourself to see if you can make a summary without us.

- Girl requires protection by man from dangerous life.
- Man carries girl to safety during storm.
- Man takes action to save girl.
- Man protects woman from storm.

This is an appropriate place to let you know about "prototypes." Characters in ERs may serve as prototypes. For example, if you come across an ER that contains a father, a mother, a brother, a sister, a girl in class, and so on, it may not refer specifically to those individuals because ERs are constructed fictions. A father may represent all men, or a girl may represent all women. As we stated earlier, ERs, like all forms of language, are symbolic, and therefore one character may symbolize all characters that have the same or similar prominent (according to the client) feature(s).

ER 2. Age: 6

My mother and I were in our house. I thought I heard some noise downstairs, and I was certain that some man broke into our basement. I told my mother that she had to call my father to nail the door shut and barricade it. She did. We were very afraid.

Most vivid: "The noise in the basement and my father nailing the door shut."

Again, look at the details, and the broad theme of the recollection. What is this woman trying to tell you? How do she and others act? Compose your headlines and come up with your own idea of how this woman perceives the world. Our own headlines:

- Girl requires protection from fearful life. (The detail "I thought" informs us about the fear, as does the word "afraid.")
- Child's unfounded fear brings others to action and alarm.
- Panicked child calmed through actions of others.
- Life scares women.

ER 3. Age: 5

When I was younger I was a really loud kid. [That part is a report.] I remember one time I was hitting my mother's pan with a wooden spoon and making a ruckus. I was making a ton of noise. My father was working on the wiring downstairs, and I heard him scream when he touched a live wire. He yelled at me, saying that he couldn't focus on what he was doing because I was distracting him. Then he said that I would never be able to keep a husband if I keep on making noise. I was despondent. I thought it would happen.

Most vivid: "My father's scream and the vision of being alone in my old age."

We're sure by now you are getting the hang of how to do the headlines. This recollection is an interesting one, and you need to look at the theme presented. Here are our headlines:

- Girl fearful of making life dangerous for man.
- Clamorous child saddened by reaction to her loud behavior.
- Rowdy child miserable after contemplating consequences.
- Noisy child worried about future.

How are you doing? Is it becoming easier to develop headlines? We will present two more ERs from this woman before we provide the summary. You are encouraged to present your summations. Remember, you are deciphering a mystery based on the clues given. What clues have you received so far? What might you be able to say about this woman if she were to give you these recollections during the course of therapy?

ER 4. Age: 5

It was my first day in kindergarten, and I expected something thrilling to happen. I saw the teacher come into the room, and she gave us all a paintbrush and a cup of water. This was new to me. I had no idea what she had in mind. I wondered what it was all about. I sat there expecting something to happen. Nothing did. I did not know what to do. I sat there baffled. I still have no idea what she wanted me to do with the paintbrush. [That part is a report.]

Most vivid: "Sitting there with a paintbrush and not having a clue of what to do."

In looking at the theme of the recollection, what do you see? Here are our headlines. You can skip ahead if you want to solve this mystery on your own.

- Girl confused in novel situation.
- Child expects excitement, experiences confusion.
- Child's lack of questions allows bewilderment.
- New situation puzzles unquestioning child.

Here is the last recollection in the series.

ER 5. Age: 7

> My teacher told the class that Santa Claus didn't really exist. I was absolutely inconsolable for the rest of the day. I remember thinking that my Christmas wishes wouldn't be fulfilled. I got off the bus and walked home slowly thinking about what my teacher said. I talked to my mother, and she told me that my father and she were Santa Claus. She said it was they who bought the presents and candy for me. Things weren't the same after that.

What does this recollection tell you about the person? This is your last opportunity to formulate an overall picture. If you have been writing down your headlines, how does this recollection fit in? Here are our headlines:

- Girl's fantasies conflict with reality.
- Girl's reality isn't as good as her fantasy.
- Girl prefers fantasies to reality.
- Teacher and parents crush girl's fantasy.
- Girl unhappy after hearing truth.

Take a minute to formulate a summary from all of the headlines you have created. So far you have worn two hats, as a news reporter and as an investigative reporter. Now you have to be a newspaper editor. Take all of your headlines and boil them down to a concise paragraph about the person.

Our Summary

I need a man to protect me from the dangers of life because women are frightened in the face of these dangers. I want my wishes gratified and feel let down when they're not. I live in fantasy with "good spirits" and "bad spirits." The reality of the situation conflicts with my fantasies or anticipations. Novel situations leave me bewildered.

From this summary we want you to make a few guesses:

- How might she view men?
- How might she view women?

- Would she prefer a male or female therapist?
- How does she see the world? Is it hazardous?
- Do others have to fulfill her wishes?
- Do others have to act for her?
- Might she come in for depression?
- How might she react to stressors in her life?
- When might she leave people?
- Does she have mature, immature, neurotic, or psychotic defense mechanisms?
- How might she move in relation to people?
- How might she move in relation to situations?
- What is she fearful of?
- What does she desire?

These are all very good questions. You may not yet have answers, but they can be answered from the interpretation of ERs. Can you see how this would be very helpful in the assessment and therapeutic process?

Are you ready for another one?

Here we present a series of ERs and possible headlines for them. Remember, this Chapter is devoted to the Headline Method, and other Chapters will be dedicated to other methods. So if you are ready, put on your investigative reporter hat once again and prepare to probe another story. The following section's ERs are all from the same man.

The ERs of Tom

ER 1. Age: 5

> My brother and I went to this department store to steal a video game. While we were there, security guards came. We dropped the video game and scrambled out of the store and through a back alley. As we were running, I could see the guards right behind us telling us to stop. I thought the security guards were going to shoot me. We all kind of split up, and I was alone. I was petrified. When my brother came back for me, he found me hiding in a tree. When I was trying to get down off of the tree, I fell. My brother and I took off as fast as we could. We jumped a fence and crossed a river. I thought I heard a shot ring out. I tried to scurry across the river, but fell down. My brother was in front of me when we ran toward our house. I thought we would be safe there. As soon as he entered the house, I saw him run right back out again. My father was chasing after him. He was angry. My father

wanted to hit my brother because he hadn't mowed the lawn. While my father was chasing my brother, I told my mother what happened. She was sympathetic. She took me in and fed me.

Most vivid: "The security guards coming, and thinking that I heard a gun shot."

This is a much longer ER than usual. This example provides you another opportunity to delve into a situation where you must piece together the clues and construct from those clues some headlines and a summary of the person. We summarize long ERs like we would sum up the plot of a movie when speaking with our friends. However, headlines are even more concise. Here are our headlines:

- Boys escape one threatening situation, run into another.
- Boy sees world as dangerous place except for sympathetic women.
- Child experiences men as punishing, women as nurturers.
- Child's theft foiled as he narrowly escapes punishment.

ER 2. Age: 7

I was on my skateboard and hung onto a car. The driver started to go faster. I thought I was going to be kidnapped. I thought that I had to get off before I got killed. I let go of the car and hit a rock. I tumbled and slid across the pavement and scarred my chin. A friend saw me and told me that he was going to call his mother for help. Thought I did not want my mother to find out, so I told him not to call his mother. If my mom found out she, or my dad, would have punished me. But my friend told his mother anyway, and his mother came out to help me.

Most vivid: "The fear of kidnapping and fear of being run over by the car once I was on the street."

How can you use the theme, the details, and the emotion contained in the recollection to provide a concise headline? Remember, you can create your headline first — and we encourage you to do just that — so that you can become more skilled at constructing headlines without us. If you want some assistance or are just curious, here are our suggestions:

- Boy hurt when joyride backfires.
- Boy escapes a threatening situation. Runs into another.
- Boy learns that excitement can become dangerous.

- Child hurt during mischief, doesn't want his mother to find out.
- Child panics when excitement turns to danger.
- Child's fear overrides excitement.
- Child fears consequences of his actions.

ER 3. Age: 4

My mother and I were in an old, rotted barn. It started to hail. I mean really hail. My mother started getting worried and was afraid that the barn would fall down on top of us. My mom grabbed me and started praying. I thought we were going to die. My aunt showed up in her truck and brought us to her house. I was scared of the hail, and my mom only got me more panicky.

Most vivid: "My mother praying for God to spare us."

We are not going to give you any more hints at what areas to look at. But we will provide our headline suggestions:

- Boy sees women both as fearful and as saviors.
- Child protected and scared by mother.
- Boy sees world as dangerous, women as protectors.
- Child fears dangerous storm.
- Boy afraid of dangerous situations.
- Women save child in frightening conditions.
- Child fears danger, gets comfort from women.
- Child finds prayer useful, rescue better.

There are two more recollections to go. Are you getting a better idea of what Tom is like? Can you see the world with his eyes?

Here is another ER:

ER 4. Age: 5

My father's friend was walking down the sidewalk while I was sitting on the front step. He said, "Hi" and asked me what I was doing. I told him I wasn't doing anything and that I was bored. He said I could come with him if I wanted to. I said I wasn't sure if I could because my mom wasn't around. He told me it was OK to just go to the corner with him to put a letter in the mailbox. So when we got to the corner, we didn't find any mailboxes. I told him I would walk with him until we found some. He told me it might be a long walk until we found a mailbox. I told him I would go further. When we got to a light, we ran into a friend of his.

He told the man to take me back home. But I wanted to keep walking with him. But he took off, and I started crying my eyes out. And I kept crying as the guy I had been walking with left. His friend got sick and tired of my crying, and he took off too. He left me at the streetlight. A long while later, my mom showed up. She was really ticked off that I left the house. She started yelling at me and then realized I was crying so hard my body was shaking. Later on at home I felt really sick, and I had a high temperature. My mom was still upset with me and just put me to bed.

Most vivid: "The guy taking off."

You should have plenty of information by now as to how Tom sees himself, others, and the world around him, and what his ethical convictions are likely to be. We're sure that you are working on a summary in the back of your head. You've got one more recollection to go. But first, here are some headlines:

- Child follows man into hazardous situation, is yelled at by woman.
- Boy learns that men lead him into danger and that women rescue him.
- Boy alarmed by abandonment, rescued by mother.
- Boy's sickness averts punishment.
- Man leads child into peril and leaves boy to be rescued, punished.
- Adventure turns into loneliness as boy leaves home.

The next is the last recollection in the series. By now you should start seeing a repetition of themes. The repetition may indicate that you have enough information and that the elicitation of more ERs may not yield much additional information. Put on that investigative reporter hat one more time and examine this last ER.

ER 5. Age: 6

My father was putting in a fence around our house. He had asked me to help him take the wooden boards out of our minivan. I totally forgot. I was playing with some sand when my father came around the corner of the house and asked me where the boards were. I told him I forgot. He went to the minivan, got a board and hit me in my left leg. I had a scar there for years. [The last sentence is a report.]

Most vivid: "My father hitting me."

By now you are probably becoming very good at writing headlines. Here are some for comparison purposes:

- Boy learns that world is dangerous and that mistakes can last.
- Child learns that men are brutal toward him.
- Child injured by father over simple mistake.
- Forgetting one's responsibility can have hurtful repercussions.

Now that you have looked at all of Tom's ERs and have come up with a number of headlines, we need you to put on your editor's hat again and refine those headlines into a concise summation. You may want to ask yourself the following questions in the mystery of Tom:

What does Tom seek?
How does he get what he wants?
Do other people help him achieve his desires? If so, who?
What is the usual result of his pursuits?
How do other people treat him when times get tough?
How does he view men?
How does he view women?
How does he see the world?
How does he cope with life?

If you can answer these questions with information from the elicited ERs, then you are on your way to becoming proficient in the use of ERs as a projective test. (Remember: Accurate interpretation requires the supervision and guidance of a clinician who has reviewed hundreds, if not thousands, of ERs.)

The information gathered is helpful in assessment and therapy and provides much information that is relevant to all forms of social interaction, whether it is between the client and the therapist, or between the client and others.

Here is our summary:

I seek excitement, often by following other men, but it often leads to dangerous situations in which I am abandoned. Women may support and protect me from this dangerous world in which men and the environment can be brutal and unpredictable. I cannot trust men to support me as women do, as they often leave me in a worse position than I was in before I met them.

Now that you have this brief summary of Tom's ERs, what do you predict would happen if he had a male therapist? How about a female therapist? There are other elements that were not included in the summary but are equally useful. What might you guess they are and how would they guide your treatment plan had Tom been your client?

Life Style of a Famous Person

The simple example we started the Chapter with should have whetted your appetite for more complex interpretations. What is presented next is a series of recollections that will be interpreted step by step until we arrive at a logical conclusion.

We are now going to examine a number of ERs from a famous person. Using the Headline Method, we offer a number of possible headlines after each recollection that provide you with clues as to who this famous person is. You should be able to see the support of each headline within the recollection. Seeing the types of headlines provided develops your ability to perceive the clues listed and gives you an understanding of what to look for in recollections.

ER 1.

> My first conscious memory is of running. I was three years old, and my mother was driving us in a horse-drawn buggy holding my baby brother on her lap while a neighbor girl held me. The horse turned the corner leading to our house at high speed, and I tumbled on the ground. I must have been in shock, but I managed to get up and run after the buggy while my mother tried to make the horse stop.

What headlines would you write about this story? What do your headlines say about the person? We have come up with a few headlines of our own:

- Boy unseated, continues to run toward secure position.
- Child learns that women may drive too fast for him.
- Boy learns life is dangerous.
- Child sees that women may not hold on to him tightly enough.
- Boy sees that when life is hazardous, he can't rely on others.
- Child thrown from vehicle, scrambles after it.

How did you do? Do you see where we got the headlines? Can you see how symbolism and metaphor play an important role in understanding ERs?

ER 2.

> [My brother] complained of a headache. The family doctor thought it was flu and ordered him to bed. [His] condition deteriorated

quickly, and the doctor was unable to find the cause. He prescribed a series of tests, including a spinal tap. After that most painful of tests had been taken, I remember my father coming downstairs. It was the first time I had ever seen him cry. He said, "The doctors are afraid that the little darling is going to die."

Again, think about what headlines to write for this story. Give yourself a chance to practice this technique and then compare your headlines with ours:

- Boy learns that life is a struggle.
- Child sees that men can occasionally express emotions.
- Boy affected by effect of brother's illness on father.
- Life is fragile and unpredictable.

All of the headlines provided are supported in the recollection. None is speculation on the part of the interpreter. Remember that when you interpret ERs you must take care not to interpret what is not in the recollection.

ER 3.

Another time when my brother was about five years old, he showed the world that he was a man by getting some cigarettes out of our store and secretly smoking them back of the house. Unfortunately for him, one of our gossipy neighbors happened to see him, and she promptly informed my mother.

You know the drill. What headlines come into you mind? Compare them with ours:

- Women make it hard for a man to be a man.
- Women spoil men's fun.
- Boy learns not to trust others.
- Woman exposes boy who tries to get away with something.
- Boy learns women cannot be trusted.

What picture are you getting of the man who gave these recollections? You must be able to take these clues and assemble them to create an image of a client, or in this case a famous person.

ER 4.

There was one time when my brother was asked to be ring bearer at a wedding. I remember how my mother had to work with him for hours to get him to do it because he disliked walking with the flower girl.

Here are our possible headlines:

- Woman makes boy do something distasteful.
- Women twist men's arms.
- Boy forced to be on same level as girl.
- Boy hates walking along with women.

You are on your own for the rest of these recollections. If you made it this far in the book, you should be capable of understanding the image that is emerging from these ERs. We'll give you one more recollection to help you identify this man's life style and possibly his identity.

ER 5.

Two days before my brother's death, he called my mother into the room. He put his arms around her and said that he wanted to pray before he went to sleep. Then, with closed eyes, he repeated that age-old prayer which ends with those simple yet beautiful words: "If I should die before I awake, I pray Thee, Lord, my soul to take."

Here are our possible headlines:

- Boy finds solace in religion.
- Child expresses faith to mother on his deathbed.
- Brother sees life as fragile in brother's death.
- Boy sees dying brother take comfort in mother's arms.

Now, let's summarize these recollections and collect the clues that will allow us to properly guess who that famous person is. We'll go through each of the recollections, taking information from the headlines to solve the puzzle.

First, we know the person is male. And he is someone who is a runner. It is important for him to be in a higher position (as is evident in his placement on the horse-drawn buggy) and will scramble to regain that position if it is lost. So we can guess that this is an ambitious person.

In addition, he is someone who thinks that life is dangerous and unpredictable so he has to hold on tight in life and not rely on others because they won't keep him safe. Also, he is impressed with what "real men" do, whether it is to smoke or show emotion. He is certain that a man can be courageous, strong, and emotional, depending on the situation.

Another hint as to this person's identity is that fact that he is suspicious of other people. For him, it is terrible to have someone tattle on you, especially when you are trying to be a real man. He holds a lifelong grudge against the woman who snitched on his brother. So it may be safe to assume that this person is highly suspicious of others and is terribly hurt when they ruin his attempt to be a real man. Therefore, we may guess that this person would take precautions to guard against people having information that might get him into trouble.

This man distrusts women who do not hold on to him tightly, who tell on people. He does see women, and for that fact religion, as able to soothe men's worries. Religion is very important to this man as a place of guidance and solace.

Assembling all of the clues from the headlines, we are able to guess at who this person might be. If you have no clue who the person is, we'll give you some options. Is it Elvis Presley? Prince Charles? Richard Nixon? Donald Trump? Mick Jagger? Prime Minister Yitzhak Rabin? German Chancellor Gerhard Schroeder? Howard Hughes? Pope John Paul II? Supreme Court Justice Clarence Thomas? Take a guess and stick to it.

Think about what you know about each person in the list and which one may have given these ERs.

All of these men are famous in their own way. However, in using ERs we need to develop the skills necessary to not only interpret them correctly, but to be able to discount clues that do not fit the overall picture presented.

Are you ready for the answer?

These are the ERs of former president Richard Nixon.

Nixon's ERs appear in *Richard Nixon: The Memoirs of Richard Nixon* (1978). What immediately impresses is that Nixon is a runner. Even when he is unseated (ER 1), he continues to run. And in view of Watergate and subsequent events, it is even more interesting that his first ER relates to a fall. Even though he is in a state of shock, he continues to run. Think back to a statement he made after his California defeat, to the effect that the press would not have him to kick around any more. One might have inferred at the time that his defeat marked the end of his political career, but he subsequently did "get up and run" again. Certainly, Nixon strove toward political rehabilitation after his defeats.

Nixon portrays himself in the ERs as being impressed with what real men do and don't do. It is personally important for him to look big and for men to be "real" men. It is even permissible to break the rules to show the world that one is a real man (ER 3). He looks down on any woman who makes it difficult for a man to be real man (ER 3). A real man resists doing the equivalent of what women do (ER 4), but women can prevail over men to do what they (men) dislike doing. A man who submits to the persuasion of a woman pays a high price (ER 4). Men are characterized as wrongdoers although they are entitled to a certain amount of wrongdoing. In order to confirm their masculinity, their maturity, and their feeling that rules don't necessarily apply to them, they may even feel required to break some of the rules. Men are also capable of intense caring, sensitivity, and nurturance on special occasions (ER 2). Life is a struggle, and even a strong man can be moved to express tender feelings for those in trouble without diminishing his masculinity (ER 2, ER 5). Nixon showed his ability to show emotion when he cried in an interview with David Frost after his resignation.

Nixon's *Weltbild* depicts the world as tragic and unpredictably dangerous, as full of crises and even catastrophic. It is altogether fitting in terms of his ERs that he titled one of his books *Six Crises* (1962). One moment you have a place, and the next moment you can lose it (ER 1). One tries to get away with doing the wrong thing, and one is exposed (ER 3). One moment it's only a headache, and the next moment one can be facing death (ER 5). In his ERs he moves from crisis to crisis. There are so many things that must be overcome. Position is important to him, but he has it only transiently. Much of the time he must run after it.

Given all of these difficulties, a true man should be able to cope with courage, strength, and sensitivity. He has to struggle against the adversities of life, and if life throws him, he may suffer from temporary shock but he continues to run. Nixon is a driver and a striver, and he can't let anyone get ahead of him. He is particularly sensitive to being left behind. A sense of urgency is evident in Nixon's references to "high speed" (ER 1), "quickly" (ER 2), and "promptly" (ER 3). Perhaps this sense of urgency is predicated upon his belief that the specter of death hovers about and may strike quickly. Because life is full of crises, Nixon must be able to be independent and self-reliant. And because the world is so dangerously unpredictable, he is not especially trusting. He is very sensitive to betrayal (ER 3) and harbors grudges toward those who betray others and act as informers. The wrong done by informers outweighs the wrong done by the person informed upon. John Dean, it must be concluded, won no points with Nixon for his revelations.

Though men do wrong, women are wronger (ER 1, ER 3, and possibly ER 4). Women are likely to be untrustworthy, malicious, and gossipy, and they often give men a hard time. They do not take care of men as well as they should. They pressure men to yield and perform distasteful tasks. From Simpson's (1988) Simpson's Contemporary Quotations we learn that Martha Mitchell, the wife of John Mitchell (the director of the Committee to Re-Elect the President), allegedly called UPI White House reporter Helen Thomas and stated that "[Nixon] bleeds people. He draws every drop of blood and then drops them from a cliff. He'll blame any person he can put his foot on."

Nixon thought that women exercise inferior judgment and let situations get out of control. Nixon's secretary, Rose Mary Woods, stated that she made a mistake while transcribing a tape for Nixon. As she reached for a ringing phone, she accidentally pushed "Record" instead of "Stop" while her foot was on the operating treadle, effectively erasing what was on Nixon's tape.

Nixon felt that others may be on your side but impotent to do anything on your behalf (ER 2) or they may be out to get you. Therefore he thought he had to be vigilant in this untrustworthy world.

In the realm of ethical convictions, Nixon is very concerned with the issues of right and wrong, justice and injustice, but we may not infer that he always does the right thing. We know from his recollections that real men have the prerogative to do wrong. Nor can we infer that what he considers to be right or wrong necessarily coincides with the views of others. However, he is a report card giver, a person who knows how others should behave. When people do not behave in ways of which he approves, he can be righteous, rigidly moral, judgmental, and vengeful. He perceives himself as moral ("I'm not a crook!"). When he sees himself falling short of his standards, he may be subject to guilt feelings, although we must observe in this connection that he veered away from taking responsibility for the Watergate events. Nixon also displays a religious bent. He extends importance to prayer and finds it efficacious in bringing internal peace to a person. He indicates that prayer is better when one does not pray alone but in concert with others (ER 5). The newspapers made much of his invitation to Kissinger to kneel and pray with him in the White House during the waning days of his administration.

This Chapter provided sample analyses that illustrate how ERs provide information that is valuable for clinical use. Our walkthrough of the interpretation of those recollections was designed to give you a better understanding of the process of interpretation. People are very complex, and so too are their ERs. We must examine all aspects of ERs, being sure not to overlook the finer points.

This Chapter focused on the Headline Method of interpreting ERs. This method was presented first because of its ease of comprehension and use. Subsequent Chapters will describe other interpretation methods and the power of ERs in understanding the client-therapist relationship, their use in marital therapy, and their influence in career guidance and other areas.

We hope that you have found this first foray into ER interpretation easy to understand and applicable to your vocational and personal interests.

Early recollections are valuable in a number of situations and can be comprehended with some supervised practice.

Summary

Mosak devised the Headline Method to clarify the teaching of holistic interpretation of ERs. When writing a headline, look at the major theme of the ER and add a dash of emotion but keep it true to the event.

Summarize lengthy ERs in a manner similar to summarizing a movie. Accurate interpretation requires the supervision and guidance of a clinician who has reviewed hundreds, if not thousands, of ERs.

4

The Typological Approach

Mastering the art of interpreting ERs is fraught with difficulties. When people first try to interpret ERs, they often "divide and conquer." That is, they take a client's recollection and try to break it down into easily understood parts. Then they interpret those parts, put them together, and attempt to gain the meaning of the entire recollection. This is similar to what Freud (1900/1950) did in dream interpretation, and those trained in non-Adlerian psychology may be especially tempted to do this.

Gestalt psychology (Köhler, 1929) at the turn of the century pointed out the disadvantages of a fragmented approach when it proposed the novel idea that the whole was greater than the sum of its parts. (Just as a movie is more than its individual frames of film.) The Typological Approach emphasizes the importance of holism and suggests that the ERs must be examined as a whole instead of being broken into smaller parts.

Ready for a pop quiz to explain what we're driving at? We'll give you an example. Let's say we are thinking of a sentence that has meaning and contains all of the following letters:

ABCDEFGHIJKLMNOPQRSTUVWXYZ

Tell us that sentence. Take your time and think about the one sentence that we have in mind. (Hint: Some letters are used more frequently than others.)

Perhaps you are thinking to yourself that anything can be made with those parts; it's the entire alphabet! True, but we are thinking of a real sentence with meaning. You are to take those parts and reconstitute not just any sentence, but the specific sentence that we created from those letters. Can you do it? (Besides, if anything can be made with parts of the alphabet, then we can make anything from parts of a recollection. This may, and probably will, lead to incorrect interpretations.)

This example should demonstrate to you that you cannot interpret ERs by parts, either. You have to look at the whole memory to get its meaning. Furthermore, you do not know what parts are more important. In this alphabet example, there are certain letters that are used more than once.

This is not a trick question; there is a solution to our question. Have you thought of it? Write it down and get ready for the answer.

Here is the sentence:

"The quick brown fox jumps over the lazy dog."

If you did not think of that specific sentence, how comfortable can you be in looking at ERs in parts?

What do you see when you look at that sentence? The answer contains every letter of the alphabet. However, when we broke this sentence down into the individual letters that constitute it, and gave you those letters, you were probably unable to reconstruct from those parts the original sentence with its intended meaning. The pitfall here, as with ERs, is that you have the whole alphabet to choose from and would therefore be able to construct whatever sentence (or interpretation in the case of ERs) you wanted!

Here is another example. Three lines like those below may be patterned into many different wholes:

These three simple lines can be made into the shapes below and many others.

and the shapes that are supposed to be here.

Each of the forms above contains the identical three elements. Their patterning into a whole transforms them into something other than their individual parts. This gives them meaning, an essence, that does not exist in their individual elements.

People often break down the sentences of an ER and interpret them one at a time in sequential order, hoping to come up with a coherent overall interpretation from several smaller interpretations. However, as in the above example, it does not work that way. The recollection must be examined in its whole, with parts supporting the entire meaning. Looking only at the parts would create a situation like looking at the Mona Lisa one color at a time, then attempting to explain the whole painting to someone!

In contrast to the early Gestalt psychologists, we hold that the whole is not only *more* than the sum is its parts, it is *different from* the sum of its parts.

First Attempts

Tenacity is of vital importance in interpreting ERs. Often people will become intimidated and discouraged by the task. Very much like every other skill in life, interpreting ERs is a learned skill that requires training, practice, and supervision to be executed correctly.

Capturing the essence or the central theme (Mosak, 1968) of a recollection or series of recollections is a complex task. Some people writing and teaching in this field take the task altogether too lightly when they invite you who are new to interpretations to "get your feet wet" (Eckstein, Baruth, & Mahrer, 1975). Such suggestions invite those who are untrained and unsupervised to violate the first rule taught to medical students, *primum non nocere* ("Above all, do no harm").

As with the Rorschach and other complicated projective tests, genuine understanding of the meaning of ERs occurs as a result of an evolving insight based upon the interpretation of hundreds of recollections and supervisory comments by one who has interpreted thousands of recollections.

The patient may have formed inaccurate interpretations with respect to self and life. These are called "basic mistakes": Overgeneralizations, exaggerations, misperceptions, faulty values, and similar phenomena (Dreikurs, 1935/1953; Mosak, 1979a). Here are a few examples of basic mistakes: "All men are rude," "Life is always dangerous," "I'm just a student," "I have to be first at all costs," "I never get a break," and "I have to please everyone."

Ellis's (1962) concept of irrational ideas is comparable to basic mistakes in that irrational ideas are unconscious assumptions from our culture and upbringing that influence our behavior and are often only noticed or scrutinized in therapy or during times of considerable cognitive dissonance. Ellis outlines a number of illogical and irrational ideas that he believes lead to "widespread neurosis." He states that there are a great many senseless ideas that are perpetuated in society, family, and institutions — ideas that are blindly accepted and assumed to be "good" with little or no scrutiny. Among these are:

"Irrational Idea No. 1: *The idea that it is a dire necessity for an adult human being to be loved or approved by virtually every significant other person in his community*" (p. 61).

"Irrational Idea No. 2: *The idea that one should be thoroughly competent, adequate, and achieving in all possible respects if one is to consider oneself worthwhile*" (p. 63).

"Irrational Idea No. 3: *The idea that certain people are bad, wicked, or villainous and that they should be severely blamed and punished for their villainy*" (p. 65).

"Irrational Idea No. 4: *The idea that it is awful and catastrophic when things are not the way one would very much like them to be*" (p. 69).

"Irrational Idea No. 5: *The idea that human unhappiness is externally caused and that people have little or no ability to control their sorrows and disturbances*" (p. 72).

"Irrational Idea No. 6: *The idea that if something is or may be dangerous or fearsome one should be terribly concerned about it and should keep dwelling on the possibility of its occurring*" (p. 75).

Do any of these "irrational ideas" sound familiar to you, or like "common sense"? These types of ideas may be common and may be easily projected onto our clients' recollections if we fail to interpret ERs accurately.

In addition, those who are seeking help and providing their ERs may be assigned a pathology that they do not possess. Or they may be understood as having a life style that does not parallel the requirements of reality. Similarly, basic mistakes that they do possess may be completely overlooked. This approach could dishearten and alarm clients who are already discouraged. Instead of receiving help from a clinician, they may be taken on a wild-goose chase and compelled to discuss issues that are not relevant to their life styles. The welfare of those seeking help is primary. Unqualified individuals interpreting ERs, or any other test without proper training, are behaving irresponsibly and unethically (American Psychological Association [APA], 2002).

Typologies

Please take a minute and think about the people whom you know that are most like you. In looking over every area of thinking and behavior, are they exactly like you? Is *anyone* exactly like you? Probably not, and this is what you need to remember when working with typologies. We are all individuals and inherently distinct from one another. We think and act differently; consequently, people do not exist in pure types and cannot be neatly categorized. Furthermore, as Menninger (1973) wrote:

> We once thought such labeling would help us better understand the nature of peculiar behavior. Perhaps it did. But it led to a kind of treatment by pigeonholing and social stratification which hurt many of our patients irrevocably. It often destroys all hope in the patient and loved ones. (p. 171)

Actually, typology runs counter to the assumptions of Adlerian psychology, which focuses on individual uniqueness, and typologies should be considered only a heuristic device (Adler, 1935a; Mosak, 1979b). Types are useful for giving us a general picture of something. For example, if someone says "car" or "house," we have a general idea in our head that allows for many variations in reality.

The type designation, as employed here, refers to the recollection rather than to the person. Thus, a "victim" type may start with a "getting"-type ER and follow it with several victim recollections. It would be a mistake to designate the person as having a "getting typology." We can characterize the victim world as we might suspect it to be, and include those who consider themselves the victim of others' carelessness or malice, and/or being the victims of themselves as they may trip themselves up (e.g., leaving the stove on, not getting their paperwork in on time). As for the getting type, we are familiar with the type of person who is always looking to get something, either tangible or intangible. They equate their worth with how much they can get. As a matter of fact, these getting types often have recollections of Christmas, birthday parties, or similar occasions when they received something. (It may help to think of the poverty-stricken 20-year-old woman who marries the 98-year-old multimillionaire as likely having getting-type ERs. Provided, of course, she is after the money and not the man.)

One may locate a category with this method, but a fuller understanding of probable behavior, attitudes, and outcomes requires knowledge of the various probabilities within types. Some probable attitudes and behaviors appear in the Adlerian literature (Ashby, 1996; Boldt & Mosak, 1997; Gregerson & Nelson, 1998; Hart, 1977; Mosak, 1959, 1968, 1970; Peven, 1973).

Those working with Adlerian theory have presented many schemes for typing people. In this regard a note of caution is appropriate. As Adler (1935a) wrote:

> In my experience I have found that each individual has a differ-
> ent meaning of, and attitude toward, what constitutes success.
> Therefore a human being cannot be typified or classified.
> I believe it is because of the parsimony of language that many
> scientists have come to mistaken conclusions — believing in
> types, entities, racial qualities, etc. Individual Psychology recog-
> nizes, with other psychologies, that each individual must be
> studied in the light of his own peculiar development. (p. 6)

Adler's earliest typology, presented in 1927, consisted of a translation of Hippocrates's humoral theory into Adlerian language (Adler, 1927/1998). In 1935, Adler constructed another type theory that described the socially useful type, those who cooperate and act, and three types who are not prepared for cooperation. Adler's (1956) types could be classified by the degree of activity (form of movement) and by the degree of social interest. Adler described a "ruling" type of individual who has a low level of social interest and either a high or low degree of activity. In a high active state and low social interest state, the ruling type may act tyrannically, sadisti-cally, or be a delinquently. (Think of a classroom bully.) In the low active state, this type may become addicted to something or someone, or the person may become suicidal. (The addiction could be to attention from the teacher, e.g., Picture a clingy child.) The "avoiding" type has a low degree of social interest and a low degree of activity. (The loner, if you will.) These types of individuals may be passive and depressive. The last type, the "getting" type, also may have a low degree of social interest and a low degree of activity. These individuals may become manipulators through charm or intimidation. (Consider the little prince or princess who wants everything presented on a silver platter.)

The latter three types are more interested in protecting their self-esteem than in meeting the life tasks in a task-oriented fashion.

Dreikurs (1947) proposed a type-like theory in his description of the goals of children's misbehavior. Four types of children's misbehavior are identified in Dreikurs' scheme: "attention getting," "power seeking," "revenge taking," and "displaying inadequacy." This classification was par-tially bidimensional in that much misbehavior could also be described as "active" or "passive" and "constructive" or "destructive" (Dreikurs, 1948). In this respect Dreikurs's view follows that of Adler, whose typing was also partially bidimensional. Adler also proposed a theory of learning types, which Way (1962) describes:

> Children, for instance, do not all learn by the same process, but
> tend to make preponderant use of one or other of their sense

organs. Teachers who employ only the voice will receive a greater response from those members of the class who are auditory types. But those others will be put at a disadvantage who are visual types and who prefer to memorize from the printed page. There are many children who feel a sense of insecurity unless they are able to see a word before having to spell it, while others prefer to have the word repeated and to learn it by ear. Likewise motor types learn best by doing and by practical repetition and illustration. (p. 254)

Kefir (1971) proposed a categorizing of people based upon their life style priorities. She named these types the "pleasers," "superiors," "comforters," and "controllers." Kefir's system and even her terminology appear to be an abbreviated form of Mosak and Shulman's (1961) typing, which was developed in the1950s.

Kefir and Corsini (1974) subsequently published a typology that is expressed in terms of dispositional sets following a scheme similar to that developed by Karen Horney (1950). Horney believed that neurotic needs could be expressed in terms of "moving away from people," "moving toward people," and "moving against people." Normal behavior exhibits some degree of conflict among these three broad categories of needs. But for the most part, some degree of balance and integration exists. Neurotic behavior is characterized by more unidimensionality that emphasizes rigid movement toward one of the three dispositional sets. Kefir and Corsini termed their sets "accord," "conflict," "evasion," and "neutral." Accord, conflict, and evasion are self-explanatory. Neutral would be described by Horney as well adjusted with the flexibility of being able to move in the other three directions as befitted the occasion. This system avoids the tendency of some who use typologies to pigeonhole individuals.

Mosak (1959) attempted to teach the value of patterning in the conceptualization of life styles through his publication on the getting type. Brief descriptions by Mosak of 14 life style types appear in Nikelly's (1971) book. Several of Mosak's students have contributed vignettes of types (e.g., Hart, 1977; Kopp, 1986; Peven, 1973).

That's enough history for now. What follows is the "meat and potatoes" of the Chapter, the types which we shall use. Mosak's type theory (1971, 1979b) elaborated on different types that are briefly reviewed here with examples of corresponding ERs. The following list of types cannot be considered exhaustive, but it does represent many of the major types encountered in clinical practice. Because type descriptions exist elsewhere, we will merely illustrate for each type some typical recollections given by people in that category. The names of the types clearly reflect the essence of the style and are therefore easy to remember. For the sake of brevity, we will refrain from including the most vivid part of the recollections.

The Getter

People with the getting style will frequently give recollections in which they get something. The something may be material (such as toys, gifts, money, etc.) or nonmaterial (such as attention, recognition, nurturance, applause, and service). Those who like to be the center of attention, or stars, may inform us of their goal through ERs. Birthday and Christmas recollections frequently appear with these getting types.

Here are some examples:

ER 1.

> I remember one Christmas morning when I was five. I got this wind-up wooden truck. I was ecstatic!

ER 2.

> My aunt bought me this purple dress for my sixth birthday and put it on me. Everyone at the shopping mall commented on how beautiful I was. A man from the local paper was there and took my picture and put me on the front page!

ER 3.

> I remember my first music recital in first grade. People were applauding for me. A woman came up afterwards and said I was another Yo Yo Ma. I was on cloud nine.

The getting type resists having something, either material or non-material, taken from them. They often feel that life is unfair when they are denied or when someone gets more than they do (Mosak, 1959).

ER 4.

> It was winter break in first grade, and my cousin and I were play-ing in my front yard. He started walking away with my sled, and I got a snowball with a lot of ice in it and chucked it at him, and hit him right in the back of the head. He started crying like a big baby.

ER 5. Age: 5

> It was Hanukkah (a Jewish holiday in which children receive gifts or "Hanukkah gelt [money]"), and my brother and I were opening presents. My brother got this cool video game, and I only got school clothes. I was so upset. I thought I was going to get something better.

These are some examples of ERs of those with a getting style. With supervised practice you'll be able to identify these types quickly and easily.

The Controller

The controlling type's ERs show "how sweet it is" when he or she and/or life are under control and how catastrophic life can be when he or she and/or life are not under control. Look at the examples below and reflect on whether the person is either in control or losing control.

ER 1.

> It was summer vacation before second grade, and I was on a plane with my parents. We were going to Disneyland, and I was looking up at the fluffy white clouds. All of a sudden the plane dropped. I felt this sinking feeling in my stomach. All I could do was clutch the arms of the seat. I thought I should be in the cockpit and flying the plane. I thought I was going to die. I didn't show people how scared I was.

This recollection is about someone who is able to keep emotions in control even when life deprives him of control. Though it appears to be a recollection from a feeling avoider; the overall recollection is about keeping everything, including emotions, in control.

ER 2.

> I remember being in first grade, and I dislocated my knee trying to get off of a bus. I was in agony. The pain was excruciating! They stopped the bus and everyone got off. I looked at my knee, and pushed the kneecap back into place. I can't describe the relief. It was great. The ambulance people came, and I told them I fixed it. They were amazed.

Clearly, the client is in control in this one. By taking control of a very unpleasant situation, the client felt better. Mark this one as a controlling-type ER.

ER 3.

> I was six. It was lightning and thundering outside. I was terrified. I was able to count the seconds between the lightning and thunder. I remember in class the teacher said that if the number got bigger, and it was, the storm is moving away. I calmed myself down.

What is happening in this ER? Through focusing on what the teacher said and counting, the client was able to focus and take control of a feeling of terror.

ER 4.

> I was in first grade, and I remember waiting with my parents to see Santa Claus. I had to go to the bathroom, and I couldn't hold it. I ended up peeing my pants in front of everyone there, and then I had to walk back through the line, past every kid and all of the parents, with pants that were positively saturated. I was thoroughly humiliated.

Evidently, this person was not in control. And not being in control for this client is embarrassing. Controlling types often have ERs with being put under anesthesia, or driving a vehicle (toy or actual), or other events in which they lose or gain control.

The Driver

The driving type can more frequently be identified through reports than through recollections. Illustrative of these reports are statements such as: "Even when I was very young, I had many jobs," "People always said of me that I was always busy," and "I never sat still for a minute." In order to have a driving style one generally must be engaged in sequential activities, and a single recollection generally fails to reflect such multiple activities. However, it may be demonstrated in a single recollection. For example, driving types reveal themselves in an ER in which they run something, as in ER 1 below, or pretend to, as in ER 2.

ER 1.

> I had this remote control car. I remember sitting on the front step
> and running the car up and down the driveway. The sun was shin-
> ing on me. I was happy, enjoying myself.

ER 2.

> I remember sitting on my father's snowmobile pretending I was
> driving it. I felt super!

The aspect of this life style that is not readily seen nor understood by
those with a driving style is the fear that one may be "nothing." The overt,
overly ambitious behavior contradicts the person's fear (Mosak, 1971,
p. 78). Those with a driving style may give recollections in which they
express both smallness and the compensatory behavior. Have you ever
seen people who were so busy that they always seem to have several
projects going at once or seldom rested? Have you ever asked them to take
a break and they immediate reject your suggestion? Then you have probably met a driving type.

ER 3. Age: 8

> I remember being in my uncle's car, and he let me sit behind the
> wheel while he drove. I held the steering wheel with both hands.
> I knew I wasn't actually driving the car, but I still felt like a
> grown-up.

This recollection clearly shows the difference between the controller
and the driver. The controller would either be doing the driving and feel
big doing it or not doing the driving and feeling powerless. The driver here
feels big even though he is not doing the driving.

ER 4.

> I was in kindergarten, and I remember getting the most number
> of stickers for completed tasks. I was so proud of my accomplish-
> ment when the teacher read out the numbers to the entire class. I
> remember flexing my muscles and looking around the room.

Here the client is telling us that he is driven and thrives on the superiority
of his accomplishment.

The Person Who Must Be Right

People who believe that they must be right in order to have a place have ERs that center on (1) rewards, intrinsic or extrinsic, for being or doing right; (2) how right they are; (3) how wrong others are; and (4) the negative consequences or bad feelings (especially guilt feelings) that accrue when one is or does wrong. Do you get the feeling that you are talking to a wall when you talk to people with this type of behavior? These are the types of people you most likely hate getting into an argument with because they refuse to acknowledge when they are wrong or even that you may be right.

ER 1. Age: 7

> The teacher came back into the room, and we had all been joking around. She demanded to know who had been talking. I was the only one to admit it. All the other kids had to write, "I will not talk when the teacher leaves the room," or something like that 500 times, but I was excused.

Here the client demonstrates that "honesty is the best policy" and is rewarded for being truthful. The client was the only person to do "the right thing." According to the client, those who don't do the right thing are punished. But you may be saying, "Hey, wasn't the client 'joking around' too?" The client also demonstrates that you can do wrong as long as you come clean about your "sins"; right makes might because the client answered the teacher truthfully.

In the next recollection the client is elevated above the rest solely because of personal integrity.

ER 2. Age: 8

> A bunch of us after school went into a convenience store. Nobody had any money, and I just went to look around, but the other kids started stealing candy and magazines. I told them they better stop and that I wouldn't steal anything because it was wrong. They laughed at me! I walked out of the store because I didn't want to be around those kids. As I was leaving, a cop car pulled up, and the officer waited in his car. When my classmates came out, he told them to stop and asked them for the receipt for the things they had. Well, they didn't have one because they stole everything. Boy, did they get in trouble, but good!

Again we have an ER that illustrates how the client is better than the others because she acted virtuously. According to the client, doing the right thing allows you to stay out of trouble.

ER 3. Age: 7

> I remember being in the kitchen with my mother and brother. She was feeding him applesauce, but he didn't like it, and he was putting up a real stink! He was banging his spoon on his bowl, screaming, and flailing his arms. When he spit it out and onto the floor, my mother picked it up and made him eat it! I was disgusted by it.

After you get past the visual image that may pop into your head, you realize that the client is telling you, symbolically, that if you don't behave properly, you may have to "eat" your mistakes.

ER 4. Age: 9

> I did something wrong in class. The teacher sent me to the principal who asked my mother to come in. I felt ashamed.

This recollection is straightforward, and by now you can figure out this recollection without our help. Good work!

Although we discuss ERs and vocations in a later Chapter, this type is ripe for speculating on careers that might be a good match, such as police officer, clergy, quality-control engineer, and judge.

The Person Who Must Be Superior

Those who have to be superior may express their goal by having to be first, best, unique, or a star. Recollections will reflect this goal or the "tragedies" ensuing when the goal is not achieved.

ER 1. Age: 8

> I got a go-kart for my birthday. The kids from the whole neighborhood gathered around me to see it. They all admired it. I was so proud that I was the only one to have a go-kart.

Though you might be tempted to label this an ER of a getter, getting is not the main theme. The getting leads to the overall theme, being admired for being unique. We could find out the true meaning of the recollection only by asking the client for the most vivid part of the recollection, which was being "the *only one* to have a go-kart." Without hearing what the client sees as the most vivid part, we are prone to misinterpreting his or her communication.

ER 2. Age: 8

> One time we had a math competition among all of the second-grade classes. It took almost all day, and at the end there were two of us left. We did so well that the teachers had to get a mathematics book from the third-grade teacher to quiz us. The other boy missed. The teacher gave me a tough math problem. She thought that I'd miss it, but I didn't, and I won the competition.

What is the client telling you in this recollection? The client is the best in math, superior to all of the other students. So superior, in fact, that a math book from one grade above the client had to be used to "separate the wheat from the chaff."

ER 3. Age: 9

> I had been the best runner in my class until this new boy came. We had a race in gym, and I came in second for the first time ever. I felt like I couldn't go back to gym again.

Here we see just how painful it is for the client to no longer be the best. The client values being superior, and being second-best is no longer a position of superiority. He may feel that he has to be the best or he is nothing. Think of the quotes of Vince Lombardi, who put so much emphasis on winning.

Early recollections of being both right and unique are particularly obvious in the superior typology as can be seen in the following ER.

ER 4. Age: 7

> One day the teacher asked the class if anyone knew where Big Ben was located. I answered "London, England." The teacher asked where I'd learned that. I was proud of it.

Occasionally some people reflect their concern with masculine superiority through their ERs.

ER 5. Age: 9

> This one day, another boy from down the street and I were talking about cars. His father had an eight-cylinder Ford Mustang

convertible, and my father had a four-cylinder beige station wagon. I thought the Mustang was more masculine.

Clients who give recollections like those listed above are telling you that they need to be superior. Furthermore, this recollection shows that the client thrives on masculine superiority. In Adlerian terms, this client has a "masculine protest," roughly translated into the notion that everything masculine is powerful and superior.

ER 6. Age: 8

> I was in a computer class at school. The boy next to me said he had an Apple Macintosh. I told him I had a Windows PC at home. I envied him; I knew the Apple Macintosh was a much better computer. I told him that there were more Windows computers in the world so they must be better, but I knew that was no argument. The Macs were just better, that's all. I felt insignificant.

Here we see that when the client does not have the best, he feels terribly inferior. Those feelings of inferiority are very difficult to bear. When the client tried to argue his way out of the inferior position, it did not work, and he felt even worse for he knows his position relative to others.

The Pleaser

Now this title appears to be self-explanatory: these people want to please. But it goes beyond that, really. They *have* to please, and they *have* to please *everyone*. Their efforts to please are also a way to keep things in control. For if you are pleased, then you will not distance yourself from them. We have all tried to please someone at some point or another. When we please, we often do not take a stand for fear of offending, or disappointing, or distancing someone. Have you seen or overheard a couple on their first date? ("Where do you want to go?" "Anywhere is fine with me. Where do you want to go?" "I don't know, where do you want to go?") Both persons are so flexible that it takes them an hour to agree on a place to go or a movie to see! The pleasing types maintain this kind of behavior to the nth degree and are dependent upon the approval of others. They bask in others' approval and shrivel when they fail to please or when they meet with disapproval.

ER 1. Age: 9

> I remember mowing the lawn before my dad got home from work one day. He was so shocked that I had the initiative to mow the

lawn without being asked. Well, of course, I knew it would make him happy (and less grumpy after work). He said, "I'm so proud of my son!" It was wonderful.

ER 2.

I was in first grade, and I brought home my report card, and it was bad, really bad. And my mother said, "Your father and I are so disappointed in you." I couldn't have felt worse.

We are all familiar with pleasers. If you ask them what they want to do, they'll say, "Whatever you want." Sometimes they are terribly frustrating to deal with, as they don't give you any feedback to go on. They try to please everyone and may overextend themselves by doing just that. Pleasers can also have a controlling element. That is, people may please in order to control the situation and keep things calm.

The "Aginner"

People who give recollections that fit in this category are typically seen as oppositional: as overt and covert rebels. They are not necessarily "bad guys." They may be idealistic fighters for principle, opposers of the status quo and of conventional wisdom. Jesus, Socrates, and Gandhi may have fallen into this group.

ER 1. Age: 4

My mother told me to eat my vegetables. I wouldn't and didn't.

Evidently people who give recollections similar to this one like to dig in their heels and hold their ground. However, their "ground" may be defined in relation to whomever they are resisting. They have been known to cut off their noses to spite their faces.

ER 2. Age: 7

My mother didn't like me eating between meals because I was so overweight. One evening before I went to bed, I sneaked some cookies under my pillow. When I turned the light off, I took them out and ate them. I felt like I got away with something, but I also felt guilty and afraid of being caught.

This recollection illustrates that one can be an aginner and be afraid of consequences. Mosak (1987) elaborates on the many purposes of guilt feelings: to avoid punishment, to avoid responsibility, to hide one's competitive urge, to make oneself the center of attention, to temper one's enjoyment of a temptation, to get away from social engagement, to gain sympathy, and so on.

As for the guilt feeling displayed in this ER, we'll just define that as good intentions the client didn't really have, because if the good intentions did exist, the cookies would never have been under the pillow!

You must remember that those who are oppositional may be against the bad as well as the good.

ER 3. Age: 9

> Some kids were picking on this little kid in the playground, and I told them they had better stop.

Here we see a demonstration of being against others that is pro-social. The majority is picking on one child. The client goes against the majority, and as a side effect, acts in defense of the "little kid."

The Victim

We are all familiar with "victims." They are the people who tell you how life treats them poorly or how they inadvertently beat themselves up. They may go out of their way to tell you just how unfair life is for them. You may get the feeling that these people are running after their slaps in the face.

Victims can be subgrouped into "schlemiels" and "schlemazels." According to an old joke (Rosten, 1968), the schlemiel is the New York waiter who spills hot soup into the lap of the schlemazel. One victimizes himself; the other victimizes others. Both have bad luck.

ER 1.

> I was in first grade. I remember I was enjoying the beautiful weather outside, looking up at the fluffy white clouds and tripping over a garden rake and breaking my nose.

ER 2. Age: 8

> I was watching this ball game. The batter swung and threw the bat. It hit me in the head. I saw stars.

Both of these ERs evoke a feeling of disaster-prone individuals. In recollections like the first one, the people are victims of themselves. In recollections like the second one, others victimize them. They portray themselves as cursed or doomed and focus on all of the negative things that happen in their lives. For example, they may say something like, "I have to drive 10 miles to pick up my kids from their grandmother's house" without being thankful that they have children or someone to watch them. Or these types of people put themselves in situations in which they are highly likely to be taken advantage of or mistreated. For example, "I keep letting my good-for-nothing brother borrow my car, and he always leaves it with an empty tank." It sounds like this person is allowing that bad situation to continue without any consequence to the good-for-nothing brother.

The Martyr

It is important to remember the difference between a victim and a martyr. They are often confused. The martyr dies for a cause or principle. The victim just dies. If the following ER,

> Some kids were picking on this little kid in the playground, and I told them they had better stop.

had ended with *"They ganged up and beat the living daylights out of me,"* it could have been the recollection of a martyr rather than a custodian of the right or an aginner. Aginners, incidentally, often find or even seek martyrdom.

ER 1. Age: 7

> It was during the 1992 presidential election campaign. One day when I came to school, these kids with a "Bill Clinton for President" sign asked me whether I was for Bush or Clinton. When I said "Bush," they beat me up.

Here we see the client standing up for a political position in the face of those with an opposing viewpoint and incurring a personal loss for it.

The Baby

A client may tell you that he or she is the "baby" of the family. It is important to note that one does not have to be the youngest child to be the baby. A person could be the first-born and still be the baby. This is because it is the *psychological position* in the family and not the birth order that determines whether or not one is the baby of the family. For example, the person may merely have been babied more than his or her siblings. Their ERs focus on smallness, ineptitude, immaturity, the requirement of assistance, nurturance, and elevation.

ER 1. Age: 5

> It was right before kindergarten began. I remember telling my mother that I wanted to be put in the high chair and given a bottle with milk in it. She picked me up, I was very small, and put me in the chair. She warmed up the milk and put it in the bottle. I felt very comfortable.

Though you may think this is similar to the recollections of a controlling type because the client is able to exert control over another person, you need to look at the overall theme. The client is communicating a preference for being treated as immature and in need of assistance.

Here are two examples given by one man:

ER 2. Age: 9

> I remember asking my father if he would put me on his lap and read the comics to me like when he did when I was younger. Well no sooner after I said it he scooped me up and put me on his lap. He read the comics to me and used the funny voices like he used to when I was younger. I felt so loved.

ER 3. Age: 3

> I awoke from my nap, and I called for my mother to lift me out of the crib. She quickly came over and picked me up.

For this client, it feels good to be the baby!

Those who have these baby-type ERs prefer to be waited on and expect others to cater to their needs and wants. Perhaps you know of a person who expects you to wait on him or her hand and foot and puts up a protest when asked to initiate some action for his or her own benefit (let alone anyone else's benefit).

The Inadequate Person

In the U.S. Air Force, an aviation cadet was labeled a "dodo," which was defined as "a large, heavy, awkward, inept, silly, non-flying bird, now extinct, of which I am a prime example." The inadequate person's ERs are those of a dodo.

ER 1. Age: 8

> One day, when I got into my class a bunch of kids were laughing at me. I had no clue as to what was so funny. My teacher came over and told me to go to the bathroom and to put my shirt on correctly. It was on backwards! I felt like such an idiot, I couldn't even put my shirt on right!

ER 2. Age: 9

> My mother asked me to walk out to the mailbox and pick up the mail. I walked out to the mailbox and came back. She asked me where the mail was. I felt like an idiot when I told her I forgot to get it. I just walked there and back. What made it worse was that my little brother, who was about 4, ran out to the mailbox and got the mail when he saw that I didn't pick it up.

ER 3. Age: 6

> I remember seeing a video game my mother put on a high shelf. I reached and reached, but I could not reach it no matter how hard I tried.

All the above recollections contain images of people who are inept and powerless. What does that tell you as a clinician? How would you treat these types of people? What might you be on guard about when giving homework or implementing an intervention?

The Confuser

The confuser confuses life and is confused by life.

ER 1.

> The first day in school. My mother took me into the kindergarten and left me. I didn't know what I was supposed to do, so I cried.

ER 2. Age: 6

> It was during an assembly at school. The teacher told me to stand in this one spot for a present. I couldn't wait to see what it was. I stood there for the entire assembly. It turned out that she wanted me to stand there for the present and then follow the rest of the class to our row of seats.

Clients who give these types of ERs are telling you that they don't comprehend the world around them. Often they will tell you that they are, or were, perplexed by a situation because they "just didn't know what to do." What might that tell you about their social interactions and effectiveness in life?

When people say they are confused, they feel as though they cannot be blamed for the mistakes they make. After all, how could you possibly be upset at someone who breaks the rules when they didn't understand the rules? Being confused can be a socially acceptable way of doing what you want without paying the price. Imagine, if you will, that a police officer pulls someone over for speeding, and the person says, "Gee officer, I wasn't clear on what the speed limit was (so how could you possibly hold me guilty for speeding)?" In addition, if someone is confused about something, say directions, aren't others put into their service by spelling out exact directions or giving them a ride? What other purposes might there be in being "confused"?

Allow us to mention a related occurrence, absent-mindedness. Perhaps a favorite of the academics of the world, being absent-minded carries two perks. First, it allows you to get away with (usually) not doing some requirement. ("Did you hand in your paperwork?" "No, gosh, I'm just so absent-minded! I'll hand it in next week.")

Second, answer the following question. Who is usually associated with being absent-minded? You remember that Disney classic *The Absent-minded Professor*, don't you? Yes, being absent-minded suggests erudition, doesn't it? All the more reason the absent-minded expect to be given some leeway: they must be working on something important and intellectual. It's not as if they are wasting their time like we commoners are. Rather, they are in deep thought, and it is quite natural to overlook some piddling little details like paperwork or taking our the garbage. Why don't we just do that for them, so we don't disturb their oh-so-important work.

The Feeling Avoider

Whatever happens, feeling avoiders rarely connect a feeling with it. Sometimes they adopt an observer's stance. Often they operate like automata or computers. Occasionally they permit life to herd them about without any feeling responses on their part.

ER 1. Age: 8

My parents took me to see the space shuttle takeoff. I just observed it.

[Feeling?] Oh, I really didn't have any feelings about it.

ER 2. Age: 7

> My teacher divided the class into reading groups. I was in the low-
> est reading group. I had no particular feelings about it.

Take a moment to think about the relationship between emotions and movement. When people are fearful, they may move away from something. When people are excited, they may move toward something. Adler (1927/1998) described these as disjunctive and conjunctive emotions, respectively. However, when people are devoid of feelings, they may not move toward or away from anything. Feeling avoiders do not generate the emotions that prompt movement.

Dreikurs (1967) put forth that emotions are inherent in being human as emotions provide "the fuel" for our behavior. Without emotions we would not have the ability to "take a definite stand, to act with force, with conviction, because complete objectivity is not inductive to forceful actions" (p. 207). Emotions, Dreikurs contends, "are the only basis for strong personal relationships to others, for developing interest and for building alliances of interests with others. They make us appreciate and devaluate, accept and reject" (pp. 207–208). Essentially, feeling avoiders do not generate the emotions that encourage movement. Feeling avoiders may see emotions as a liability, especially in business situations in which it pays to be poker-faced, or they may believe emotions to be feminine and inferior.

The Excitement Seeker

Some people either seek excitement regularly or when life becomes overly dull, routine, or boring. The latter are often referred to in psychology as commotion makers. The excitement may be either internal or external. People who seek excitement often produce many sexual recollections. While a single recollection may help classify a person as an excitement seeker, most people who are classified as excitement seekers have a *sequence* of exciting ERs.

Farley (1986) indicates that people have an optimal level of psychological arousal that they try to maintain, either by increasing or decreasing activity. Excitement seekers are those Farley refers to as having the Type T (or Big T) personality.

ER 1. Age: 7

> There were these woods in front of my house. I thought I would be
> like Indiana Jones and explore the woods with some kids from my
> neighborhood. We went looking for treasure. We cut a path in the

tall weeds, and I found a small snake. It was cool. We had to cross this stream. So I got a bunch of saplings and put them over the creek. We walked over the saplings, but one kid fell in and got soaked. He had to walk back alone. We jumped the fence to steal some apples for lunch. The farmer yelled at us, and we took off. I skinned my knee as his dogs chased us off the property. It was wild!

This recollection is undoubtedly that of an excitement seeker. The mix of emotion and action throughout the recollection reads like an adventure novel. Reread the recollection and examine the twists and turns, the dramatic highs and precarious situations.

The Social Interest Type

This is the ideal type by Adlerian standards (Adler, 1935a). Their recollections are laden with instances of contribution, of cooperation, of compassion and caring, and of belonging (Mosak, 1991).

ER 1. Age: 9

> My family was having dinner at a restaurant. It was some special occasion, and my dad said that I could order anything I wanted. I ordered one of my favorite, and one of the most expensive, meals, Alaskan King Crab legs. I very, and I mean very, rarely had this type of dinner. When it came to our table it was a huge serving. I thought, "Cool, I can take it home and have it over the next day or two!" However, when we left the restaurant, I saw a man in a wheelchair asking for some money for food. I gave him my still-warm take-home bag full of crab legs. I thought he needed it more than I did.

ER 2. Age: 8

> I was in my aunt's car. She was driving. My cousin was in the front seat, and I was in the back. We had just gotten these toy airplanes from McDonald's. They were really cool. My cousin held his out the window and pretended it was flying. I guess he didn't think about it, but the wind blew the airplane out of his hand and onto the road. He was very upset. I gave him my toy airplane to make him feel better.

You may be saying, "Hey, wait a second, these appear to be very close to the pleaser kind of ERs. Why not qualify these as pleaser-type ERs because in both examples the client is pleasing someone?"

It's a good point. But the above ERs are considered to be of the social interest variety because the client acts in the best interest of others (yes, pleasing them, but doing more than that) and without seeking approval or to calm a situation in which the client would be rejected. See the difference? Any of the preceding types in practice may be invested with social interest depending upon whether the person's behavior is on the useful or useless side of life (Adler, 1956). Because, for Adlerians, types are not classifications, there are not a finite number of types (Mosak, 1979). The illustrations above are merely some common examples.

BASIS-A and Mosak's Typologies

Cooley (1983) proposed that understanding people's life styles would enhance psychologists' ability to help clients bring about change. In an effort to expedite the process of determining life style, Wheeler, Kern, and Curlette (1993) created the Basic Adlerian Scales for Interpersonal Success — Adult Form (BASIS-A) Inventory. This measurement was designed to assess life style themes correlated with Mosak's typologies (Wheeler, 1989).

The BASIS-A has five scales that the writers correlated with Mosak's types (Curlette, Wheeler, & Kern, 1993). They found that the Going Along scale is similar to Mosak's need-to-be-good type. The Taking Charge (TC) scale is equivalent to Mosak's controller type. The Being Cautious (BC) scale is comparable with Mosak's victim type. A low Belonging/Social Interest Scale (BSI) is associated with Mosak's inadequate type.

Merits and Cautions

For the voyager taking the initial trip to the terra incognita of ERs, the Typological Approach provides a "port of entry" that is usually easily navigated. Though it may not be as easy as the Headline Method presented in the last Chapter, it provides few problems in the understanding of the central theme of the recollection (Mosak, 1977b). Yet, for those who fail to understand the theoretical assumptions underlying an Adlerian theory of types, the task may prove problematic. An Adlerian typology is not constructed merely for taxonomic purposes and labeling. Consequently, one may discover overlap among some types, a situation that factor analysis studies may eventually help clarify (see Mullis, Kern, & Curlette, 1987; Wheeler, Kern, & Curlette, 1986). Adlerian life style themes can also studied for their correlation with other assessments or demographic variables (for example, see Di Pietro, 2003) in an effort to clarify what relation, if any, exists between life style themes and other measures.

The overlap among types may be seen in different ways. For example, people who wish to control may do so through being right. The victim is also in a sense a getter, as the victim is always getting the short end of the stick. Early recollections may also reveal a composite picture of several types. In one ER, the client is not only an excitement seeker but also a victim, both schlemiel and schlemazel, and a getter. Lowe (1977) indicated that there could be more than one theme in a single ER.

Even in those instances in which interpreters can identify only the type from the ER, they need not stop at that point. Since descriptions of those types do exist (Boldt & Mosak, 1997; Hart, 1977; Mosak, 1959; Mosak, 1977; Peven, 1973), reference to these writings will provide some clues as to what may further be searched for in the ERs or may provide hypotheses for investigation in personality assessment or psychotherapy.

As we've said repeatedly, you cannot understand a person's life style by interpreting only one recollection. Therefore, in using this approach, you should classify the type to which the ER belongs and should avoid limiting the person to this classification. As noted above, a recollection classified as a getting ER may be that of a getter, a victim, or a pleaser.

Placing the ER into a type classification — for example, labeling respondents as pleasers, tells us what they are or have rather than what they do. It can provide a thumbnail sketch of the individual, but not a comprehensive picture. We are more interested in, for example, pleasers' lines of movement rather than their label.

A diagnostic label, as described in Chapter 1, cannot provide us with detailed information that encompasses the entire person. Labeling a person as a type is a bit like labeling a car a "sedan." If you rent a car, and the representative tells you that you have a sedan, what questions would you ask? What kind of sedan? What color? How fast does it go? How big is it? How good is it on gas? Does it have manual or automatic transmission? As well as other questions.

A label is a quick reference to something, someone, or some process and should be used only for quick, not in-depth, indication. Walk down the hallway of some emergency room, and you'll most likely hear sentences like these:

"There's a gall bladder in the next room, and a broken leg out in the lobby."

"We've got a bypass at noon, and a lung resection at 2."

"There is a herniated disk down the hall."

The references are made to the most relevant feature of the people that needs to be examined and taken care of. It is only after the "gall bladder" comes in for surgery that the surgeon finds out about the person. Age, race, medications, general health, allergies, and other valuable information about that person is gathered and communicated because more detailed information is relevant and necessary.

Interpreting the ERs as labels loses for us the sometimes rich meaning of many of the details that are in them. However, types can provide a quick reference just as "gall bladder" does.

A mechanical knowledge of ER interpretation does not suffice. Many graduate students being introduced to the interpretation of the Rorschach Inkblot Test make diagnoses of schizophrenia on the basis of test indicators without ever having seen a schizophrenic. They are as often wrong as right in their diagnoses. Firm grounding in psychodynamics is essential if error is to be minimized. One may encounter difficulty in interpretation or commit error and harm a person if one has insufficient knowledge of personality dynamics. For example, what do you make out of the following ER?

> My father told me to wash my hands before sitting down at the dinner table. I washed and washed, and they all had to wait for me.

Classifying this person as a controller may indeed be correct, but one should also entertain the possibility that this person may use his control in the form of compulsive hand washing.

The following recollection may at first glance appear to be that of an observer.

> I was in kindergarten around Halloween time. We were all dressed up in costumes. I was looking around the room at everyone's costume. I clearly remember glaring at the teacher going through the lesson plans at her desk. She was dressed as a witch. She looked like a real witch! I was petrified. I ran out into the hallway and saw three more girls who were dressed as witches. I ran into the boys' bathroom, and a couple of my friends calmed me down.

However, more centrally, the man may actually be making a pronouncement about women. They are all "witches," and he can't get away from them fast enough. His only safety is to retreat into a part of the world that is totally masculine and to be comforted by men, who may be seen as nicer and safer.

Typologies are useful as shorthand for understanding a group, but not as a pigeonhole for individuals. The understanding of the central theme of a recollection begins with the determination of the personality type portrayed in the ERs. It is the type that is predominantly shown in the ERs that helps the clinician understand how clients see themselves, others, the world around them, and their ethical convictions.

Kopp (1986) put forth that many typologies focus on the negative and designed a typology that is more optimistic in its orientation in an effort to parallel the Adlerian style of focusing on the positive. To that end, we present a full series of ERs that focus on comprehensive understanding rather than labeling. These ERs are from a 45-year-old female.

Example of a Type in a Series of ERs

ER. 1 Age: 7

> I remember this one snowstorm we had. I told my parents that I was going to shovel the entire driveway right down to the black asphalt for them. As I was shoveling, it kept snowing, and it seemed as though the more I shoveled, the harder it snowed. I didn't think I would be able to reach my goal. I remember my mom called me in for some hot chocolate. After I was done with the hot chocolate, I went right back to work. Well, I was able to shovel the driveway right down to the asphalt. It took all day, but I did it. I felt great. When I came in, my father gave me a great big warm hug.
>
> Most vivid: "Looking at the driveway after I was done. It was all black, and the snow was all white."

In this recollection we see that the client has much persistence and that it pays off for her. She has a sense of accomplishment after a hard day's work. She demonstrates that she is a hard worker who has social interest. After all, her parents would get more use out of the driveway than she. Women and men, as represented by her mother and father, are seen as supportive. The world is represented as both warm and cold. Warmth as demonstrated by her parents, and the cold represented by the snow. In addition, for this client the world is black and white. If you have stick-to-it persistence, then you will get warmth and affection.

ER 2. Age: 7

> I was in gym class, and we all had to climb these ropes up to the ceiling. I started climbing, but I remember my arms were tired and I gave up. The other kids mentioned how I went the least amount of the way up the rope. I felt bad. The boys' gym teacher, Mr. Haggerty, came over and told me I was one of his favorite students and not to worry about what the other kids said. I felt better after that.
>
> Most vivid: "Stopping so low on the rope."

Here the client is saying that she cannot achieve. That apparently contradicts the previous recollection in which she fights an uphill battle and feels great. This is an example of the if-then condition that exists within some recollections, and some people. The client stated, indirectly, that if she is persistent, then she will accomplish her goals. However, if she is not persistent, then she fails and is picked on by her peers. Men in this second recollection are seen as caring and having a big heart. They can soothe her. Also, it is somewhat of a competitive world as she is compared to others. To the loser goes the criticism.

ER 3. Age: 5

> I remember being in kindergarten and walking around the room. The boys and the girls were separated. The boys were playing together, and the girls were playing together. As I walked around the room I noticed that the boys' area was very messy and the girls had a very neat area. The boys asked me to play with them, and when I went over there was a peanut butter and jelly sandwich on the ground, which one of the boys picked up and took a bite out of. He then offered me some of the sandwich. I thought that was nice, but yucky. I walked to the girls' area where they had been playing for a while, and they made room for me next to the blocks.
>
> Most vivid: "How messy the boys were and how neat the girls were."

In this recollection the client tells us that men are messy but nice, and women are neat and accommodating, especially for the new girl on the block.

ER 4. Age: 9

> My mother told me that I was not doing well in math and spelling. She was very nice about it and encouraged me to do better. Well, once I found out I was not doing well at math, I knew I had to work harder. The next day there was a big math exam. I studied day and night for that exam, and I got an A on it. I was so happy. I told my parents when I got back home, and they gave me a hug. I knew then that I would study for the next spelling test until I got every word right.
>
> Most vivid: "Getting that A on the exam and thinking about all of the hard work I did to get that A."

In this recollection the client is stating that she has some inferiorities, but she is able to roll up her sleeves and persevere. It is through persistence and hard work that she can achieve. When she achieves, she is rewarded with affection.

ER 5. Age: 5

> I couldn't tie my shoes. I asked my mother to show me how, and I kept at it all day. She would correct me from time to time as she looked over. She made sure to bring her laundry and other chores into the kitchen to watch me. At the end of the day I was able to tie my own shoes. I was so proud of myself. She made me chocolate chip cookies after I showed her.
>
> Most vivid: "Seeing the tightening of the laces when I did it right."

In this recollection the client is telling us, again, that persistence pays off. She is also stating that women are supportive and flexible (her mother moved her work into the kitchen to watch her). Also, she indicates that to the victor go the spoils. She earned her chocolate chip cookies through her hard work and determination.

ER 6. Age: 9

> There was this boy in my class who was very cute. This other girl and I liked him quite a bit. She and I tried to win him over; it was a rough competition. [That part is a report.] We both liked him, and I didn't want to lose him to her, so I called his house after school about 20 times, and his mother told him not to talk with me. He ended up dating the other girl. I felt like a loser.
>
> Most vivid: "Him telling me that his mother told him not to talk to me anymore."

In this recollection we get a better understanding to the downside of the client's persistence and an indication of her current problem. The client's persistence has paid off in the previous recollections but has actually gotten her further away from her goal in this recollection. The straightforward understanding that she could have anything she wants if she is persistent enough does have its limits. In this recollection and more generally (it is the reason she is in therapy), the client takes her persistence too far. She tells us in this recollection that it is a competitive world and that persistence does not always get her what she wants. Sometimes it backfires. Prior to coming in for therapy, she was e-mailing an ex-boyfriend numerous times a day in an effort to get him back. He replied that she needed to seek counseling because she was harassing him.

Now that you have some of the information from the recollections, what type would you assign this client's perceptions and behavior?

In addition, can you see how there is a positive and a negative to functioning? It is true in this case. Persistence gets both rewarded and punished. Furthermore, can you observe the client's perception of herself, the world, others, and interactions among men and women?

Have you come up with a type for this client?

We would describe this client's mind-set and behavior as that of the driving type. She believes that persistence and determination (drive) will allow her to succeed in life and get her what she wants. However, at least in one area, she has been too persistent, and that is a problem.

Now you can understand the importance of assessing the positives as well as the negatives of human functioning. The drive to succeed may make this client do homework and follow through on assignments. In short, persistence and drive may help her reach therapeutic goals.

Summary

The recollection must be examined in its whole with parts supporting the entire meaning. The whole is not only more than the sum is its parts; it is different than the sum of its parts. Because people are unique, there are conceivably as many types as there are people. It is important to remember that types refer to behavior, not the person. We prefer not to label people.

The getting types frequently give recollections in which they get something or have something taken away from them.

The controller types give ERs that show how sweet it is when they and/or life are under control and how catastrophic life can be when they and/or life are not under control.

The driving types can more frequently be identified through reports than through recollections. In order to have a driving style one generally must be engaged in sequential activities, and a single recollection generally fails to reflect such multiple activities.

The right types have to be right in order to have a place. These people tend to have ERs that center on (1) rewards, intrinsic or extrinsic, for being or doing right; (2) how right they are; (3) how wrong others are; and (4) the negative consequences or bad feelings that accrue when one is or does wrong.

The superior types may express their goal by having to be first, best, unique, or a star.

The pleaser types are dependent upon the approval of others. They bask in others' approval and shrivel when they fail to please or gain disapproval.

The aginner types are typically seen as oppositional, as overt and covert rebels. They are not necessarily "bad guys."

The victim types tell you how life treats them poorly. They may go out of their way to tell you just how unfair life is for them.

The baby types have ERs that focus on smallness, ineptitude, immaturity, the requirement of assistance, nurturance, and elevation.

The inadequate person types view themselves as inept and inferior.

The confuser types confuse life and is confused by life.

The feeling avoider types rarely state a feeling. Sometimes they adopt an observer's stance.

The excitement seeker types either seek excitement actively or when life becomes overly dull or routine or boring.

The social interest types have recollections that are laden with instances of contribution, of cooperation, of compassion and caring, and of belonging.

Kopp wrote that many typologies focus on the negative. He designed a typology that is more optimistic in its orientation in an effort to parallel the Adlerian style of focusing on the positive.

5

The Life Style Convictions Approach

Previously you learned how to interpret individual recollections, one at a time. In earlier Chapters we summarized the themes of individual recollections without providing an overarching depiction of the person. Now we will present a number of sample cases and illustrate how multiple recollections present more detail for interpretation. We provide a full interpretation at the end of this Chapter using the Life Style Convictions Approach.

We present this Chapter as a workbook because we believe people learn more quickly when they interact with the material (thinking, guessing, reviewing, etc.) than when they are lectured (through either the spoken or written word). It should be pointed out that the summary of the ERs could give us the core of the client's personality. It is not equivalent to the method by which we administer and interpret the Life Style Inventory (Mosak & Shulman, 1988), a method that allows us to gather physical development, gender guiding lines, sibling constellation, family atmosphere, and so on. In other words, while the information gleaned from ERs is a central and vital part of understanding, it is limited in scope by its inability to provide comprehensive information about such important factors as socioeconomic status, biological maturation (commencement, duration, influences on attitude and behavior), an exhaustive list of who was part of the family and their influences, as well as many other important factors.

The life style convictions fall within the self-concept (e.g., what I am, who I am, what affects me), the self-ideal (what I should be to have a place in the world, to be significant, to belong), the *Weltbild* (my picture of the world), and the ethical convictions (my personal moral standards and what I believe to be appropriate conduct for myself and others as well as the consequences of ethical and unethical behavior).

What we are going to do in this Chapter is to take each recollection and give the likely self-concept, self-ideal, *Weltbild*, and ethical convictions as indicated by that recollection. Not all areas will be represented in every recollection (which is another reason we need more than one ER for proper interpretation).

We'll start with recollections in which only one or another conviction is given. After we have become familiar with the process, we will tackle more complicated recollections. The following is a relatively easy ER from a man.

ER 1. Age: 7

> I remember that my mother came into my school on my seventh birthday with treats for the class. I was so happy that it was my birthday and that the whole class would be celebrating it with me. My mother brought some really great treats, much more than the other kids did. I loved being in tune with the whole class. But when she starting passing the candy out, the kids started jumping and screaming for it.
>
> They were all grabbing the candy, and my mother was really angry. She said, "You kids better settle down, or I'll take all of this candy back to the store." I was so embarrassed. She was overreacting, and I couldn't help but think that I would never be able to get back in with the other kids again.
>
> Most vivid: "My mother yelling at the kids and the feeling that I was going to be an outsider."

What do you make out of this recollection? What life style conviction is the client telling you here? Here are some possible choices however, there is only one most correct answer.

- Self-concept: I am a victim of women.
- Self-ideal: I should do something so that women don't threaten my place.
- *Weltbild:* Women threaten my place.
- Ethical conviction: I am a bad boy.

We will now discount all of the inappropriate answers until we get to the right one.

The self-concept is incorrect as there is no statement, direct or indirect, to support it. If you have chosen to speculate on self-concept, you may be projecting more information than what is presented in the recollection. Self-ideal is incorrect as well, as there is no such desire indicated in the recollection. The ethical conviction seems mistaken as there is no shame, guilt, or any other emotion that indicates that the client thinks he is a bad boy (or man). The *Weltbild*, however, seems correct: The client states specifically that his mother was "overreacting" and that he "would never be able to get back in with the other kids again."

ER 2. Age: 5

> I went to Catholic school, and the nuns ran a really tight ship. [That part is a report.] It was picture day, and they asked us to get all dressed up. I came in my best white shirt and blue tie. Well, they scheduled my picture to be taken after recess. During recess I was playing in the schoolyard, and I fell and got dirt all over my shirt. I tried to wash it off, but I only made it worse. When I came in from recess, one of the nuns saw me, and she was furious. She was absolutely livid! She yelled at me for what seemed like an eternity. I was terrified.

> Most vivid: "Seeing the dirt on my white shirt and knowing that I was going to get chewed out, but good!"

What is he telling you? You have been given a recollection that indicates possibly two components. Here are four possibilities:

- Self-concept: I shine when people see me, and Self-image: I should be in pictures.
- Self-image: I am a mess, and *Weltbild*: Life is harsh.
- Self-ideal: I should be neat, and Ethical conviction: I should be bad.
- Self-concept: I am terrified by the consequences of my wrongdoings, and Ethical conviction: If I do wrong, I get hollered at.

If you chose the first option, you perhaps focused on "best white shirt and blue tie" and "picture." However, that option fits only if you ignore the rest of the recollection. The second is an interesting one in that it can be arrived at only by inference: The recollection presents no direct evidence that the client sees himself as a mess or life as harsh. If you chose the third option, how did you justify the apparent opposites stated? Is being "neat" also being "bad"? Probably not. That brings us to the last option. Since it is the only one left, obviously it's the correct one. But what makes it accurate? First, the client says he is "terrified" by his actions. Second, he is "hollered at" for doing something wrong.

Here is another recollection from the same man.

ER 3.

> In kindergarten, an old nun had us write numbers from 1 to 20. I got stuck at 13, so I took out a book and looked up the numbers in the book until I found the next number. I did it on the sly. I was checking to make sure it was right. I felt like it was cheating, and I felt terrible.

Most vivid: "Looking up the numbers. Trying not to get caught."

Imagine you are assessing this man, and he gives you this ER. It is your responsibility to interpret it correctly. The reward for a job well done is better comprehension and pursuing a correct path in therapy. Reread the recollection and come up with a conviction in his life style. This time, however, we will forgo the multiple-choice format and look at each component, deciding what fits. It should be easier this time as you already have a previous recollection from this man.

Remember, ERs are a reflection not of childhood but of current adulthood. Is this client telling you that he is afraid of nuns? No. So what is the overarching theme of this recollection? If you wish, turn back to the previous recollection for a clue. What is the client doing? He is checking numbers "on the sly," and he feels "terrible." What does this indicate about his life style?

Again we observe his ethical conviction, and that ethical conviction is "I am terrified or I feel terrible about the consequences of my wrongdoing." However, this recollection differs from the previous one. In the first recollection, he tells us that his wrongdoing is innocent. However, in the second recollection, his wrongdoing is deliberate. He is clearly acting covertly (a modifying detail; see Chapter 8 for more information about details). So while we are able to say that the central theme is the same, the second recollection modifies and expands our interpretation.

What do you make out of the presence of the nun and the number 13? What symbolism *may* the man be presenting to you? Is it a religious or superstitious reference? That is, does the client feel as though he gets "stuck" on thoughts of religion or superstition? Might this man "psych himself out" and not be able to perform in life because he focuses on these things? Possibly, but to interpret him this way, we would need more ERs supporting that idea.

The next recollection comes from a woman:

ER 4. Age: 9

> One day my brother and I were in our red wagon in the backyard. Our father was going to come out of the house and pull us around the backyard. My younger brother, who was about three at the time, was sitting in front of me and playing with my Frisbee. I really don't recollect why I wanted to slug him. I just wanted to. Anyway, I told him not to throw my Frisbee, because if he did, I was going to slug him. I see him take the Frisbee and wind up and chuck it across the lawn. I pounded him in the back of his head, and he started crying and screaming.

What are the key elements she presents in the recollection? Remember that most, if not all, ERs contain at least one metaphor. Would the recollection be the same if she were sitting in front of her brother? She specifically states that she is behind him (essentially in the back seat). Therefore, we may say that she takes a back seat with a man. What part does the house play in the recollection? None. Though we should keep this location detail in the back of our minds, it is not directly relevant to the recollection. If we look at the overall theme of the recollection, we have a clear self-concept and *Weltbild* conviction.

Let's investigate the recollection for clues to components of her life style.

What is the most important part of the recollection related to the self-concept? First, she tells us that she "wanted to slug him." Therefore, we have an idea what her goals are. Notice that the feeling comes prior to her statement to him; it is not as though her brother threw the Frisbee and *then* she wanted to hit him. She tempted her brother to do something. Though she did not say, "I dare you," the implication exists. If her stated goal was to hurt him, we must look at her actions prior to hurting him that would have allowed her (justifiably in her mind) to hurt him. We find one such action: the threat that she lays down. Therefore, in the recollection, the client invites her brother (interpret it as "men") to do something so she can then hurt him (interpret it as "them").

What is the *Weltbild* component that the client shows us? We know that she set up a trap for her brother (again think of it as "men"). Her brother then did exactly what she wanted so that she could abuse him. The brother, as far as we know, had no clue that it was a trap. Therefore, the *Weltbild* conviction illustrated in the recollection can be interpreted as "Men naively go along and fall into my traps," as that is what the brother did.

She adds to the recollection:

He cried, then our neighbor came out of her house, and she couldn't open her garage door while holding some packages. So I jumped out of the wagon, ran across the yard, and assisted her, but I knew I wasn't really a nice little girl.

So what should we make out of this additional clue? Is she telling us that she puts on a front for others? Yes. Therefore we can add to our conception of her: I may act like a nice little girl, but I am not, and I know I am not. That is exactly what she is doing in the recollection. She knows darn well that she isn't "really a nice girl," as she is just putting on a façade of being nice. She hurts men and helps women.

She gives another recollection:

ER 5. Age 8:

I was in the backyard with my parents. I was at the picnic table. My mother was shucking corn, and my father was pulling weeds from the garden. They were working very hard. Earlier in the day I was at the store, and I saw this huge flat-screen television that I really wanted for my room. It cost several thousand dollars. I asked my mother for it, and she ignored me. I walked out to the garden and asked my father. He ignored me too! I asked them both at once as I screamed out my demand for the TV. I remember my father turning to me and saying that I was ungrateful and obnoxious. I realized he was right. I quietly walked into the house alone.

Most vivid: "My father turning to me and telling me I was ungrateful and obnoxious."

What do you think this client's self-concept and self-ideal are? Look at the entire recollection. What does it tell you about her? She wants something, and she wants it now. She is ignored by her mother and upbraided by her father. It is only then that she realizes that her actions are unbearable for others. Therefore, we can guess that her self-concept is: I want what I want, and I am impatient to get it. In addition, I am obnoxious without knowing it, until others (possibly men) point it out.

For this client, what is her self-ideal? What does she want to accomplish? In her mind, others should fulfill her desires. Furthermore, she realizes that she can be obnoxious to others, and that it is not good. Therefore, her self-ideal (what she aspires to be) is that she should not be obnoxious because that drives people away and keeps her from getting what she wants.

The next recollection is from a young man:

ER 6. Age: 7

> It was summertime, and I had to go to the bathroom desperately.
> I really had to go. I ran into the house and up to the bathroom.
> My sister was in there. It was the only bathroom in the house.
> I kept pushing on the door until the latch gave way. She was on
> the john, but I really had to go. I dropped my shorts, and I tried to
> make it into the toilet. I urinated all over her. She was soaked.
> I don't recall any feelings.

Most vivid: "The sheer relief when I emptied my bladder."

So what might be this man's self-concept and *Weltbild*?

Think about metaphors in ERs. Remember that during the time prior to language development we learn, think, and communicate in metaphor. It is a skill that we carry throughout our lives, even after we develop the ability of comprehensive language. Metaphor is something that we use in tandem with our spoken, verbal, and written language skills.

With that in mind, we can see the client's self-concept more clearly: I piss on women. Not only does he piss on women, but it doesn't even bother him: "I don't recall any feelings." So why might this man not care if he pisses on women? How does he see women (his *Weltbild*), and how would that justify (in his mind) his actions toward them? When you look at the recollection, what is his sister (interpret that as "women") doing?

He has a goal in this recollection. He desperately needs to go to the bathroom. However, he is, at least temporarily, held back from his fulfilling his needs by his sister. Therefore, his *Weltbild* can be interpreted as: Women get in the way of my satisfying my needs.

The next recollection comes from a woman:

ER 7. Age: 7

> I was in first grade, and we had "Pioneer Days." It was when all of
> the students got dressed up in costumes like we were in the Old
> West. Well, I had on this beautiful dress and was showing it
> around when a reporter from the local paper came into our class-
> room. He came directly to me and told me that he wanted to take
> my picture to put in the next day's paper. I was so pleased that he
> picked me. It was between me and another student, and he chose
> me! I was excited and happy.

Most vivid: "The reporter picking me instead of anyone else."

Look at the word "chose." The client is chosen for a happy and exciting event. If she were not chosen, would she have been as happy or excited? Probably not. Therefore, we can interpret this recollection to provide some information about the client's self-ideal. In this case we can say that in order for her to have a place she should be specially selected. Her self-concept is of somebody who is special and is recognized as special and that being selected is what makes her excited and happy.

She offers another recollection:

ER 2. Age: 8

> I remember being at a museum of science someplace, and there was a demonstration of static electricity. Another girl and I were picked to go on stage and touch a metal object to have our hair stand up on end. I was so pleased when the presenters called me up to the stage. I was a bit scared being called up because I had never done anything like that. The two of us walked up to the stage laughing. We were ecstatic that we got picked to go.

Most vivid: "Being chosen among all those people in the audience."

This ER compounds the conceptualization we received in the first recollection. Her self-ideal is that in order to have a place she should be specially selected. It is not that she is unique or has some special talent, per se, but rather that someone else selects her. Even though she is scared of a novel situation, she is happy because she was "picked to go" on stage.

As you read our interpretation and summary of the recollection, you must remember that you need several recollections to find out what clues are replicated, and that you summarize all of the recollections collectively rather than summarize each recollection individually.

Just looking at this summary, you may get some idea of how the client will behave in therapy, what some of the client's interactions are like with other people, and what the client values in life.

Series of ERs From One Person

Up to this point we have provided one or two recollections from different clients as a means to get you familiar with the Life Style Convictions Approach. You are now asked to look at all of the ERs from one case. Go through each recollection and give your ideas for the self-concept, self-ideal, *Weltbild*, and ethical convictions. We want you to imagine that you have received the following recollections as though a client gave them to you. We'll give you one clue: The client is a middle-aged female.

ER 1. Age: 6

I remember one summer day. It was absolutely beautiful outside. We were on my dad's boat, my dad, my sister, and me. We were on a lake that was peaceful and scenic. I remember my dad was driving the boat, and he made a turn into a narrow creek. Well, the trees on the side of the creek were tall and thick with branches and leaves, and they blocked out the sun. It became very dark. I remember feeling uncomfortable. All of a sudden a mammoth bird swooped down, and he pooped all over my beautiful blue swimsuit. I was petrified; I did not know how many more would come. My sister was laughing at me. I don't remember anything after that.

Most vivid: "The darkness of the creek and the bird coming right at me."

ER 2. Age: 9

I was playing in my friend's backyard. There were a few of us girls there. It was very dark out, and I was out well past the time I should have been home. Well, in their backyard they had one of those super-powerful lights that focused on one area, and when I was bending over to pick up a toy, the light went on. I was the only one lit up. I thought, "Oh boy, I'm in trouble now. My mom must be here." I was so terrified that I couldn't move.

Most vivid: "The light on me and the feeling like I was in deep trouble."

ER 3. Age: 8

We were in gym class, and it was co-ed. The boys were playing basketball, and the girls were playing volleyball on opposite ends of the court. A couple of us were bored playing volleyball and decided to watch the boys play basketball. We snuck up into the control booth that overlooked the basketball court. I sat behind the controls. I made sure not to turn the lights on so that people would not see us. I flipped the switch that raises and lowers the basketball net. The boys were trying to put the ball through the hoop at all different heights. It was great to be able to make them change what they were doing on the court. I felt powerful.

Most vivid: "Watching the boys try to get the basketball in the hoop at different heights."

ER 4. Age: 7

I remember being in church getting communion and the priest dropped the wafer on the wet floor. Even though I knew the floor was dirty, I picked up the wafer and put it in my mouth and swallowed it. I knew that God was watching. I felt like it was my duty to follow through, and while I didn't feel good about doing it, I felt like a loyal and responsible person.

Most vivid: "Putting the wafer in my mouth and feeling like it was the right thing to do."

ER 5. Age: 8

I was playing with a bunch of other kids at the end of our street. It was one of those streets that they were supposed to connect to another road, but they never did, so it just kinda stopped. We were dividing up into two teams to play Wiffle-ball. I remember I wanted to be on both teams, so I told each captain to pick me and that I would do a great job. They talked to one another, and neither one picked me. They played in a nearby field while I stayed at the end of our street, alone.

Most vivid: "Being left alone on the street."

ER 6. Age: 7

There were a bunch of boys who were playing video games at a store. I walked past them, and they were really nice to me. They gave me compliments and all that sort of stuff. I left them and continued to look around the store. As I walked back to where they were, and I heard them picking on some girl, calling her a "dope" and "ugly," but when I looked around the corner, there wasn't any girl there. I soon realized that they were talking about me. I felt deflated.

Most vivid: "Realizing they were calling me names and not some other girl."

ER 7. Age: 5

I remember waiting on line to see Santa Claus. I was behind this girl with very pretty, long blonde hair. When Santa put her on his lap, he told her how pretty she was, and how he was sure that she was a "good little girl this year." Well, I knew that I was a good little girl too. When I got to Santa and was on his lap, he didn't tell me that I was pretty or that I had been a good girl. I thought that I would not get any presents because he was not able to see the good things that I did. I really thought it was unfair.

Most vivid: "Waiting for Santa to call me a 'good girl,' but he didn't!"

ER 8. Age: 7

I remember being in class and the teacher said that the person who does the best on the spelling test would get ice cream. I studied as hard as I could. I knew I was going to get ice cream, especially because some of the other kids did not study at all. We took the test, and I did the best. Then the teacher said that we had all done well so that we all would get ice cream. I was angry. I should have been the only person to get ice cream because I did the best.

Most vivid: "The disappointment when the teacher said that everyone would get ice cream."

There are the eight ERs from one client. Have you written down your understanding of the client's self-concept, self-ideal, *Weltbild*, and ethical convictions?

We will now review our answers for each of the recollections in turn. You will want to use the skills you have developed thus far. This particular set of recollections is rich with metaphors. We have identified a few for you.

In the first ER, we see that the client understands that no matter how good things start off, if a man is in the driver's seat (metaphor) he will eventually take a wrong turn and put the client "up shit creek" (another metaphor). Furthermore, the client does not receive empathy from other women when she is shit on. She ascribes a gender to the bird, male, when it is more likely the case that she did not know the gender of the bird, and it could just as likely have been female. Is she telling us that men shit on her? The client perceives that when things go bad, they do so quickly. Also, she loses her beauty when things go wrong. She is not as "beautiful" after things happen and does nothing to help herself. She is too scared to act.

Therefore, from the first recollection we might get some idea of her self-concept. First, she is not in control, and when she is not in control, things go bad quickly. Her *Weltbild* may be described as the attitude that the world is unpredictable. Even though things start off "peaceful and scenic," she is soon up a creek. Also, she may have the view that when a man is in control, he will put her in a dangerous situation, and she will be shit upon.

In the second recollection, we see that as long as the client operates in the shadows, she can have fun. However, if she is put into the spotlight, she is "terrified" and immobile. She may feel as though she is put into the spotlight when she is down and least prepared for it. Also, the client gives the impression that she likes to push the envelope by staying out "well past the time [she] should have been home." In addition, we get the impression that the client feels as though women can call attention to her rule breaking.

From this recollection, we see that the client's self-concept is "If I break the rules, I get caught," and "If I am put into the spotlight (metaphor), I am terrified." Her *Weltbild* may be "Women spot my rule breaking." One of her ethical convictions might be, "If I break the rules, then I get caught and singled out."

Her third ER adds some dimension to our understanding of the client. Here she is telling us that she likes to be in control as long as she is able to do so from the shadows. In addition, she likes to raise the bar for men and, in a sense, make them jump through hoops.

Here we get an idea of the client's self-ideal, the way she should be. According to this recollection, she should be in control, as long as she can do so from the all-concealing shadows. She should also be in a position to make men jump through hoops (metaphor). She demonstrates that she enjoys being in control and that it gives her a sense of power. We can also view the client's *Weltbild* in that life is more enjoyable when women are in control of men.

In the fourth ER, we see some ethical convictions. The client is telling us that even though men drop the ball, so to speak, it is her obligation to pick it up. Furthermore, she is to swallow (metaphor) whatever men give her, no matter how dirty it is because it is her responsibility. However, it appears that she engages in such "loyal and responsible" behavior only when God is watching. Therefore, we might say that when she is in plain sight, she fulfills her duties, but don't expect her to do so when she is in the shadows. Her *Weltbild* is that men are not to be trusted to give her the good things in life.

In the fifth recollection, we see that when the client tries to please everyone, it is a dead end, and she winds up alone. Her self-concept may be, "I must please everyone." Her self-ideal may be to please everyone. Her *Weltbild* appears to be that others will leave you if you try to play a game with them (being a double agent to please both sides). Furthermore, she may have learned the truth of the adage You can't please all of the people all of the time.

In the sixth ER, the client is telling us that boys (men) play games with her emotions. They may say something pleasant to her when she is around, but she shouldn't turn her back on them because they will, figuratively, stick a knife it in. Therefore, her *Weltbild* is "Men shouldn't be trusted because they like to play games (with my emotions)." Also, "Men raise my spirits, and then bring me down."

In the seventh recollection, we see another component of the *Weltbild*: "Life is unfair. People (men) don't see my good deeds, and, consequently, I will not receive the goodies in life." Also, "Other women get more attention from men than I do."

In the last recollection from this client, we have additional evidence of her *Weltbild* that the world is unfair and that her specialness and hard work are not noticed. Essentially, she feels that life is unfair because even those students who did not work as hard as she did also received ice cream. Furthermore, the client believes that part of the unfairness of life is when people, in this case the teacher, change the rules on her.

Now you have a large amount of information about this client. What might she come into therapy for? What are her strengths and weaknesses? How would you describe to a colleague this client's perception of self, others, the world, and her ethical convictions?

All of the above questions are very important and practical in conducting therapy. Early recollections can provide us with a wealth of information about clients' life style convictions. This information can be used to make therapy more effective and efficient.

Summary

This Chapter illustrated how to use the life style components in ER interpretation. The summary of the ERs is not equivalent to summarizing a whole life style. Early recollections may provide some insight to the client's life style, particularly in regard to some areas. With the Life Style Convictions Approach, it is important to take each recollection and give your ideas of the self-concept, self-ideal, *Weltbild*, and ethical convictions represented there. This will help in understanding the client on different levels of functioning, emotion, and cognition. Most, if not all, ERs contain at least one metaphor. Therefore, it is important to become familiar with how metaphors are presented. This skill may be best honed through the supervision of a clinician who has interpreted hundreds or thousands of ERs. Remember, not all components can be found in every ER, and that is why we cannot provide a comprehensive picture of the individual from just one recollection.

6
Sequential Analysis

This Chapter looks at series of ERs from individuals and then teaches you how to do a sequential analysis. In other words, we are going to use the abilities you developed in previous Chapters to solve a mystery.

Up to this point you have learned the importance of details, types, and how to go through with a fine-tooth comb each recollection for clues about a client's self-concept, self-ideal, *Weltbild*, and ethical convictions. We are now going to use these skills comprehensively to develop a summary of ERs. These summaries are a result of interpretation, but not the final use of them.

Think of ERs as a mystery metaphor. Clients are mysteries to be solved. Early recollections are the clues they provide. Some clues can be a "goldmine" (Dreikurs, personal communication, 1969). As a clinician you must have a sharp eye to perceive these clues. Next, you have to define what these clues mean. For example, if Sherlock Holmes were to find a matchbook at the scene of a crime with the matches torn off from the left side of the matchbook, he might induce that the killer was left-handed. The clues in ERs can be just as subtle. We hope we have trained you well to find and define clues in ERs.

Yet Sherlock Holmes might say, "Having the clues is not good enough, Watson. We need to string these clues together to form a picture!" This applies to the use of ERs as well. We must examine the clues in the recollections to find a common thread or threads. Those threads are then used to weave detailed pictures of clients.

Once we have woven a rich tapestry of clues that creates images of clients, we must act on it. A Sherlock Holmes novel does not end with his interpretation of clues, and our work does not end when we solve the mystery of who clients are. It is how we *act* upon that knowledge that defines the usefulness of the ERs.

We must apply our solution to the mystery in the therapeutic process and other "venues." When Sherlock Holmes pursues a murderer after having solved the mystery, he predicts how that criminal will respond to the environment. Though most of us are not working with criminals, we too predict from the ERs how clients will act within certain contexts. We have some information about our clients' mistaken beliefs. That is, in regard to psychopathology it is how the clients' thoughts and behavior get them into trouble. Early recollections provide us with comprehension of clients' interfering attitudes and belief systems, in DSM-speak, an Axis II disorder. Furthermore, we are able to understand how those interfering attitudes and belief systems have led to their difficulty (that is, how their personalities [e.g., a pleaser] have led to their presenting therapeutic problem [e.g., depression]). For those of you familiar with the DSM, we are looking at how sometimes the Axis II disorders lead to Axis I disorders. However, not all personality disorders lead to an Axis I disorder. That is, someone can be a victim type but not have clinical depression. Again, it is important to remember that ERs are used for functional assessments, not for diagnoses.

Early recollections are also able to describe the positive things that people do. For example, look at this ER and think about the positive qualities the person demonstrates.

> I remember being in first grade helping a classmate put on his boots. They were black rubber rain boots, and his foot wouldn't slide in. He was very frustrated. I grabbed two old plastic bread bags and told him to put them on his feet and then slide them into the boots. He did it, calmed down, and made the bus on time.

This recollection shows you the positive aspects of a person: ingenuity and social interest. And isn't it better to have information about a full spectrum of functioning rather than just the negative stuff? Early recollections are better able to describe a wider range of functioning than diagnoses can, because diagnoses focus solely on one aspect of functioning and thought. How many diagnoses provide information on the positive aspects of clients? We need to use our detective skills to find the good as well as the bad. This will broaden our understanding of the client and provide a more comprehensive picture of the individual.

Just as Sherlock Holmes can predict from the clues he finds, we can predict from ERs how clients will interact with their therapists, what lines of work they might be interested in, whether there is good personality match between a couple headed for marriage (known as life style matching), and a broad range of other things. Perhaps the most important understanding is how to treat clients therapeutically. That is, what might be their underlying motivations; how might they respond to particular interventions; and how might we best interact with them in therapy.

A Walkthrough of Sequential Analysis

Case 1

Read the following sequence of ERs from a 36-year-old woman and look for a common thread.

ER 1. Age: 7

> I remember walking home from school, and I saw this kid kicking around a blue and white coffee can with red lettering. I asked him what he was doing. He said that there was a frog inside the can. I was aghast. I thought that he shouldn't be doing that, and I told him so. He didn't listen, and I told his mother what he did. He got in trouble when he got home that evening.
>
> Most vivid: "Telling him he shouldn't be kicking the can with a frog inside."

ER 2. Age: 8

> I was in a department store with some other kids. I saw this really pretty pink pencil. I really wanted it, and so I put it under my jacket and told the other kids not to say a word. Well, I forgot to take off the security tag, and the alarm went off when I left the store. I was so embarrassed. The store clerk asked me what I was doing, and I told him that I forgot to pay for it. I got into trouble twice. First, for taking it, and second, for lying to him. He was behind the aisle when I told my friends not to say anything. He asked me if I knew I was doing wrong. I said, "Yes," which made it even more intolerable and awkward.
>
> Most vivid: "Being caught for doing something I knew was wrong."

ER 3. Age: 6

I remember I was in an assembly at school waiting for the play to start. I had to go to the bathroom real bad, but I knew that I wasn't supposed to talk during the assembly. I ended up wetting my pants. It was embarrassing. I recall them putting newspaper on the floor to soak it up. I felt so embarrassed.

Most vivid: "Seeing the disappointment in the teachers' faces after I wet my pants."

ER 4. Age: 8

I was in church, and I saw this one lady go up for communion. As she got to the priest, she put her hand out to take the wafer. I knew that she was wrong; the real way to do it was to have the priest put the wafer in your mouth. That was the right way. I thought that she wasn't going to Heaven.

Most vivid: "Thinking that she didn't do it right. The priest had to put the wafer in her mouth."

ER 5. Age: 7

I remember it was during a church festival, and a girl cousin and myself were picking up these balloonlike things off of the pavement and blowing on them. We were having a good time. My mother came out and slapped me and said never to do it again, that is, pick up germy things on the asphalt and put them in my mouth. I felt I'd done something wrong, but I didn't know what. I think she didn't need to slap me. That was over-kill.

Most vivid: "My mother slapping me."

Remember, sequential analysis involves going through a whole set of recollections and putting them all together in a summary of the ERs. We look for a thread that runs through the recollections. The thread is a central theme, and every recollection may deal with it. Therefore, it is important to be attentive to any common elements.

How to proceed? First, always look for the "thread" because it is the statement or set of statements that helps us to integrate all of the recollections. The task is to find a unifying or central theme. Sometimes identifying the thread is a piece of cake because it is so transparent. Other times it is like finding a needle in a haystack.

Take your time and reread the recollections. There is only one common thread illustrated in all of the above recollections. So what do all of the ERs have in common? What is important for this woman? Let's take a brief look at the recollections before we give you our answer.

The boy in the first recollection gets caught doing something cruel to an animal and gets punished. In the second recollection, the client gets caught for lying and stealing. In the third recollection, the client is embarrassed for doing something wrong. In the fourth recollection, the client thinks the woman in the church commits a mortal sin. In the last recollection, the client's mother burst her bubble (so to speak) when she and her cousin were enjoying themselves.

Having given you those clues, you should be able to identify the common thread among those clues. Are you ready to compare your answer to ours?

If you look at the recollections, it is easy to see that all of the ERs relate to right and wrong. Each recollection is merely an elaboration upon the previous ones. Whether we use the Typology, Headline Method, or Life Style Conviction approaches, the thread is obvious. It has to do with right and wrong. Did you see that? If not, reread the recollections and look for the clues presented. How might the knowledge of the client's emphasis on right and wrong be useful in understanding the client and creating a treatment plan?

Second, we need to look at the cast of characters presented in the above recollections. Who does the wrong? Inspection of the recollections tells us that everyone does wrong — young and old, male and female, and the client herself. Sometimes in other sets of ERs, we find that only men do wrong; in others, only women do. In some cases such as this, everyone does wrong. Sometimes everyone does the wrong, but the client doesn't. Sometimes the client admits being or doing wrong, but everyone else is wronger still. Sometimes the client admits being or doing wrong but at least has the decency to feel guilty, whereas others do not. Sometimes the client feels that doing wrong is not that bad. What is bad is getting caught at it.

Third, we must look for any modifications or elaborations of the theme. For example, our client is an innocent wrongdoer at times (in ER 5, she does wrong but doesn't know what). We also know from ER 4 that she is preoccupied with wrongdoing and exaggerates it. Similarly one sees this process in people who have actual symptoms and exaggerate them, magnify them, or conjure up additional ones. She also tells us what happens to wrongdoers. They are invariably found out or caught. She also tells us she feels shame or guilt when her wrongdoing is exposed.

Fourth, we look for reconciliation. That is, when we have two or more seemingly contradictory ERs that we cannot make sense out of, we must find how they connect because of the unity of the personality.

Dreikurs (1966), in discussing "two points on a line," commented that we need to have only two points to draw a line and that once we know the line, we can know the remainder of the points that make up the line. Therefore, when one piece of information about a client appears to contradict another, we must find two points that would connect these (apparently) conflicting pieces of information. We must look for a pattern that includes all of the points (facts) that we have. With every additional piece of information we compare that to the pattern to see if it fits. If it does not fit, we look for a different pattern to explain all the facts.

An example of two points on a line can be seen in the following example:

> A man told his therapist that he was "the world's greatest idealist." The therapist then asked the man if she had a magic wand and could grant the man any wish what would it be? The man immediately replied, "A million dollars!" The therapist scratched her head and said that did not sound like a statement "the world's greatest idealist" would make. Without missing a beat the man replied, "If I had a million dollars, I could afford to be the world's greatest idealist!"

As you can see from the above example, people have creative ways of thinking. We must find the unique lines that each client draws by identifying the points that constitute his or her life's philosophy. Though some pieces of information may seem contradictory to us, they are not to the client. We must perceive the world as the client sees it. Early recollections help us identify how people comprehend themselves and the world around them.

Take the following two ERs:

ER 1. Age: 9

> I was outside of school, and these boys came over. I did not know who they were or what they wanted. Before I knew it, I got hit with a piece of metal and had to go to the hospital and get 10 stitches in my chin.

> Most vivid: "Getting hit and getting stitched up."

ER 2. Age: 6

> It was early Christmas morning. I was up before everyone else in the house. It was still dark. I started to unwrap my presents to see what I got. I received so much, including an electric train set that I asked Santa for. I was in high spirits.

Most vivid: "Unwrapping the electric train set."

What do you make of these recollections?

Let's use the Typological Approach to make some sense out of these recollections. In the first recollection, we can say that this ER is a victim-type recollection. But would we be right?

If we look at the recollection as getting cut and some stitches, we might develop a slightly different perspective that makes the second recollection understandable and in accord with the first recollection. In the second recollection, the client clearly is not a victim. He gets an electric train. So how do we reconcile an ER in which it appears that the client is a victim with a recollection in which the client is clearly not a victim?

The best way to reconcile the differences is to change our interpretation of the recollections. So what is the common thread in both recollections? Our answer is that the client is a recipient, a beneficiary of whatever life has to offer, whether it is positive or negative. In the first recollection, he *gets* cut and *gets* stitches. In the second recollection, he *gets* an electric train and other gifts. The evidence never lies; we just have to develop our perception well enough to distinguish those clues.

Fifth, we resort to specification. We can think of that as the clue inside a clue. Look at both recollections again. How might you categorize the client's getting behavior? What does the client have to do to get something? Nothing.

In both recollections, whether the client is the target of aggression or a beneficiary of a gift, the client is a passive recipient. The client does nothing in both and receives something! So what do you make out of recollections of that kind? How might the client behave in therapy? How might the client see the world?

Others and the world act upon the client, according to these recollections. The client is a passive object who does nothing to influence what happens. In Freudian terms, he is the oral-passive-dependent person. We could liken him to a baby bird that does not have to find his food or even chew it. The food should be found, chewed, and then deposited into his mouth: a definite oral-passive-dependent person.

If, however, he were to give either of the following two ERs, our interpretation would change.

ER 3.

I helped my father deliver papers, and he gave me $10.

ER 4.

I said something to this kid, and he punched me in the nose.

In both of these, he is still the recipient, but he does something that influences his getting.

The same type of reconciliation can be done using the other approaches for interpreting ERs.

Sixth, we have the conditional interpretation. Look at the following example from Mosak (1958):

ER 1.

We had a cookie jar on the top shelf in the kitchen. I couldn't reach it by myself, so my uncle lifted me up, and I got the cookie jar.

ER 2.

I was sitting on top of a fence. Suddenly, I lost my balance, fell off, and broke my jaw. (pp. 304–305)

In the first recollection, the patient describes her dependency upon others, especially men. In the second recollection, she describes what happens when she relies on herself. Only disaster can ensue; she cannot stay "on top." This woman felt that she could only be elevated, "lifted up," by a man, and she married one who gave her status and material possessions. When her husband left her and deprived her of her status and his strength, she could not bear living alone and attempted suicide.

These ERs demonstrate the conditional interpretation of "if-then" statements. *If* a man elevates her, *then* she can get the goodies. *If* she relies on herself, *then* she falls. Makes sense, doesn't it?

Seventh, we look at the details. In ER 1 from the first set of recollections given in this Chapter, we learn that the client includes color detail — "a *blue* and *white* coffee can with *red* lettering." Color details in ERs suggest an eye for art, beauty, or the appearance of things. The significance of color details (as well as other details) is discussed in Chapter 8.

Eighth, we look for symbolism. An example from Mosak (1958) follows:

ER 2. Age 5:

> When my mother died. She was lying in the coffin. Suddenly she picked herself up and hugged me (p. 309).

Obviously the memory is fabricated, and it may provide a clue that the client may be psychotic. Nevertheless, we see the symbolism of the client being a passive recipient of the center of attention. The client is telling us through the recollection that even death will not deny him special attention that only a mother could give? Is the client destined to a life of isolation because no one else could give the attention a mother could?

Ninth, as discussed throughout this book, we sometimes get a metaphor for a person's life style in one or more of the recollections. We have presented a few examples; here is another:

ER 1.

> I was out swimming, and before I know it I was in over my head.

This one is easy. You tell us, what metaphor is the client using? (Big hint: Recollections like these indicate that clients get in over their heads.)

ER 2.

> It was Thanksgiving time, and it was snowing, and I was playing with these boys in our front yard. We were building a giant turkey made out of snow. I was enjoying myself, and then all of a sudden one of them said something rude. I got up and walked away. I never looked back.

Do you think that this client may give up boys (men) cold turkey?

ER 3.

> One time the neighborhood kids were playing hospital. Some of us were surgeons, some of us were nurses, and some of us were patients. I was an orderly, and I had to carry people into the hospital. It wasn't so bad, except for whenever I had to pick up and bring in one of the girls, they would stick their arms straight out and it would make it difficult for me to carry them. I dropped a couple.

Is this client telling us that women are a cross to bear and that if they make things too difficult for him, he'll "drop" them?

Tenth, we look at the feelings. As previously reported, we don't concern ourselves with the feelings in ERs the way others (e.g., Waldfogel) do. We keep in mind that feelings are cognitively based. However, we may discover a thread with respect to feelings. If the person finishes each ER with "I cried," we learn that the person's solution to or posture in life is to be a "crybaby." We may also treat feelings as conditional statements: Under these circumstances, I feel happy; under these, I feel sad. For example, if I get, then I feel happy, and if I lose, then I feel sad. Another example of the "if-then" contingency would be *if* I win, *then* I feel happy.

Always keep in mind the most vivid part of the recollection for the client because the essence of the personality resides in that part. The rest may be important, but it is more peripheral.

Case 2

Now you have the basic skills to craft a sequential analysis from a series of ERs. There are three more case examples that will help you develop some familiarity with the process.

Below are six ERs from one individual. Your task is to read each recollection and gather the pertinent clues from each that will capture the client's convictions.

ER 1. Age: 5

> There was this one time, late at night, I was in the backyard after a housewarming party my parents gave. We didn't have a big backyard, but I couldn't find my way back to the house. It was a new house, but I should have been able to find my way back. I was frightened, and I called out into the night for someone to help me. My uncle found me and picked me up, dusted off my pajamas and took me to my parents. I was so relieved that my uncle found me. It was so kind of him to go out looking for me.
>
> Most vivid: "Being alone and lost."

From this and other recollections presented in this section, write down your impression of the client's self-concept, self-ideal, and *Weltbild*. When you have your answers, compare them to ours.

We interpret this client's self-concept to be: "I am a frightened, lost soul who can't find my way." The self-ideal is: "In order to have a place, I must be rescued and cared for by a man." The *Weltbild* is: "Men are kind and take care of me."

If you did not have those answers, or something similar to them, reread the recollections and find the clues that suggest what we have interpreted. If you are happy with your choices, move on to the next early recollection. As you read it, think about how it fits with the previous example.

ER 2. Age: 6

> There was this festival at the local church. I was walking around with my mom, and we saw all kinds of things. We walked past the haunted house attraction. I never saw one before, and I was too afraid to go in. I wondered what it was like on the inside. My mom and I walked into the haunted house, and then I discovered it was not as frightening as I imagined it to be.

> Most vivid: "Not knowing what to expect."

Make your choices. Once you are comfortable with them, compare them to our interpretations.

We understand the self-concept to be: "I am a pessimist, and I don't know in advance what's going to happen." What is the client's self-ideal? We believe it to be: "If I don't know what's going to happen, I fear something bad will happen." Finally, we have the *Weltbild* interpretation. The client's picture of the world is: "Life is not as bad as my anticipations make it. The novel makes me uneasy, mother's companionship doesn't reassure me."

We hope that makes sense. If it doesn't, review the recollection. By now, you should be getting some inkling as to what the client thinks about others and the world, and you may be able to predict how that person would act in therapy and what the presenting therapeutic problem is most likely to be. Let's see if the remainder of the recollections confirm our interpretations.

ER 3. Age: 5

> My class was going on a field trip. I was not familiar with the place we were going. I asked my mom to come along. She didn't. She just left me off at the front door of the school. I didn't know where we were going or what I was going to do there.

> Most vivid: "My mother leaving."

We have interpreted the self-concept from this recollection to be: "I do not know what to expect when confronted by the novel." Furthermore, the *Weltbild* may be seen as: "Women are not there when I need them."

By now you might be right on track in comprehending the client. Here is another recollection.

ER 4. Age: 9

> I was on the school bus riding home with all of the neighborhood kids. I really had to go to the bathroom, and I was doing a pretty good job of holding it in. When we got off of the bus, we had to walk to our houses. I was able to hold it in and not run to my house. I thought I was going to make it, but as soon as I got in the door, I peed my pants in front of my family. I couldn't make it to the bathroom. They made me clean it up. I was so embarrassed. They kidded me that I needed diapers.
>
> Most vivid: "Losing bladder control in front of everyone."

Just tell us the self-concept that is shown in the recollection. Here is our interpretation: "I can't completely control myself, and it embarrasses me. My lack of control will show, so I have to admit it. I have to clean up my messes."

How did you do? Two more recollections to go, and then we'll summarize the ERs by looking at the common threads.

ER 5. Age: 8

> There was this one mean kid in the neighborhood that no one liked, including me. I was talking to my mother about this kid, and she said, "You can take him. You're bigger than he is." I couldn't believe my ears. I was scared at even the idea of fighting this kid. I told her that I wasn't able to beat this kid up. Just then he knocked on the door. My mom pushed me onto the front step, and I heard her lock the door behind me. I knew then that she wanted me to fight him. I was too scared, so I made like I was his buddy because I knew I wouldn't fight him. My heart was beating a million miles an hour.
>
> Most vivid: "Deciding it would be healthier to be friendly to him."

You know the drill. Write down your guesses. But this time we are going to make it more challenging. Write down the client's ethical convictions. Now compare your answers to our interpretations.

For self-concept, we have: "I am afraid of fighting. The mere thought of it frightens me." For self-ideal, we have: "In order to have a place,

I shouldn't fight, especially with bullies, and I shouldn't listen to women who encourage me to do so."

Next, for the *Weltbild* (remember, that's the client's picture of the world), we have: "Women egg me on to get into trouble." And for the last area, ethical convictions, we have: "It's wrong to be a bully."

Do your interpretations match ours? Are they close?

There is just one more recollection to go.

ER 6. Age: 8

> It was our "School Olympics Day." I was a pretty good runner, and some of the other students suggested that I run in the 100-yard dash. Now only the best runners wound up in the 100-yard dash, and I was one of six competitors. I looked at the other runners, and I knew that at least three of them were probably faster than I was. I was panicky. I told my teacher that my finger ached, even though it didn't. She told me to see the nurse after the race. She and I debated whether I should run the race first or go to the nurse first. I ran the race and came in last. But then I had to play out the lie that my finger hurt, and I still had to go to the nurse even though I didn't need to. Later I felt like such an idiot for the whole stupid thing.

> Most vivid: "Having to run the race in spite of what I told the teacher."

We interpret the self-concept to be: "I am afraid of competition. I am a pretender. I engage in debate with others when I don't want to do something. When on the spot, I try to fake my way out with illness, even though I know I'm not good at it."

We hope your suggestions for the self-ideal match ours: "In order to have a place I shouldn't lose. I shouldn't give in. I have to fake it although it makes me feel silly." As for the *Weltbild*, our interpretations are: "Competition makes life difficult for me" and "When competition get tough, I get scared."

It appears as though in order to accomplish something he must be sure. He doesn't operate without guarantees.

So how did you do? Do our interpretations make sense?

Once we have gone through the recollections in this way we need to sew the common threads together to create an image of the client. What follows is one interpretation of this client's ERs:

I'm a confused little boy who doesn't know where I am and wander around aimlessly and frightened unless there is a big person around to support me. I'm deficient, scared, and most of all scared that others will find out. Even when I know the answers, I am so distrustful of my abilities that I either louse things up or I find evasions so that I will not have to meet the task. I am afraid of confrontation, and even if others are confident of my ability to handle it, I am not. I am afraid of the novel, of competition, of confrontation, of being lost. However, anticipations are often worse than what actually happens.

Men are kind and take care of me. Women make life difficult for me. They try to place me in difficult situations in which my performance and masculinity are on the line. The best I can do is try to evade their pressures and retreat.

Do you see how ERs can tell you much about a client? These things are important, especially in therapy. The first step is to understand how people perceive the world, the interfering attitudes and beliefs, and their coping mechanisms. Having that knowledge makes you a better clinician.

You are now on your own. For the last two case examples we are going to present the ERs along with our interpretations and an overall summary at the end.

Case 3

ER 1. Age: 7

A bunch of us were playing kickball in my front yard. My mother was watching us from the kitchen window. She must have seen something that she did not like, and she opened up the kitchen window and started screaming at everyone. I thought that whatever she saw, she is making a mountain out of a molehill. All I could think about was that all of the neighborhood kids wouldn't want to play with me anymore. I would be ostracized for sure.

Most vivid: "My mother screaming her head off."

Self-ideal: My place depends upon what women do.

Weltbild: Women are shrews and make it problematic for a man to have a place. Women overreact.

ER 2. Age: 8

I remember talking to this kid at school, and he invited me to his house on the other side of town to play some video games. He had a dog, and the dog looked real hungry, so I gave him a chocolate bar that I was saving for after dinner. I also figured that it would save my friend the trouble of feeding him. I told him, and he thanked me. However, I didn't know that chocolate can be poisonous to dogs. The dog's eyes became all bloodshot, and he stopped moving around. They had to take him to the vet. My friend was all upset, so I decided to go with him to the vet to keep him company. Well, it took longer than I had anticipated, and my parents didn't know where I was, so they called the school, called the parents around the neighborhood and even called the police. When I got home, I got into so much trouble. I think I was grounded for five years.

Most vivid: "Seeing the dog's bloodshot eyes and being grounded."

Self-concept: I am an innocent commotion maker. I help others.

Self-ideal: I should avoid making commotion. I should stay close to home.

Weltbild: Life is a matter of reward and punishment, and you can't have one without the other. People are unfair because they overly punish for the "crime." People reward and punish.

Ethical convictions: Even when I start off right, I wind up doing wrong. Thus I can get rewarded and punished for the same deed. My punishment is too harsh.

ER 3. Age: 8

There was this pretty girl in class that I had a crush on. One day I was talking to a bunch of kids, and I told them I thought she was cute. They told me that she liked another boy. I figured that she didn't like me because I wasn't that bright in class.

Most vivid: "The kids telling me that she liked another boy."

Self-concept: I am inferior to other men and am willing to infer it even if there is no explicit evidence.

Self-ideal: In order to have a place, I should be smarter.

Weltbild: Women know that I am inferior even if they don't state it directly.

ER 4. Age: 7

It was during the first Friday in second grade. The kids called it Freak Friday because all of the skinny kids (freaks), especially those with glasses, were targets for the bullies. I was so scared that I was going to get beat up. I remember giving my lunch money to a big kid if he would walk next to me and stop any of the bullies from picking on me. Long story short, nothing happened that day. I remember feeling that I absolutely needed a bigger boy with me because I was unable to defend myself. That made me feel like I was one of the girls instead of a boy.

Most vivid: "The fear of getting beat up by the big guys."

Self-concept: I can't defend myself in the masculine world.

Self-ideal: In order to have a place, I require protection because I can't defend myself.

Weltbild: There are bullies in the world. The worst calamities are those that never happen.

Remember that no summary is ever complete. It is a thumbnail description, so feel free to add anything you see that we may have omitted. Early recollections are multifaceted and thus capable of many interpretations. Having said that, here is our understanding of the client from the clues presented in the ERs:

Women especially tend to make me feel that my place is precarious. Even when this is not so, I can read it in their words. The reasons I have no place are that I don't always please, I don't always do the right thing, I am not always adequate. I am not masculine enough, and I am not smart enough to protect myself. I am an innocent commotion maker, but I pay for it nevertheless. I am a person who enjoys helping others, but that may lead to negative consequences.

Case 4

ER 1. Age: 4

I was in a department store with my parents. I was real little, and I could not see over or around the cabinets in the store, and I lost sight of my folks. I thought that I would never see them again. Then I thought that one of the store employees would take me home and that I would have to join their family. I just sat there and started crying and crying and crying until they found me. Once I saw them, I felt like a great weight had been lifted off of me.

Most vivid: "Not being able to see my parents."

Self-concept: I am lost, cannot find my way, and can only cry.

Self-ideal: In order to have a place, I must not be lost.

Weltbild: Life is dangerous. Things are never so bad that I can't make them worse in my own mind. However, all's well that ends well.

ER 2. Age: 8

It was the first time I used the riding mower by myself. No one was home. I started up the tractor and began mowing the lawn. I looked at the grass and the trees and the flowers and the people walking by. Things looked so different from up in the seat. I was soaking it all it in. I remember the joy of being able to do it on my own. And I was doing a good job.

Most vivid: "Being in the seat rather than having to sit on my father's lap as he drove the tractor."

Self-concept: I am an observer. When I am independent, I feel good.

Self-ideal: In order to have a place, I should be independent. I should be on top of things.

ER 3. Age: 8

We had some fields near my house. A friend of mine and I were in the fields on a hill. I thought it would be cool to start a campfire. We started a fire with a lighter I had, and it kind of got out of control. Just then the guy who owned the field showed up. He was furious. I took off and headed for home. I suspect he had to put out the fire. I never told anyone about that.

Most vivid: "The fire getting out of control."

Self-concept: I make mischief and run.

The possible consequences of my mischief scare me. (This is also an ethical conviction.)

Self-ideal: I must consider the consequences of my mischief, or I must avoid making mischief.

ER 4. Age: 7

It was after lunch and I had to go to the bathroom. I accidentally started to go into the girls' bathroom, and the guys' gym teacher [male] grabbed me by the ear and pulled me out. It hurt so much I started to cry.

Most vivid: "Realizing I was in the girls' bathroom."

Self-concept: I do innocently wrong. (This is also an ethical conviction.)

Self-ideal: In order to have a place, I should know or be careful where I'm going.

Weltbild: People (men?) punish me for doing the wrong thing.

Ethical convictions: If I go into the girl's private area I will get punished.

ER 5. Age: 5

One day in kindergarten I was skipping around the classroom rhyming words out loud. I must have done something wrong because the teacher told me not to do it again, and she put me in the corner of the room, way away from everyone else. I was frightened. I was there for an awfully long time until this nice woman told me I could join my class again. I was so relieved.

Most vivid: "The woman rescuing me from the corner."

Self-concept: I am an innocent wrongdoer. Even though I'm just having fun, others think it's bad. Even when I'm ostracized, I can be reinstated.

Self-ideal: In order to have a place, I shouldn't make mischief.

Weltbild: Women punish me. Women rescue me.

Ethical convictions: If one does wrong, one may get ostracized.

ER 6. Age: 8

This kid and I pushed this other kid out of his chair in the cafeteria. One of the lunchroom assistants saw us do it, and we were hauled into the principal's office. I remember the other kid was petrified as we sat outside the principal's office. Once we started talking to the principal, he kinda told us not to worry and it wasn't that big of a deal. It was just to get our attention.

Most vivid: "The principal telling us that we did something wrong, but it was no big deal."

Self-concept: I do something wrong.

Self-ideal: I shouldn't do wrong, but it's no big deal.

Weltbild: They apprehend me. Crime doesn't pay. Others are more scared than I when they do wrong.

Ethical convictions: What I do wrong is no big deal, but the authorities feel I should be kept in line.

ER 7. Age: 8

The bully on the street took some kid's bike and started riding it around and wouldn't give it back. So I took a fistful of gravel and sand and chucked it at him as he rode by. He ran into a telephone pole and got hurt. I was scared.

Most vivid: "Chucking the fistful of gravel at his head."

Self-concept: I am willing to take on tough guys. I do wrong.

Weltbild: Even tough guys can be handled and have their downfall.

Ethical convictions: I do wrong and am scared. It's OK to do wrong, but one should consider the consequences.

ER 8. Age: 7

In school we had coed soccer teams. One evening during soccer awards held in the school auditorium I was to be awarded MVP [most valuable player], and they placed me on one of those stands where the first-place person is highest, then the second-place person, and then the third. Well, my parents were in the audience, and as I was standing on the highest platform for first place, I realized that the girl who was on the second-place platform was blocking the spotlight from reaching me. The next thing I knew she fell down and cut her lip. My parents could see me after that.

Most vivid: "The girl blocking me."

Self-concept: I need to be in the limelight, and people (or perhaps women specifically) who stand in my way take a fall.

Self-ideal: I should be in the limelight, even if that means others lose face.

Weltbild: Women get in my way.

Interpretation:

I am a mischief maker, attracted to wrongdoing, and because I am a mischief maker, I often wind up the victim. I want to explore the world, observe it. I want to be independent and do what I want to do without interference. Most often life interferes with that aim, and when life catches up with me, I run scared.

People don't get along well with me nor I with them. I give them a hard time; they give me one in return. I commit punishable offenses because I don't do the things others think I should. Even if I am ostracized for it, it will only be transitory. My mischief is no big deal. It is best, however, to keep it from public view or else I may get punished.

Other men are also mischief makers, and though we all may be fearful of the consequences, they are more scared than I. Other men may be bullies. I can't handle them through direct confrontation, but I can handle them through making mischief.

All in all, I want to be independent, a big shot, do what I want without interference, and be my own person. What scares me is that this posture places me in the dangerous position of being lost in life and requiring the intervention of others.

We hope this Chapter has provided some insight as to how ERs can be analyzed sequentially and convey pertinent information about clients. Early recollections present clues. It is up to the clinician to see and interpret those clues properly.

Summary

Sequential analysis involves going through a whole set of recollections and putting it all together in a summary of the ERs. We look for a thread that runs through the recollections. The thread is a central theme, and every recollection may deal with it. We also look at the cast of characters presented in the recollections for general themes, such as "men elevate me." In addition, we must look for any modifications or elaborations of the theme. These modifications or elaborations may provide a more three-dimensional understanding of the client.

Then we look for reconciliation between two or more seemingly contradictory ERs that we cannot make sense of. Because of the unity of the personality — that is, because people do not contradict themselves in ERs — we must find how the apparently incongruous ERs connect. Then we try specification, to look for a clue inside a clue. Afterward, we have the conditional interpretation, in which the client may have an if-then condition, such as "If men are nice to me, then I am happy; if they are mean, then I am upset."

Additionally, we look for the details given in the recollection, such as color, position, and elevation, which provide more information about the client. Symbolism is often used in ERs, and each recollection should be inspected for symbols that provide clues about the client. Similar to symbols are metaphors, which also provide clinical information. An examination of the feeling given with the recollections may add to the interpretation.

7
Sample Analyses

Congratulations, you've made it about halfway through the book! This is a good place to give you a general overview of some of the concepts presented, a brief review of relevant history, and a sample case that we can analyze. Think of this Chapter as a mini midterm review. The purpose of this Chapter is to review key concepts and integrate those ideas with a quick review of someone's ERs.

Brief Review

Early recollections have served as the major assessment device for Adlerian psychologists since Adler's pioneering article of 1933. Adler indicated that for every person, the ERs are "The Story of My Life." When we elicit people's ERs, we obtain a glimpse of their life styles — that is, how people uniquely think, feel, and act, and their ethical convictions, particularly within certain contexts.

A large body of literature exists, and Dudycha and Dudycha (1941), Mosak (1958), Mosak and Mosak (1975; 1985), and Olson (1979) have compiled references to articles on the topic of ERs. As a review, we present the following assumptions underlying the use of ERs as a projective technique:

1. Early recollections express rather than repress. Thus, instead of viewing ERs as screen memories as Freud did, Adlerians view them as

a projective technique. Ruth Munroe (1955) refers to them as the first projective technique.

2. Memory is selective, and people retain into adulthood those ERs, that reflect their *current* outlook on life and themselves. Another way of saying it is that we can detect people's life styles from their ERs.

3. A recollection need not be true. The mere fact that a person says, "I remember . . . " defines it as an ER (as long as the event reportedly happened prior to the client's 10th birthday). Many recollections are partial or complete fabrications remembered in a way that reveals the current life style. Memory is a matter of construction rather than reconstruction (Bartlett, 1932).

4. Adlerians regard only singular incidents as ERs. Memories of a more general kind, such as "I used to go to the movies every Saturday when I was a kid," are not treated as ERs, although they may be clinically useful.

5. If a client gives you a recollection such as "My family said that when I was a kid . . .," it is a family story. Family stories do not originate from the client and therefore cannot be used as ERs, although they too may possess diagnostic significance.

6. According to Adlerians, the interpretation of a dream cannot be accomplished without knowledge of the dreamer (Shulman, 1973). However, knowledge of the person who gives the ERs is not required for their interpretation. In this way the method differs from other attempts by psychobiographers or psychohistorians who attempt to formulate diagnoses of people without examining the people themselves.

7. Since personal knowledge of the client is not mandatory, Adlerians can examine the ERs of persons whom they are not treating to acquire a picture of their life styles. This makes possible the supervision of a client whom the supervisor does not know.

8. Adlerians who have conducted experiments to investigate whether one can assess mental health from ERs have generally been unable to make this assessment. One can have the same life style in both the abnormal and normal state. A person who, for example, must be first can do so by becoming a superachiever or through maintaining that he is Jesus Christ, or by being the first in line, or the first to achieve something. According to Dreikurs (1935/1953), one could use the same life style either on "the useful side of life" or on "the useless side of life." For example, one can be an "aginner" and go against the injustices of the world and help others, or just be the most difficult person you would never want to sit next to on an airplane.

The concepts of "the useful side of life" and "the useless side of life" may best be explained with examples. Most everybody is familiar with the great achievers in history (e.g., Gandhi, Leonardo da Vinci, Jane Addams, John Lennon, George Washington Carver, Golda Meir, Thomas Edison, Albert Einstein, Chuck Yeager, Miguel De Cervantes, Harriet Tubman, Yo-Yo Ma, Michelangelo, Steve Jobs, Mother Theresa, Ludwig van Beethoven, Margaret Mead, etc.). These are people who put their talent toward being productive on the useful side of life. However, there are people who devote their energies into being superior on the "useless" side of life.

Many good examples of superiority on the "useless" side of life are chronicled and displayed in such media as the Guinness World Records (n.d.). Venues like that dedicate themselves to the oddities (for the most part) of human successes; in which we can see examples of being superior on the "useless" side of life. For example, people who have the most rhinestones on their body or the most clothespins on their face. Or, people who can smoke more cigarettes at one time than anyone else or build the biggest house of cards in the world. These achievements do elevate these people above the crowd, and they draw attention to these people for what they do, but really, are these talents and recognition on the useful side of life?

The remainder of the Chapter will present samples of ERs and analyses of them. Please read the following ERs and summarize them. We have presented a summary at the end of the recollections that you may compare your answers with.

Early Recollections of Travis

ER 1. Age: 3

> I remember looking out of my kitchen window and seeing my two neighbors fighting. They were a married couple that always fought. She picked up a rake and swung it at his head. He started to bleed all over the place. They continued to argue until he fell down. I thought he died. I was scared stiff. I ran into my room and hid under my bed.

> Most vivid: "The blood all over his face and on the street."

Look at the overall theme of the recollection. What is happening, and what are the prototypes of men and women?

ER 2. Age: 5

My sister and I were outside playing, and she took a sharp flat rock and threw it at the boy next door. Hit him right in the forehead, and he started bleeding like crazy. She was laughing like a hyena! She thought that she could have pitched for the Dodgers. She hid behind some trees and kept on laughing. I thought she was going to wet her pants, she was laughing so much. I jumped the fence to help out the boy next door. I looked into his house and looked at his mother. She saw the whole thing and didn't even bother to come out and help him.

Most vivid: "My sister's insensitivity."

What does this client think of men and women? How are their interactions portrayed?

ER 3. Age: 5

My father got me a puppy for my fifth birthday. I was in kindergarten and went to school a half a day. My chore was to clean up the dog's area before and after school. Apparently, the dog had diarrhea that day and made a big mess in the box that we had for him. When I got home from kindergarten, I asked my mother what smelled so bad. She said, "I'll show you." She took me into the kitchen where the box was and put my face right into the dog's diarrhea. It was all over my face, in between my teeth, and I swallowed a whole bunch. I kept trying to spit it out, but she kept smashing my face into the bottom of the box and smearing it back into my mouth. I can still feel it in my mouth.

Most vivid: "My mother pushing my face into the dog's diarrhea."

What is the metaphor in this recollection?

In this sample of three ERs, we have presented a client who is trying to communicate something. Remember, whether or not these events actually happened makes no difference because they are used as a projective technique to indicate the client's current functioning.

Here is our summary of the client's ERs:

Women are crazy and just try to make a man eat shit. Men are innocent — they don't do anything to provoke it, but they catch it anyway. They can't protect themselves; they can only fear the craziness of women. Though people don't care for me, I care for them. I can't bear to see anybody hurting, and I will do my best to take away their pain.

Does our interpretation make sense? If you compare the summary to the recollections you will see that every sentence is supported in the recollection. This leads us to our next point and a very important one at that.

You can interpret only what the client presents in the memory; otherwise you are projecting your own life style onto the client's ERs.

8
Details in ERs

In every great mystery, details play a pivotal role in the solution. The same thing applies to unraveling the individual mysteries of our clients. This Chapter reviews the different types of details found in an ER and their contributions to its meaning (Dreikurs, 1967). Details in ERs add nuances to the interpretation because they can illuminate what is important. There are many types of details, such as color, location, tactile, vocational; even the omission of details can provide information about your clients. Throughout this book, in order to focus on what is being taught in that section, some of the ERs will be truncated.

Recollections of Trivial Events

Early recollections are treated as projections; consequently no trivial ER exists. What appears insignificant to a clinician may have considerable meaning for the client. The ER of a seemingly trivial event often deals with important people or issues. What might you make out of this recollection?

> I was in my uncle's car by myself. I was in the driver's seat and turning the wheel and pretending I was driving.

For those of you who say, "Everyone has done this in their childhood," you are missing the essence of the recollection. It is not whether it is "normal" or universal to do so, but rather why is it coming up now, many years later, as an easily remembered event. What does this tell us about the client?

Here are a few options you may or may not have thought of. Go through them and decide what is the best answer.

- I am alone in the world.
- Men are in the driver's seat.
- I pretend I can do what real men do.
- Children are in control.

You must remember that you cannot tell much about a person from just one ER. However, this recollection is offered by the client and therefore does reflect on his current functioning. What is presented is an important issue to the client. We just have to decode the metaphor.

Though you may think that all of the above statements are possible, there is one that stands out as best. Let us go through each clue and see if it fits.

The option of "I am alone in the world" focuses on only the first part of the recollection, forcing us to throw away the remainder of the information available. On that basis alone, it is not an appropriate choice.

You may believe that "Men are in the driver's seat" is correct because there is a metaphor involved; however, that choice is not appropriate because he is a child in the recollection. A man would have to be in the driver's seat for that option to be true.

"Children are in control" seems unlikely. Since ERs are a projective of current functioning, it's not referring to children (unless he's a frustrated father), and besides, the child in the recollection is not in control of the car. It remains stationary, demonstrating that he is not controlling it. The best choice is "I pretend I can do what real men do" as it takes into account the entire recollection and is exactly what he is doing in the memory. It suggests that his ambition is to be able to do what adult males do, but in his projection, he sees himself as a "pretender." Trivial ERs may reveal as much about our clients as dramatic recollections do. Sometimes they are more revealing, as suggested by Corsini in the introduction and previously by Mosak (1958).

Tactile Details

When clients tell us recollections that contain tactile details, they are indicating that they may have a sensual response to tactile stimuli, and they may be more sensitive to their inner feelings (Peven & Shulman, 1983). For example,

I remember this one time I was holding my teddy bear and feeling the warmth and the softness of the fur as I ran my fingers through the brown fur.

In our example, "softness" (or other tactile clues) indicates an awareness of contact with other things or people. Here there are two meanings for feeling, the first being tactile awareness — that is, a sensitivity to touch or to how things feel when touched (such as rough, smooth, wet, warm, fuzzy, etc.). Another meaning for feeling when presented in ERs has to do with inner feeling or emotion. Knowing this information, you may approach therapy with clients who give you this type of response a little more aware of their attention to inner feelings and sensitivity.

The first example has been presented previously:

ER (dramatic) — There was a fire in the town we lived in. Three quarters of the town burned down at night. All kinds of homeless people were brought to my house. There was an old man, a Parkinsonian, burned all over. He was treated in my house. I felt sorry for him. (Mosak, 1958, pp. 307–308)

Here are two more examples:

When I was about four years old, I was walking barefoot on my driveway after a heavy rain. There were worms all over the driveway. I remember feeling the squish of the worms under my feet and in between my toes.

I had to be about four or five and I was in the bathtub. I remember feeling the heat of the water on my skin, especially as I ran my arms through the warm water. I could feel the warmth and the resistance of the water as I pushed my hands through.

Similar to Rorschach interpretation, tactile detail may also indicate a need for affection.

Vocational Details

We'll discuss the relationship between ERs and vocation later (Chapter 12). For our current purpose, we'll touch only upon occupational inclinations from ERs.

Adler (1937a), Orgler (1939/1963), and Mosak (1958) have pointed out that people in various vocations may reveal their occupational choice in ERs. Adler (1929/1964) in *Problems of Neurosis* indicated that physicians retain at least one ER about the themes of death, illness, or injury. The recollections of Freud, Adler, and Jung (Mosak & Kopp, 1973) and of Dreikurs (Terner & Pew, 1978), and the findings by Lashever (1983) support this hypothesis.

An example of a theme of death, illness, or injury can be seen in the following recollections:

> I remember my father bringing this injured puppy into the house. I remember pouring milk into a saucer to nurse it back to health.

> My grandmother had cancer. I remember going to the hospital one time and seeing all of these older patients in wheelchairs in front of the television.

> I was in first grade. They brought in this man who lost his hands as a boy. He told us we could do anything if we put our minds to it. He then used his wrists to draw a beautiful picture of me. I was fascinated and inspired.

The last recollection is interesting as it is inspirational. The client may keep it as a reminder that anything is possible if you put your mind to it. This also reminds us that positive recollections exist and that they allow broader comprehension of individuals — at least broader than just focusing on their pathology, as other methods do.

The following ER has a vocational clue. Though it may be readily apparent on your first reading, take your time and read it more than once. The toughest part may be filtering out all of the nonclues; therefore, try to focus on what is important to the client.

> I was in my room counting the ceiling tiles. After I completed counting them, I re-counted them to make sure I was accurate the first time. I thought it was interesting how I got the same number twice. I was happy I was right.

What occupation might you make out of this ER?
Here are some choices of occupational inclinations:

- carpenter
- accountant
- interior designer
- quality-control engineer
- warden

Make your selection of a likely career.

First, ask yourself what the theme of the recollection is. Is the client building anything? No. So if you chose a carpenter, take another guess. Is the client designing anything? No. Scratch interior designer. Perhaps a warden? Clearly, the client is in a room and pleased. But that is not that answer for the reason that being in the room does not please the client. Those of you who selected an accountant were right on the money, so to speak. The client is happy counting. Isn't that what accountants are supposed to do?

But what about a quality-control engineer? Ah, you're on to us and to the flexibility of career selection. Though ERs may allow us to see an individual's talents and interests, they do not specify a single career selection. They merely point to a direction of interests which may be further explored in vocational guidance. There isn't just one good career choice per person.

Here is another example:

> I had to be eight or nine, and I remember my father taking me out deer hunting one year. He shot a deer and took out a sharp knife from its leather holster and gutted the deer right in the field. I thought it was so cool the way he used the knife.

The "I thought it was so cool" gives us an indication that the client might be a surgeon, as he specifically references the use of the knife. Or perhaps a serial killer. Clearly, the client enjoys the event described in the recollection.

Read the Chapter on ERs and vocation (Chapter 12) for a more comprehensive examination of the use of ERs and career guidance.

Omitted Details

Occasionally ERs are given that on the surface appear innocuous and straightforward but have an element that requires us to prompt for more information. That information may yield what Dreikurs (personal communication, 1969) called a "goldmine." We must at this point remind you how important it is to be a clinician and not a scribe. A good clinician will ask follow-up questions. Imagine the important information that we would miss had the clinician not further queried the client in regard to the following ER:

> My family and two neighbors were sitting around the dining room table. It was a festive occasion. Everyone smiling, everyone pleased. Father was home. (Mosak, 1958, p. 303)

At first glance, we may believe that we have a complete memory minus the most vivid part. It is an interesting recollection, but why do you think the client gave that last sentence? After all, "My family" would seem to imply that the client's father was there. Clearly, the narrative would make just as much, if not more, sense if that last sentence was not given. Obviously something is omitted. The astute clinician will notice the odd inclusion and question.

Why is the father mentioned specifically? The clinician found out that the client's father had just been released from a sanatorium. The client's family was of the Christian Science faith, which disapproves of such hospitalization. The omission of a detail is a clue in and of itself.

What is omitted from the following recollection?

> Age 5 — Saturday morning. I'm coming out of the hospital. My uncle and aunt were there to get me. (Shulman & Mosak, 1988, p. 184)

Why was the client in a hospital? And why were his aunt and uncle picking him up there, rather than his parents (the client had previously indicated that he lived with his parents). After investigating this point further, the clinician found out that the client's father smothered the entire family with pillows, and the client was the only one to survive. The father was subsequently executed.

One last example of an omitted detail comes from a 40-year-old man:

> I remember it was a cool autumn day, and I was in the kitchen with my mother. We were making cookies and talking. My father was going to come home shortly, and we were going to surprise him with some fresh, hot, chocolate-chip cookies. I can still remember what the kitchen looked like. It was blue and brown, and we had a wooden kitchen table with six chairs. I could hear the birds chirping and the kids playing in the street. I could smell the cookies [see olfactory details later] as they baked in the gas oven. My mother and I were talking, and she hit me. I felt sad.

Most vivid: "Being hit."

Why does the client omit the mother's motivation, and what might this mean? Is the client not able to see how his actions get him into trouble? Of course. Is he telling us that he sees others as acting against him with no rhyme or reason? Yes. Might this client feel that his best intentions are not recognized? Yes.

Take a moment and think about why a person who gives recollections like these would come into therapy. They may come into therapy on their own ("other people don't understand me and criticize me"), or they may be urged to begin (or continue) therapy by their spouse, relative, coworker, or boss.

We hope this illustrates the importance of querying the client. Don't neglect to ask questions. Otherwise you may miss a wealth of information.

Geographical, Location, and Positional Details

Every part of the recollection can be informative. We must pay attention to the details no matter how commonplace they may appear. The position of the client (and others) in ERs provides clues as to the client's stance toward life (Dreikurs, 1954).

A geographical detail names a specific location, for example, a city, town, or country. The following ERs contain geographical details:

> When we lived in London, I remember this one day walking into a store and seeing eggs sitting on a shelf. I thought it was so odd that they were not refrigerated like they were when I lived in the States.

> When we lived in Australia, I remember seeing this kangaroo jump in front of our car. I was so scared.

The inclusion of geographical details prompts us to query clients for more information. Such details may point out movement, for example, as in the following ER:

> When I was five, my father lost his job. He said we would have to cut back. I remember one day moving from a beautiful, idyllic paradise in the Hamptons to a small apartment in dreary Plattsburgh, New York. I was irritated, bored, and dejected.

Here the client is telling us how she had to move out of the "Garden of Eden."

Location details are those that include a reference to a particular type of place. Here are some examples of location details in ERs:

> I remember being in the detention room at school and having the teacher tell me to "shut up." I was so embarrassed.

> I really, really had to go to the bathroom at school. I got out of lunch, and I couldn't hold it any longer. I ran into the bathroom

and couldn't find the urinals. I was panicked. I started peeing my pants. Just then I realized I was in the girls' bathroom.

The location given in the first ER, "in the detention room at school," may suggest questions such as "How often were you in trouble at school?"

In the second recollection, could the man be telling us that he puts himself in the wrong place at the wrong time?

Positional details indicate position relative to others metaphorically (e.g., up, down, ahead, behind). Here are some examples of positional details:

I was at school, and we were playing king of the hill, and the girls were on top, and I was on the bottom.

When I was a child, my family lived in Canada. Every day my older brother and I used to take the ferry across the bay to get to school. [That part is a report.] One day when I was about seven, my brother and I were walking to the dock to get the ferry. He was way ahead of me and was able to catch it. I missed it.

In the first recollection, the client may be telling you that in his life currently, women are on top, and he is at the bottom. In the second recollection, this client's brother (or perhaps men in general) may be ahead of him in some way (such as starting a family, being smarter, etc.). However, metaphorically, the client may feel as though he has missed the boat — that he is not far enough ahead in life to join others and move forward with his life.

Knowing that geographical, location, and positional details metaphorically describe clients' current perceptions, what might you understand about the person who gave this ER?

Age 8 – I was sitting on the curb watching the other kids play ball across the street. I didn't go over. (Shulman & Mosak, 1988, p. 184)

Look at the positional clues the client has presented in the recollection. First, the child in the ER is apart from the other children. He is sitting, observing others play. Second, the phrase "across the street" provides a pertinent positional detail. The ER suggests that the speaker is an outsider who can only watch others enjoy life rather than enjoy life himself.

Here is an ER with a clear positional detail:

I remember being upstairs in my house and looking down upon the construction workers who were working with their hands

digging and pouring the concrete for our swimming pool.
I remember they were all sweaty and dirty.

Do you think this person looks down on those who do manual labor?
Probably.

Feeling Details

In Chapter 2, we discussed the necessity of asking for clients' feelings at the time of the event the ER describes. As was discussed earlier, the feeling can be a crucial detail in understanding the individual. Furthermore, if we gather ERs at different times in therapy, we may see noticeable change in the feeling that the event elicits. For example let's say you twice got ERs detailing this event, once at the beginning and once at the end of therapy.

I pushed my sister down for taking my toy truck. I felt powerful.

What might you think about this person? Let's say this man has been ordered by a court to get therapy in a spousal abuse case. Fast-forward to the end of therapy. You are now given this recollection:

I pushed my sister down for taking my toy truck. I felt ashamed.

How might you feel about your therapeutic intervention? Do you think that you helped the client develop feelings of empathy? Maybe, but you have a bigger problem: If you focus on the feelings, they have obviously changed. However, if you focus on the behavior, you notice the abusive behavior continues.

How about this change in the ER:

My sister took my toy truck, and I decided it was better if we play together with it. We played together in the sunshine. We were very happy.

This is a big change from the original recollection and goes one step further. The violence that occurred in the first recollection never happens in the last one. It demonstrates that the client has a different attitude about how to interact with females.

However, a change in emotion does not necessarily indicate a positive change. Suppose a client tells you this recollection at the beginning of therapy:

I remember one time in first grade I was walking around with my zipper down. I didn't notice it until the end of the day. I was so embarrassed.

And say he gives you the following recollection at the end of therapy:

> I remember one time in first grade I was walking around with my zipper down. I didn't notice it until the end of the day. I didn't feel ashamed.

The change needs to be queried for more information. What created the change? Did the client get over the embarrassment, or does this client just not give a care? How would you feel if this client was court mandated for therapy after multiple arrests for pedophilia?

Affect in ERs may also show how the person reacts toward the world. Consider these recollections, all from the same person:

> I was with my family on a plane flying over some city. I looked out of the window, and I was petrified.

> I remember some kid telling me at school that if I drank soda pop my teeth were going to fall out. I was very scared!

> I had to sing a solo in front of the entire student body in our school's auditorium. I was frightened to death!

> I remember watching the movie *Jurassic Park*. When I saw all of the dinosaurs I remember not being able to move. I thought they were going to get me. I was so afraid!

These recollections are given to illustrate the importance of getting the feeling of the recollection at the time it occurred from your clients. This client is clearly frightened in every recollection. This demonstrates a tendency to be frightened about life's difficulties and to refrain from engaging in activities or problem solving.

Affect as Expression of a Value

We can get an idea of what the client values by considering the feeling, or lack of feeling, associated with the recollection. For example,

> I remember going into my friend's house. He was very wealthy. His family had a huge-flat screen TV, a DVD recorder, and a great stereo. I had the best time.

Think about what the client is trying to tell you. Keep that idea in your head as you read the next recollection. When you are done, compare the two recollections to discover what the client values.

I had to attend a public school, and I was watching this movie on this old, cheap movie projector that broke down right at the best part of the movie. I hated that.

What does this person value? Friendships? Television? Stereo? Movies?

These are only part of the picture. Though he does have a good time with his friend, it is not friends that he values; after all, he has classmates at school but does not mention them as friends. It's not television or a great stereo, specifically, that he values, as those are only part of the whole picture. Movies fall in the same category. What he values is wealth. It is wealth that is able to buy that huge TV and great stereo. It is the lack of wealth (the old, cheap movie projector that broke down) that the client hates.

Absence of Affect as a Response

Looks at the details for clues to solve the mystery that your client presents you. What might you make of this recollection?

I had to be about five years old, and I remember looking in the mirror at the scars on my face.

Feeling: "I really didn't have any feeling."

We have provided a very short recollection to make it easier to find a clue. What can you see in the above sentences? How do you interpret the client's lack of feeling? Could that lack of feeling indicate a coping mechanism that the client often uses? If you had scars on your face, wouldn't you be frustrated, angry, fearful, sad, or at the very least, miffed? In querying the feeling associated with the recollection, we may learn the client's coping style. In this case we have a feeling avoider (Mosak, 1971), a person who turns a blind eye to distressing situations. How might this type of person feel if his or her marriage was on the rocks? How might feeling avoiders view others and their emotional responsibility to them? Might their children feel as though they are not heard? Would they give the presentation of being "cold"?

Often, feeling avoiders believe feelings (whether theirs or others) to be liabilities, and those clients avoid feelings at all costs. As a matter of fact, when you ask them for feelings associated with their ERs, they may provide thoughts rather than feelings.

Suppose a client gives you the following recollection:

I was in kindergarten. I was in line with other students going to the lunchroom, and I wet my pants.

When asked for his feeling at the time, the client says,

I thought I was going to be in big trouble.

Though you *could* speculate on your client's feelings, you should not do so. Nor, however, should you accept thoughts as feelings. At times like these, we have to push the client to give us an emotion rather than a thought. However, do not push a client for a feeling when he or she says, "I didn't feel anything," or something similar. When clients give us that type of answer, then that is their answer. Pushing them to create an emotion moves us away from an accurate interpretation of the recollection.

Affective Detail as Revealing the Meaning of the Early Recollection

When clients give you a feeling for their recollection, it can provide much more information than the recollection alone. In this section you will see how the feeling will explain the whole memory and perhaps give you an entirely different understanding of the person.

Let's start with the first part of a recollection:

My father and I made this great go-kart. It was the coolest thing on the planet. One day I went to the shed to take it out, and it was gone. I was completely enraged, livid. Later, I found it in the woods smashed to pieces.

As you can see, this recollection has an emotion attached to it (enraged, livid). This may indicate that the client was angered by the actions of others who took the go-kart. Lesser clinicians would stop there as they believe that they have the emotion for the entire recollection. However, let's query for a feeling for this recollection.

Feeling: "I felt much better, because if I couldn't play with it, nobody else should."

Without the associated feeling we would not have gotten the true interpretation of the event, the delight in fairness, which is the actual theme of the early recollection. The client turned a defect into something positive. The client may be thinking, "If I can't have it, they shouldn't either." This is an example of how clients turn a minus into a plus (Mosak & Maniacci, 1998)

This example also highlights the importance of properly associating multiple emotions within an ER. Often clients will give more than one emotion to a recollection. It is our responsibility to clarify which emotion is connected to what part of the recollection. For example, if a recollection has both happy and sad emotions given by a client, you must determine what part was happy, and what part was sad. This is just an extension of our normal inquiry when we ask for an emotion at the time of the event in the recollection. Sometimes, the client gives several emotions for one recollection. Clarify each emotion and how it relates to the recollection.

Do not accept an emotion if the client states it from the present tense looking back at the event as part of the recollection. Suppose, for example, the client says,

> I remember I was nine and my father telling me that I couldn't get a motorbike. I was outraged.

Suppose he then adds,

> You know, looking back at it, he was right. I would have killed myself on one of those things.

We accept the first part because that is an ER of a specific event prior to the client's 10th birthday. However, we do not accept the second part because it is not an ER but a reflection from today as the client looks back at the event.

Changing Affect in ERs

Given that ERs are a projection of current functioning, it makes sense that current emotions will appear in recollections of earlier events. Therefore, we need to consider the client's current mood when asking for the feeling at the time of the recollection. If your client is depressed, the affect of the recollection may (and probably will) be contaminated by the client's current mind-set. Correspondingly, when that depression subsides, the memories will have a more optimistic affect. However, you must keep in mind that affect associated with the ER is different from the theme. The themes (such as "I should get," or "I must be in control," or "life is dangerous") should remain the same while the affect may change.

The If-Then Contingency

The *if-then* contingency has been demonstrated many times earlier in this book. Dreikurs (1966) elaborated on the unity of the personality and "two points on a line." Dreikurs's idea was that if we have two points (such as someone's thoughts or behavior) we can connect those two points with a line. That line will have an infinite number of points that describes the client's behavior in different situations. Our task is to draw an accurate line. There is *always* a line. We just have to find it.

Because of the unity of the personality, individual ERs cannot contradict each other; people do not act or think in contradictory ways, even though it may seem like that at some times. This is in accord with Festinger's (1957) contribution of "cognitive dissonance" (discussed in Chapter 1).

A person is a whole unit who thinks, feels, and acts in concert toward goals. Therefore, if you have two ERs that appear to contradict each other, that means you must dig deeper for an understanding that resolves the contradiction.

Mosak (1958) gives as an example two ERs that illustrate this point clearly:

> I remember that I was under three, and the lady next door picked me up over the fence to take me home.

> My uncle gave my sister 10 cents to kiss him. Then he made me the same offer. I ran out the back door and all the way home. (p. 305)

In the first recollection, people are supportive. In the second recollection, people appear threatening. So now you may be saying, "These are contradictory ERs. Where is the unity of the personality?" But if you apply the *if-then* condition to the above recollections, clarity emerges. Reframe your understanding of those ERs, and the client, and think of the client's mind-set as, "*If* the person is a woman, *then* I'll be supported. *If* the person is a man, *then* I'll be threatened."

Let's say you get the two following recollections:

> It was Christmas Day, and I got this wooden toboggan. I was exhilarated, I ran around the house and jumping up and down shouting "Toboggan! Toboggan! Toboggan!"

> I wanted this golden retriever that my neighbor was selling. I ran home and got my mom to show her the dog. She said I couldn't have it. I was so depressed. I was inconsolable.

Though these ERs may appear to contradict each other (good feelings/bad feelings), the if-then contingency removes that impression. In this case, *if* the client gets something, *then* there is exhilaration. And *if* the client does not get something, *then* there is depression. This is reflective of the "getting personality" (Mosak, 1971).

Most Vivid Details

As we demonstrated in Chapter 2, when we gather a recollection we always want the client's feeling at the time of the event and the client's impression of what the most vivid part of the recollection is. The most vivid part of the recollection helps the clinician to discover the essence of the recollection.

> I was in the driveway with my parents on a very sunny day, and we were washing the car. It was this red station wagon with simulated wood siding and a folding seat in the back where all of us kids would like to sit. I remember my brother taking out his orange skateboard, and I was trying to hit him with water from the hose as he went past. It was such a hot day that he kinda liked it. I asked him for the skateboard, and I sat on it and pushed myself around. Well, the driveway was kinda steep and wet, and I couldn't stop, and I ran into the mailbox and chipped my tooth. I was furious.

This is a long recollection with many details given. Upon reading it, you may see why it's so important that we ask for the detail that is most vivid to the client. If we do not, we run a very high risk of misinterpreting the recollection based on our own projection about what we believe to be the essence of the recollection. For example, we might well assume in this case that the most vivid part is running into the mailbox and chipping a tooth. But that assumption is in fact incorrect. The client said that the most vivid part was "not being able to stop."

What might you deduce from this? Basically, the gist of the ER consists of the client being furious at losing control and the consequences related to losing control (chipping a tooth). The losing control can also be seen in relation to the part of the recollection that precedes the accident. That is, here we have a client telling about a sunny day in which he engages in collective family activity and has fun. Could the message be, "When all is right in the world, and I am enjoying myself with others, I lose control and hurt myself (and possibly lose face)"? And if you were treating this client, you would find out from the client what might be about to go out of control or was currently going out of control, and why being in control may be seen as essential.

You can see the importance of getting the most vivid part of the recollection from the client. Failure to do so greatly hampers our ability to make correct interpretations of the recollections provided. The most vivid part focuses our understanding and paints a clearer picture of the client.

Color Details

Remember that what is important to the client will be displayed in the ER. Those things that are not important, the client is not sensitive to. So if in an ER a client gives a color detail, this generally indicates some artistic or aesthetic interest (Mosak & Kopp, 1973; Sweeney & Myers, 1986). Clients who give color details in their ERs believe that they have taste or style (whether or not it is true).

Things that are important to us surface in different ways. For example, if we are to ask for directions from a gourmand, we might get something like the following: "Go past the hamburger stand, make a right at the ice cream parlor, and it's two doors down from the chocolate brown house."

In other words, we communicate what is important by what we choose to focus on and relate to others.

Pay attention to the color details in the following recollection:

> I was in kindergarten, and I was on stage wearing a green and yellow dress. Behind me was this blue sky made from construction paper and beautiful white clouds made of cotton.

Clearly, color is important to this client as it is so prominent in this recollection. Our clinical experience suggests that artists and those people with strong aesthetic inclinations will include color detail in their ERs.

Olfactory Details

Olfactory details are not very common in ERs. People who have a highly developed sense of smell or no sense of smell at all often give olfactory details. What follows is an ER from a physiologist of the senses.

> It was the first time I saw the sea. I don't remember seeing the sea first. I only smelled it first and heard it; then I saw it (Mosak, 1958, p. 307.)

Modifying Details

Information that is included in a recollection that seems to be irrelevant to the memory may be a modifying detail. If elements of ERs are stated but not relevant to the narrative, then clients include them for psychological reasons. Look at the following recollection:

> It was wintertime, and I was watching a scary movie with my brother. We were petrified.

Why does the client include "wintertime"? Does the client sees the world as a cold place? If it were not important, then why would the client even mention it?

Here is another example:

> I remember playing soccer in the backyard one day. I was having a great time. It was sunny. My family and all of the kids from the neighborhood were there. I scored a goal and won the game. My father wasn't home yet.

We suspect that the last sentence got your attention. It doesn't seem to fit, does it? Might you suggest that the client's father was not home from work yet? Sounds reasonable, but that would be our projection and that is why we need to follow up on such modifying details. Upon further inquiry we find out that the client's father was in prison for tax evasion and did not return home until the client was 12 years of age. How might that influence your understanding, as well as your interview, of the client?

Metaphor Details

Understanding the use of metaphors is very important in comprehending ERs. As we said in Chapter 1, during our formative years there is a relatively large temporal window in which we have not yet acquired language; most of our interaction is in a different symbolic construct, metaphors. Correspondingly, metaphors appear throughout our lives and in many areas. We dream in metaphors. We express ourselves in metaphors through music ("she's my baby"), writing ("winter was near"), everyday speech ("I'm coming unglued"), computer terminology ("on the web"), and many other communicative media.

As a matter of fact, all languages have figures of speech and are symbolic as the words are not the real things, but only represent them. An apple can have dozens of names among a number of languages, and each word is nothing more than a representation. Metaphors are symbolic and are inherent in communication, including what is communicated in ERs. There is usually at least one metaphor in each ER.

Kopp (1995) indicated that ERs can function as metaphors for a life situation, problem, or a variety of other things. For example, what metaphor is used in this woman's recollection?

> I used to live on a farm. And one time my neighbor invited me to her birthday party. This was after a big storm came through on the night before. . . . I was cutting through the field to get to her house, and it was very muddy from all the rain. I ended up getting

> stuck there and being unable to move without losing my shoe.
> I ended up not going to her house for the party. That was OK.
> I really didn't want to go anyway.

Do you see a metaphor in that recollection? Before we give our answer away, let us continue with Kopp's (1995) elaboration on metaphors in ERs. He wrote that these types of metaphors differ from linguistic ones as spoken metaphors use an image to communicate the meaning of the situation. Early recollections must meet certain criteria to be metaphors. These criteria include the ability to carry over the meaning from the area of imagery (that is the image from the client's youth) to the situation in their current life.

Therefore we can consider ERs as metaphors based on their timing. That is, ERs are metaphors when they can be seen in relation to a current problem, symptom, or feeling. So in regard to the above recollection, have you come up with a metaphor for this person?

Let's give you a little information about her current problem. She is in therapy because her husband says she doesn't want to do anything with him. He feels as though she is no longer interested in him, and he suspects that she is depressed.

It appears to us that she is a "stick in the mud."

Here's another example:

> One summer day, I remember being really, really mad at my mother. But I thought that I would play it cool, and I figured that if I didn't talk to her, she wouldn't know how angry I was at her. I went into the kitchen and put a lot of ice and fruit in the blender, I turned it on and all of the fruit sprayed all over the kitchen. My mother screams from the other room. "I know you're mad at me, but don't make a mess in the kitchen." I was dumbfounded. I was like, "How did she know I was mad at her?"

Can you think of a metaphor that is appropriate for this ER?

It appears as though this client may have a difficult time "keeping a lid on it." In this recollection the metaphor is also seen in the theme. He cannot keep a lid on his emotions, and he cannot keep a lid on the blender.

Always look for at least one metaphor in each ER. Knowledge of clichés, platitudes, euphemisms, and similar sayings helps us to comprehend and summarize ERs. Let's look at a quick list of ERs and metaphors that may be associated with them.

I remember being in a museum and seeing JFK's desk chair from the Oval Office. I came close to it but was unable to touch it.

Hidden metaphor: Seat of power.

I remember running on the beach in my bikini. One foot was touching the hot sand, and the other was in the cold water. At first I liked it, then I didn't.

Hidden metaphor: She runs hot and cold.

I remember trying on these very comfortable boots that were really expensive, and my mom told me I was more interested in looking good than being good. I thought she was right.

Hidden metaphor: If the shoe fits, wear it.

One day my father took me to the ice rink. He was so tired from work that he fell asleep on the bleachers while I was skating. He was so boring. I thought, "I'll never work so hard that I'll miss the fun stuff in life."

Hidden metaphor: All work and no play makes Jack a dull boy.

My sister and I were in our mom's car. She was behind the wheel beeping the horn, and I was in the seat behind her wondering when my mom was going to finally come out and take me to soccer practice.

Hidden metaphors: Women are in the driver's seat. Women toot their own horns. I take a back seat to women.

One Thanksgiving I remember sitting around a table, and my father complained that the skin of the turkey was too crisp and brittle. My mom cried hysterically for the rest of the day.

Hidden metaphor: Women have a thin skin.

I remember this one time swimming out into the deep end of the pool. I almost touched bottom, but I ran out of air and almost didn't make it to the surface. I thought I was going to die. I was terrified.

Hidden metaphor: When I get in over my head, I get frightened.

> I remember this one time when I was in the dentist's office. She was drilling a cavity I had. She removed the drill, and I shut my mouth when she went to put the drill back in. She hit my chin with the drill and it really hurt.

Hidden metaphor: If I keep my mouth shut with women, I'll end up taking it on the chin.

> I remember this one time when I was in this school play about a farmer with this barn. Inside the barn were all of the boys from the next grade or two up dressed in pink costumes with snouts and curly tails with their faces in a trough.

Hidden metaphor: (Older) men are pigs.

As we have seen, metaphors are an important part of ERs. Therefore, we must sharpen our skills in recognizing what clients say to us metaphorically in the memories of their youth. Sometimes an ER can be summarized in one phrase.

Summary

Details in ERs add nuances to the interpretation. There are many types of details, such as color, location, tactile, vocational. Even the omission of details can provide information about your clients. Tactile details indicate sensual response to tactile stimuli and perhaps sensitivity to inner feelings. Details in ERs may also be of use in vocational guidance. When clients omit details in ERs, it is up to us to be good clinicians who think and ask about those omissions.

The position of the client and others in ERs may provide insight into the client's stance toward life (e.g., above others). Location details reference a particular type of place (e.g., a school). Feeling details indicate how a client experiences an event, and they can be used to evaluate change from pre- and postintervention ERs. Feeling details can also provide information about clients' values. Absence of feeling may indicate clients' coping mechanisms.

Early recollections cannot contradict each other because the individual is a unified whole. If you have two ERs that appear to contradict each other, you must look for a hidden consistency that would dispel the contradiction. An "if-then" contingency among ERs frequently resolves the contradictions.

Getting the most vivid part of the recollection helps the clinician to discover the essence of the recollection. Not asking for the most vivid part of the recollection runs the risk of having our life styles projected into the clients' ERs.

Color detail indicates an aesthetic eye. Metaphors are frequently in ERs, and part of the interpretive process includes discovering and understanding the metaphors presented. They are a form of communication.

9
ERs and Diagnosis

Diagnosis focuses on the "negative" behaviors of an individual. Nevertheless it is the standard by which therapy begins. And, unfortunately, nomenclature diagnosing is very common in psychology, perhaps too common. Rogers (1942) stated,

> The psychiatrist's training has been notoriously weak in any basic training in the psychological development of the normal individual, and he has been handicapped by the fact that his training concentrates to such an extent upon the organic problems of the individual that insufficient time is given to the psychological aspects. (p. 258)

Menninger (1973) also finds difficulties with the manner in which psychiatrists do diagnosis. He wrote, "It is apparently a human propensity to identify others by a single, perhaps conspicuous attribute" (p. 170). In psychiatry, he said, this propensity found expression in the word "insane," which was eventually divided into a number of ways to be insane, with special designations. Menninger wrote:

> Lists of names to call patients! Lists from which psychiatrists may (must) choose a word to describe the configuration of symptoms exhibited by each of his patients! These are names he may use to identify his patients' afflictions, and they become the names by

which he must label his patients, and even by which the patients are designated. (pp. 170–171)

There are many reasons psychologists diagnose clients, and we suspect that it goes back to the medical model of functioning. Back to the days of calling everyone who came into a therapist's office a "patient." Back to the days when everyone who practiced therapy was an M.D. rather than a Psy.D. or a Ph.D. This Chapter examines the meanings and purposes of diagnosing, as well as the use of ERs in functional assessment.

We also discuss in this Chapter the inherently different perspectives of the diagnosing procedure versus the process of gathering and interpreting ERs. We believe diagnosing to be more along the lines of labeling the negative characteristics of individuals. Early recollections provide more information than do diagnoses because they offer a broader understanding of people that includes both the positive and negative aspects of a person. They also give evidence of each person's unique perspective in regard to self, others, and the world, as well as that person's uniquely held ethical convictions. It is for those reasons that ERs can be considered a functional assessment.

Is Medical Nomenclature Appropriate for Psychological Issues?

Though diagnosing is very useful for medical problems, we believe that nonmedical issues such as psychological functioning need a more robust system of understanding the individual. Medical doctors have a convenience that psychologists, counselors, and therapists do not have: the simplicity of cellular reaction and observable physical malformations (e.g., a broken bone). Though there is a huge variability in the types of physical conditions that exist, there is an inherent similarity within each narrow medical diagnosis. That is, one person's broken leg or dislocated knee will look very similar to other broken legs and dislocated knees; one case of lung cancer will generally appear comparable to other instances of lung cancer. As a matter of fact, if a diagnosis is too broad, it may be further simplified by being broken down into particular types. For example, there is not just cancer but melanoma, carcinoma, leukemia, bone cancer, skin cancer, prostate cancer, and so on. Because of the physical composition and reaction of cells, there is an innate consistency within each diagnosis. However, for the holistic psychologist, people should not be broken down psychologically into parts. We should deal with the whole person.

Psychologists have to deal with the inconsistencies of people. There are at least four areas that need to be examined in the development and maintenance of psychological disorders. First, is the disorder a result of an organic syndrome? That is, is there some biochemical, neurological, or other condition that is causing the disorder? It is unethical to provide psychological treatment instead of medical treatment for a medical problem. Any medical causes for psychological disorders must be ruled out prior to psychological intervention.

Second, if a psychological disorder is not biochemically caused, we need to look at the other remaining factors. What happened prior to the disorder? In a case like depression or anxiety, there are a number of factors that the client and/or the therapist may link to the onset of the mental condition. This adds a variable that the clinician must take into account.

Third, what is the person's interpretation of the event? How does life style come into play in the development and maintenance of a psychological disorder? Each life style is different, and that adds another variable to the diagnosing equation.

Fourth, what are the contingent elements to the psychological disorder? For example, does the disorder or even the diagnosis of the disorder bring financial or social benefits to the client, or does it allow the client to put others (friends, family members, the state, etc.) in his or her service? This question examines the purpose of the illness and adds yet another variable to the equation. With such variability in the development, interpretation, and maintenance of psychological disorders, we get an idea of how inadequate the medical model is when applied to psychological conditions.

We have another bone to pick with the diagnosing of individuals who come in for therapy. We view each person as a unique individual with distinctive reasoning, goals, ethics, and worldview. As such, we believe that diagnosing leads to pigeonholing individuals, much like calling a rhombus a rectangle; it's close, but fails to take into account the unique structure of the shape. The DSM forces clinicians, to some degree, to put oval pegs in round holes. This leads to "common mode error," a problem that translates into "garbage in, garbage out." If we begin our journey with a client on the wrong foot (inaccurate labeling or an incomplete understanding of functioning), how might the course of therapy progress?

Yet another problem in the labeling process of diagnosing is the haunting thought of how a diagnosis can follow someone for too long. Diagnoses are told to clients and insurance agencies. Clients then refer to themselves in discouraging terms, as diagnoses always focus on weaknesses rather than strengths (e.g., "I'm manic depressive"). Furthermore, clients may use the diagnosis to excuse their behavior (e.g., "I'm ADD, so I can't focus on my homework."). In addition, if a client tells friends and coworkers the diagnosis, it may lead them to misunderstand the client, focus on his or her maladaptive functioning, and marginalize the client from the group. Also, we must remember that those who are not familiar with psychology may not know the actual criteria that go along with a diagnosis. How many times have you heard people mistake schizophrenia for multiple personality disorder? (Have you ever heard the school playground poem "Roses are red. Violets are blue. I'm a schizophrenic, and so am I"?)

For these and other reasons, we prefer functional assessments that can be derived from ERs. Functional assessments paint a brighter, more detailed picture of individuals, but they cannot be used to formulate nomenclature (DSM) diagnoses. Though we may be able to determine from ERs that someone is prone to being depressed, there are several types of depression, and it is therefore very unlikely that we can derive a nomenclature diagnosis from ERs.

DSM diagnoses have an inherent instability. This can be demonstrated by their "Chinese menu" structure. Clinicians have to determine which of the available criteria for a diagnosis is present in an individual for a diagnosis to be made. For example, for a client to be diagnosed as having a major depressive episode, he or she needs to meet at least five of nine criteria. Accordingly, you can have two people who are both diagnosed with a major depressive episode yet have only one symptom in common!

In regard to the validity of personality diagnosis, Yalom (1989) writes,

> Others, and among them I include myself, marvel that anyone can take diagnosis seriously, that it can ever be considered more than a simple cluster of symptoms and behavioral traits. Nonetheless, we find ourselves under ever-increasing pressure (from hospitals, insurance companies, governmental agencies) to sum up a person with a diagnostic phrase and a numerical category.
>
> Even the most liberal system of psychiatric nomenclature does violence to the being of another. If we relate to people believing that we can categorize them, we will neither identify nor nurture the parts, the vital parts, of the other that transcends [sic] category. (p. 185)

ERs and Functional Assessments

Early recollections allow us to get an overview of how clients *function*. We can assess how clients perceive themselves, others, and the world, and we can see what their ethical convictions are. Perhaps more important, functional assessments through ERs also focus on the positive aspects and strengths (adaptive functioning) of individuals. All of these are perhaps more important and more extensive than what we would get from a DSM label. That is one of the reasons why this book was written. We wanted to demonstrate the ease of gathering ERs and their clinical usefulness.

We are hardly alone in concluding that ERs cannot be used to arrive at DSM diagnoses. Ferguson (1964) studied ERs within the context of Adlerian theory. She gathers ERs from 10 people labeled as normals, 10 labeled as neurotics, and 10 people labeled as psychotics. From those ERs three Adlerian clinicians wrote life style summaries. Seven additional clinicians, including Freudians, eclectic therapists, and other Adlerians, correlated life style summaries to the recorded ERs. All 10 clinicians attained significant accuracy in correlating the ERs to the life style summaries. Some attained an accuracy rate beyond the .0001 level of significance! This finding demonstrates that life style summaries based on ERs are easily transmissible to a diverse population of clinicians.

As you may have suspected from our priming earlier in this book, of the five clinicians (two eclectics and three Adlerians) who attempted to make diagnoses of psychopathogy from information from the ERs, not one of the them was able to make an accurate nomenclature diagnosis better than chance. This demonstrates two things. First, and rather obviously, you cannot make DSM diagnoses from ERs. Second, the intrinsic variability in the DSM system of diagnosis introduces a moving platform on which we cannot build a stable understanding or a clear picture of a diagnosis. That is, this "Chinese menu" of symptoms from which the clinician must choose particular symptoms for diagnosis eludes a lucid, definite pattern, and thus it may pose difficulty for any assessment other than the DSM. That is, the DSM will correlate best with the DSM, and anything else will not be as accurately correlated with it. It would be like taking a "bullet train" and trying to make it run on the Chicago elevated train tracks. It just won't work (and could be very dangerous if you tried!). In other words, just because two things appear similar does not mean that they are interchangeable. Though people may be tempted to make DSM diagnoses from the information gleaned from ERs, they should not.

Early recollections may demonstrate a pattern of thinking that is in accord with symptomatic pattern, yet is not sufficient to arrive at a DSM diagnosis. Jackson and Sechrest (1962) looked for a relationship between ERs and neurotic symptoms. They found that ERs with themes of trauma, illness, accidents, and fear were found in clients with anxiety. They also found that clients who were diagnosed as obsessive-compulsive recalled strong prohibitions and more themes of sex. In addition, they found abandonment themes in depressed patients, and themes of gastrointestinal distress in persons with gastrointestinal disorders.

Though not diagnoses, these findings indicate a pattern of thinking. Mosak (1958) presented the following recollection:

> Age 5: When my mother died. She was lying in the coffin. Suddenly she picked herself up and hugged me. (p. 309)

Mosak states that this recollection gives us the clue that the client is psychotic. The client considers himself "the center of attention, the passive recipient of the affection of others, and an individual so special that even the impossible is not denied him" (p. 309).

You must remember that the presence of certain patterns in diagnostic categories does not preclude their presence in other diagnoses. So the presence of, for example, sexual themes in ERs does not necessarily indicate obsessive-compulsive behavior; people with very different diagnoses may also have ERs with sexual themes.

That a functional assessment gathered from ER analysis is discordant with a DSM diagnosis does not mean that it is irrelevant to clients' current functioning. Just the opposite is demonstrated by Eisenstein and Ryerson (1951), who wrote that the first memory is an informative diagnostic statement. They contended that when clients give their earliest memory (usually from the third or fourth year of life), no matter how seemingly insignificant that memory, it is a choice that is influenced by their presenting symptom or complaint and that this first memory reveals information that the client is unaware of revealing.

Eisenstein and Ryerson saw in that first memory a condensed statement of clients' inner orientations. Because it is created prior to ego formation, yet is recalled after the personality has developed, it can be especially revealing: its selection may clarify the client's problems and early defense mechanisms, and its theme may mirror the client's current situation and current coping mechanisms. According to Eisentein and Ryerson, this indicates a high degree of correlation and they encouraged clinicians to correctly identify and interpret the first memories in a way similar to dream interpretation.

This Chapter was written to reestablish the understanding that ERs are relevant to current functioning but should not be used for DSM (nomenclature) diagnosis. They are nevertheless very powerful instruments for functional assessments of clients. We prefer functional assessments for several reasons. First, functional assessments speak of what clients do and how they think in both adaptive and maladaptive ways. Second, the variability of individuals, mental disorders, and social contexts negates much of the accuracy that supposedly exists in nomenclature diagnosis. Third, nomenclature diagnosis is a holdover from times prior to current psychological intervention and is more representative of the medical model than of a system focused on intra and interpersonal functioning. Some concepts just do not translate well from one arena to the other.

Summary

While diagnosing is very useful for medical problems, we believe that non-medical issues such as mental disorders need a more robust system of understanding the individual. Early recollections may be used for functional assessments, but they cannot be used to formulate nomenclature (DSM) diagnoses. There are many problems with the standard diagnostic procedure, which is based on the medical model. Early recollections allow the clinician to get an overview of how clients function. You cannot make a nomenclature (DSM) diagnoses from ERs. Also, the intrinsic variability in the DSM system of diagnosis introduces a moving platform on which we cannot build a stable understanding or a clear picture of a diagnosis. Early recollections may demonstrate a pattern of thinking that is in accord with symptomatic patterns.

10
Client-Therapist Relationship[1]

The therapeutic relationship is a social one, and much more than a sterile one-up, one-down monologue. How clinicians act in therapy influences how clients act and vice versa. Perhaps more important, how clinicians and clients view that social interaction can provide a great deal of clinical information Such as how clients act in therapy demonstrates transference patterns and has an effect on therapeutic outcomes. One of the important assessments that a clinician can make is how clients will perceive therapy and the therapist. Early recollections can provide information about the interpersonal relationship between the clinician and the client.

Mayman and Faris (1960) found that earliest childhood recollections may provide information about transference patterns carried into therapy sessions and possibly reenacted in personal interactions. Mosak's (1965) article on predicting relationships between clinicians and clients presents a second view based on Adlerian rather than Freudian principles.

This Chapter provides examples of how ERs can be used to predict the relationship between the client and clinician. Life style variables are examined as we guide you through interpreting several case studies. How people act in therapy may be no different from how they act with others outside of therapy.

---

[1] With permission of the University of Texas this Chapter is adapted from Mosak, H. H. (1965). Predicting the relationship to the psychotherapist from ERs. *Journal of Individual Psychology, 21,* 77–81.

Consistency in Behavior

People act in accord with their life styles in or out of the therapy session. Freud was one of the first clinicians to understand the connection between patient and analyst. The Freudians' conception of transference is the displacement of a person's unresolved conflicts, dependencies, and aggressions onto a substitute object. Alfred Adler was also aware of clients' perceptions of their doctors but explained those perceptions as preexisting life style factors.

Adler wrote (1913/1927):

> I expect from the patient again and again the same attitude which he has shown in accordance with his life plan toward the persons of his former environment, and still earlier toward his family. At the moment of the introduction to the physician and often even earlier, the patient has the same feelings toward him as toward important persons in general. The assumption that the transference of such feelings or that resistance begins later is a mere deception. In such cases the physician only recognizes them later. (pp. 336–337)

If therapists could predict a client's attitude, could they avoid this "later" recognition? Sure, but how?

Early recollections, according to Adler (1913/1927), are people's reminders about their own limitations and what situations mean. Adler believed that there were no such things as "chance memories," as people remember only those things that have a bearing on their situation. Furthermore, they do not have to be true memories, since ERs are used as a projective technique. As such, gathering ERs enable clinicians to understand clients' life styles.

Below, we'll analyze ERs from two clients with these points in mind. The first is a 40-year-old man with a history of poor interpersonal relations. This fellow acts like the "nice guy" he thinks he is. However, he feels others treat him poorly. This does not make any sense to him. He believes that if he is nice, others will reciprocate his kindness. His recollections paint a more detailed picture.

Case 1

ER 1. Age: 7

> I was in the video arcade playing a game and waiting for my father to pick me up after he was done shopping. I saw him come into

the arcade, and he started talking to a female security guard. He was talking a bit too close to her and started to touch her arm. She pulled away. He tried to touch her again. I was angry with him because he was wrong.

Most vivid: "My father touching the security guard's arm."

What is going on in this ER? How are people interacting?

ER 2. Age: 8

I was riding my skateboard down some stairs, and I tried to jump onto the railing, but I missed and cracked my head on the concrete steps. I was awake but out of it. My mother saw me and ran over to help. She put me in the car and took me to uncle's office. My uncle was a veterinarian. I had no clue why she didn't take me to a people doctor.

Most vivid: "Thinking to myself, 'Why am I being taken to a vet instead of a human doctor?'"

Does the client comprehend the actions of others? Is he a victim of himself?

ER 3. Age: 9

One day we had a really bad connection on the television. So I thought I would go up on the roof and tinker with the satellite dish. My mom came home and saw me on the roof and started yelling at me. She said she would call my father (they were divorced at the time) and tell him that I was out of control. I told her that she always threatened to call him but never did. I was rather mater-of-fact about it. I figured she needed to learn to follow through on at least one of her threats. Anyway, she made me come down from the roof and put me in my room. I was grounded for a week. I was saying to myself, "Geez, I was only trying to help her."

Most vivid: "Thinking she never follows through on anything. What kind of parenting is that?"

Here we see the client getting himself in trouble through not understanding how to interact with others.

ER 4. Age: 8

One day my aunt bought me a Dennis the Menace comic book. It didn't have Spiderman, or Superman, or Batman. I read it and did not let her know that I hated it.

Most vivid: "Seeing the comic book that I didn't like."

We don't see any positive interaction here either, do we?

ER 5. Age: 6

One time I was at this girl's birthday party. I went to give her a birthday kiss, and she slapped my face and knocked me over. I fell on a sharp rock right on my butt. My mother and father were there and saw it. I started to cry. My father laughed as he walked over and made me drop my pants as he cleaned up the blood.

Most vivid: "Getting slapped."

The client's interaction with men is no better than with women. A female knocks him on his behind after he tries to be affectionate, and then his father adds insult to injury by the public display of his rear end.

ER 6. Age: 6

I was in kindergarten and we were going to have a field trip. I had to ask my parents for $20 to pay for the trip and lunch. My mother gave me $20 and put it in my back pocket and buttoned it. She told me not to take it out of my back pocket because she did not want me to lose it. I ended up opening my back pocket, and I lost the $20. I called my mother from school and told her that two bullies took my money. She called the school and when the principal asked me what happened I crossed myself up and when I got home my father grounded me for a week.

Most vivid: "Crossing myself up."

In this recollection, the client brings about his own punishment through poor social interaction. There are two admissions of incompetence. First, he took the $20 bill out. Second, he lied and "crossed" his stories.

ER 7. Age: 7

One day my father bought a DVD player, and I was so fascinated by how it would take in the DVDs that I started to see what it would take and not take. I put some pennies in there to see what would happen. Nothing did. So I put more in. Still nothing happened. Later that night when my father came home to watch a DVD, he put the DVD into the player, and it got jammed. He scratched the DVD and broke the DVD player when he tried to get it out. A couple of pennies came out of the machine while he was working on it. He asked me how the pennies got in there and I told him I put them in there. I thought he was going to kill me after I told him!

Most vivid: "How livid my father was."

A penny for your thoughts? What might you guess about his in-session behavior? What might he think about others and how might he make himself the victim of therapists or of himself or both?

Clearly this client victimizes himself and others and is victimized by others in turn. He does not perform well in social exchanges. As a matter of fact, he makes people think about inflicting serious injury on him.

The Client's Life Style

Early recollections mirror people's current mode of perception. Therefore, we can use them to distinguish several major trends in personality. In the above case, we see that in every ER somebody acts incorrectly, intentionally or not. People are not getting along and spoil things for each other. The client is one of those wrongdoers. Even when he tries to do something right, it ends up all wrong. He tries to please but only ends up suffering.

This client's ERs provide clues to his life style. He paints a picture of a social critic who finds fault with everything and everybody, including himself, although he has better intentions than others. None of the ERs demonstrates positive social interaction. Therefore, we can comfortably predict that he is a pessimist who may "run after his slaps in the face." He anticipates suffering after some social exchange.

Predictions

How might this person perceive and use therapy situations? We can formulate several tentative hypotheses. The client might

1. criticize therapy, the therapist, and his progress;
2. perceive the therapist as another person who will make him suffer;

3. attempt to provoke the therapist — not intentionally, of course, but to make him (the client) suffer. Then he could be critical of the therapist and feel morally superior to him;
4. devote himself to the recitation of incidents, past and present, in which others have abused him, humiliated him, and wronged him;
5. distrust the therapist and distrust the possibility of a good human relationship with him;
6. try to ingratiate himself with the therapist and then be disappointed when the therapist fails to meet one of his implicit or explicit demands;
7. attempt to lie his way out of a tight spot. He would probably do so clumsily, though, since he would expect to be found out;
8. withhold certain information from the therapist until he feels he can trust him with it.

Outcome

During therapy, the client's behavior confirmed several of the above hypotheses. He consistently inquired of the therapist whether therapy was really helping him (1).

At other times he would attempt to ingratiate himself with the therapist by telling him that therapy had been helpful but that his wife and children really needed the treatment (6).

He devoted most of the initial period of treatment to a recitation of how his mother abused him, how his wife and her family wronged him, how his children misbehaved, and how his employees took advantage of him (4).

He withheld speaking of his own misdeeds until much later in treatment, and then with a sheepish grin since he was apprehensive that the therapist might disapprove of him (8).

When he terminated treatment, he grudgingly admitted making some gains but was still focusing on the world's abuse of him (1 and 4).

As we can see from this example, gathering ERs during clients' intake should help us predict the potential client-therapist relationship. This is a testament to the ERs' benefit-to-cost ratio.

Case 2

Occasionally the question of whether a certain type of therapist is preferable for a particular client assumes importance. Frequently we ask ourselves whether the client might relate better to a male or female therapist, though there are differences of opinion as to how crucial a factor this may be. This decision is difficult to make at the initiation of therapeutic contact since we have so little reliable information about the client at that time. Early recollections may be useful for determining what type of therapist (e.g., gender, ethnicity, age) might be best for a client.

We will not tell you anything at this point about the man who gave us the following recollections. Read each one and determine if the client would likely have a preference for a therapist of a particular gender.

ER 1. Age: 5

It was recess, and all of us were out in the schoolyard playing. There were a bunch of girls playing jump rope. I remember getting pushed over and this one girl sitting on my chest. I couldn't take a breath. I felt like my life was being squeezed out of me. It was intolerable!

Most vivid: "Not being able to breathe."

Here the client is telling you of a repulsive experience. There is no mention of a man in this recollection. For this client, he is a pushover with women, and when a woman is around, it feels to him that all the life is snuffed out of him.

ER 2. Age: 6

My sister and I were playing ball in the front yard. The ball got out of control and went into our neighbor's yard. They had a big dog, a German shepherd or something like that, and the ball was close to the fence. I knew I could reach without getting near the dog. As I was leaning over the fence, my sister pushed me into the yard, and the dog bit me.

Most vivid: "My sister pushing me over the fence and into the dog's territory."

It appears as though women push him into "harm's way." As with the previous recollection, men are not present. Bad things can happen when you interact with a woman.

ER 3. Age: 4

My mother bought some jelly doughnuts. I ate four or five of them. Later that night I felt miserable. I ended up having diarrhea and pooped my pants. It stunk pretty bad. I put on cologne to cover it up, but my mother found out and made me clean it. She marched me into the laundry room and showed me what to do. I was so sick. I couldn't believe she was making me clean it up; she always did the laundry.

Most vivid: "My mother telling me I had to clean up my mess."

Women make him clean up his shit, and he believes women should clean up his shit.

ER 4. Age: 9

I told this girl that I felt like an outsider. All of the other kids were good-looking or popular or were rich, and I had nothing to offer any girl. I felt like a loser. She looked me in the eye, and I thought she was going to say something consoling. She told me I was a real loser. I was crushed. I wanted to leave school right then and never return.

Most vivid: "Her telling me that I was a loser."

The client puts himself in a vulnerable position with a woman, and she "crushes" him. Her rejection is so embarrassing that he does not want to return to school.

ER 5. Age: 7

I remember I was at my uncle's house. There were a lot of family members there. They were all sad. Someone told me my aunt had cancer. I thought it was funny, and I started to laugh. I couldn't stop laughing.

Most vivid: "Not being able to stop laughing. The more I tried to control it, the harder I laughed."

A female relative has cancer, and the client laughs.

ER 6. Age: 5

I was in gym class. I hit this girl who was calling me names, and she fell straight back like a domino. The girl's gym teacher [female] came over and started talking to me. She asked me if I knew what I did wrong. I said, "Yeah, I know." But I really didn't. It was fair because she was bugging me.

Most vivid: "Saying to her that I knew when I really didn't know."

The client insults a girl, and then feigns knowledge to a woman.

Are you getting an understanding of the client and how sees and acts with women? How would this client act with a female therapist?

Predictions

From this brief diagnostic material it was possible to guess the client's probable attitudes toward a female therapist. Consistently the ERs depict a little boy being overwhelmed and hurt by women. In addition, in ER 3, he attempts to cover up the malodorous part of himself, but even in this instance, a woman finds him out. As with the client in the previous section, we can offer several hypotheses of what would likely occur were this client assigned to a woman therapist. The client may:

1. perceive a female therapist as a threatening, potentially overwhelming person;
2. take perverse pleasure if something adverse happened to his therapist;
3. provoke the therapist to see whether she makes trouble for him since he feels he is the victim of women;
4. attempt to cover up his deficiencies, his "sins," and his "ignorance," at the same time expecting to be found out;
5. make some "innocent" sexual advances toward the therapist and, if "accused" of such behavior, attempt to leave therapy;
6. devote much of his therapeutic time to elaborating upon the theme of how women overwhelm and hurt him;
7. feel that "you can't do business with women."

Outcome

You can see that in the above case the client should be assigned to a male therapist because he would not be receptive to a female therapist. After some time in therapy, the client might be better able to lower his walls and be assigned to a female therapist. That would give the therapist an opportunity to see whether the client is better able to handle female guidance as a result of therapy, and this could be demonstrated by gathering his post-therapy recollections. A client like this may not show up for a second session if he is assigned to a female therapist immediately after intake.

Summary

How clinicians act in therapy influences how clients act, and vice versa. Perhaps more important, how clinicians view that social interaction can provide a great deal of clinical information. How clients act in therapy demonstrates transference patterns and has an effect on therapeutic outcomes. Early recollections can provide information about the relationship between the clinician and the client. Alfred Adler was aware of clients' perceptions of their therapists, and explained those perceptions in terms of preexisting life style factors.

Prediction of the probable attitudes of clients towards their therapists could prove of assistance to therapists of any orientation. Choice of a suitable therapist may also be facilitated. Early recollections could aid in these predictions.

11
ERs in Marital Therapy

According to the National Vital Statistics Report (2001) from the Centers for Disease Control and Prevention, the divorce rate in the United States is approximately 50%. In other words, if that rate continues, for every two marriages that occur this year, there will be one divorce (and that does not count other forms of breakups, such as separation, annulment, and so forth, which are not measured by the report).

There are a number of reasons why divorces are much more common today than in the past. First, it is far more accepted in modern society for people to divorce. Many years ago, people, especially women, often refrained from getting a divorce because they did not want to be branded a failure or "used goods." Second, women are now in the workforce in greater numbers and are better able to support themselves if they wish to live independent of their husbands' incomes. That is, they may not have to stay married for financial support. Overall, it is easier to get a divorce (legally, socially, and financially) than it has been in the past.

Though it may seem odd to begin a Chapter on marriage by discussing divorce and separation, we believe that an understanding of the life style components that are so influential in marital discord will assist in our understanding of marital harmony.

This Chapter will explore the unique social situation called "marriage" and how married couples interact. The importance of personalities in attraction and conflict will be discussed. Also, we will investigate how using ERs to determine personality characteristics can be very effective in marital therapy.

Development, Neurosis, and Marriage

Oberndorf (1938) states that neurotic symptoms indicate a failure of a child to resolve parental attachment, that is, to develop "normally." He adds that it is a mistake to believe that marriage by itself will alleviate the neurotic symptoms that develop in childhood and continue to exist in adulthood. He suggests that people with neurotic thoughts and behavior have a restricted ability to love and excessive need for attention that can disrupt marriage. Therefore, it is up to the therapist to bring to the clients' attention these factors that maintain neurotic behavior and create social discord.

Mittelmann (1956) echoes Oberndorf's work in the statement, "The habitual attitudes of a spouse may contain the original reaction to a parent or other infantile experience" (p. 84). The relationship between childhood development, neurosis, and marital interaction should not be discounted. Mittelmann writes, "Neurotic circular interpersonal reactions among individuals who are in close and intimate contact are an important component of the neuroses, and may follow one of several patterns" (p. 81). Mittelmann gives several examples, including couples in which one spouse is aggressive and the other dependent. Another example is a relationship in which one spouse is emotionally detached and the other has an open demand for affection. The demand only makes the other spouse more distant. A person who is terribly dependent and views his or her spouse as omnipotent may feel continual disappointment and depression when the spouse cannot live up to that expectation.

There are many areas in which neurotic symptoms may interfere. Problems with intimacy are one of the telltale signs of neurosis and personality clashes. Eisenstein (1956) wrote:

> "The sexual symptom is only one of many indicators of individual emotional problems which find numerous avenues of expression in a marriage. Disturbances in the sex life are related to the individual neurosis, the neurotic choice of a mate, and the resultant type of neurotic interaction between partners" (p. 101).

As we will demonstrate, complementary features and clashes of each spouse's personality play an inherent role in marriage instability as well as cohesion.

"You're Better, Our Marriage Is Worse!"

The early practice in marriage counseling was to counsel only one spouse. Freud (1950b), for example, held that "the analytic situation allows for the presence of no third person" (p. 3). It was assumed that once one spouse's functioning improved, the marriage would get better. The result would be that one spouse might change, and the other would continue to think and act as he or she always did. Dreikurs (1946) cautioned that counseling an individual for a marital problem was counseling for a divorce. He reasoned that the one in treatment would make changes. The one not in treatment might then not be able to adjust or would resist adjusting to the new behaviors of the spouse in therapy.

A marriage is a social situation with each partner often playing one-half of a symbiotic role. (For example, in location: one spouse works outside of the house, and the other inside.) Therapy is designed to, among other things, create change. As a result, if one spouse goes into therapy and the other does not, the marriage changes by the shift in the balance of the relationship.

Let's look at an example of one spouse who is always tired and frustrated by giving in to the other spouse and seeks therapy to remedy that problem. The marriage may become out of balance if the one who is in therapy learns to not knuckle under to the other. Meanwhile, the spouse who is not in therapy may continue to expect to be waited on and have the partner cave in. Consequently, that spouse may become frustrated and angry in the marriage.

So you may ask, "Does therapy break up marriages?" Our answer is "No, people decide to break up their marriages." That is, when couples come to marital therapy, they may do so as a precursor to divorce. In other words, their relationship (also think of it as their personalities or life styles) is not a good match, and they may discover that in therapy, which may lead to their divorce. Prior to entering therapy, the couple may only have been perpetuating a bad match, barely keeping their marriage together. How this relates to this book in particular is that we believe that marriages are an interleaving of personalities (or life styles). Gathering ERs from each spouse helps determine where the couple might conflict and where they symbiotically exist. In this regard, marriage is very similar to other interpersonal contexts. Some coworkers we like and get along with; others we wrangle with. Why do we like some and disagree with others? It often boils down to whether we have similar goals and harmonious (although not necessarily the same) life styles. We have a balance with those we get along with, whether it is at work or at home. The interesting part is that the balance may not always be a healthy one. Certainly parasitic and abusive relationships may be balanced and unhealthy.

Can you think of a symbiotic relationship that can be maintained that is not healthy?

Harmony and Conflicts of Personalities

We must remind you at this point that psychological disorder does not necessarily doom the marriage. As a matter of fact, psychological disorders may play a *cohesive* role in keeping the marriage together.

How? Well, for example, if a husband considers himself a great provider, and the woman is a "getter," they have a match. Another example is a woman who is a "victim," and a man is a victimizer; they may play complementary, but unhealthy, roles. Or a psychotic and a caretaker. In other words, there is a match for every person, although that match may not be healthy.

You may want to think about why Hollywood marriages are notorious for their ephemeral existence. At first you may ask, "Well, here we have two people in the same business, with lots of money and admiration, so why in the world do they separate so darn often?" Does it have to do with conflicting personalities?

We think so. For example, when you have two people who want to be in the spotlight, one spouse may have to take a backseat to the other. It may be difficult for a person who wants to be in the limelight to allow the spouse to get all of the attention. Remember, like poles of a magnet repel each other. Each spouse is competing for attention, and some get tired of the one-upmanship game. Besides, nothing makes the front pages of tabloids more quickly than separations and new relationships. Therefore, in these Hollywood-type marriages, separations and new unions allow an escape from the competition of attention and the acquisition of new attention with the news of the latest relationship. It's an interesting way to prolong one's time on center stage. In such instances, it is the similar personalities that repel one another. So maladjustment or psychological disorder, in and of itself, does not ruin the marriage; it is the conflict of life styles (personalities) that ruins a marriage. Get the picture?

Don't think so? How about another example? What if one spouse is an excitement seeker, and the other spouse is so anxious that he or she refuses to leave the house, let alone engage in anything exciting? What if a married couple comes to you, and you find out they both "have to be right all of the time." That sounds like a recipe for conflict, doesn't it?

However, there are plenty of compatible couples in which one spouse complements the other, providing a balancing role to the marriage. For example, if one spouse is a tyrant and the other is a pleaser, there exists, in its unique fashion, a reciprocal relationship. There is also the example of the healthy, well-balanced marriage in which each spouse provides a caring role that promotes mutual concern, mutual respect, and cooperation through (sometimes unique) contributions. There are plenty of these well-balanced and reciprocal marriages. Think about the people you know who have been married for a while and how they act in relation to their spouse. How might those husbands and wives provide something for the other that balances their relationship?

Life style matching is not as similar to a "love connection" as many people may think. As we saw above, some matches are symbiotic but not healthy. As Dreikurs (1968) said, "We are so accustomed to using the term cooperation only for constructive interactions that we overlook the fact that one cannot even fight without the other's full cooperation" (p. 87). In such relationships, each person has a similar method of operation (arguing) and continues to engage in mutual activities (fighting). And that is the cooperation in an apparent quarrelsome situation. If there was total discord, one would want to argue, and the other would walk away. It is how people see themselves and others as well as their goals in life that are the key components of matching life styles.

Dreikurs continues:

> When we enter a relationship or when we break it up, we act in accordance with goals that we have set for ourselves and that are reinforced by our partner. We share secret aims and expectations which guide us like a compass. We respond only to those stimuli which fit into our plans and recognize only those opportunities which confirm our expectations. We feel attracted when we meet someone who offers us, through his personality and his intentions, an opportunity to realize our own goals. We play a very important part in evoking and stimulating in the other person precisely the behavior that we expect and need. (pp. 87–88)

Therefore, the roles played in the "dramedy" of relationships influence the roles evoked by the other person in the relationship. That is why it is best to treat married couples together, rather than to treat one spouse. To treat one spouse is to upset the balance in the marriage. It is important to remember that each spouse plays a supportive role, and the treatment of one spouse changes the dynamic of that relationship.

Dreikurs states:

> Matching of the life styles does not mean identity of the life styles. On the contrary, opposites often attract each other because they complement each other. An aggressive, determined person may

want a mate who is willing to be led and supportive, just as a passive, submissive person needs one on whose strength he or she can rely. A creative person, who is likely to go astray, needs and wants someone who is solid and realistic, with both feet on the ground. One who tries to please in order to have a place will choose someone who demands, often in a selfish way, admiration and submission. It is the role that each one plays in life that fits him to the role which the other plays. (p. 88)

So perhaps you can see why the counseling of one spouse may further disrupt a marriage. The roles played by each person need a counterpart. If a role changes, and the counterpart does not change, there is disharmony.

So you may ask, "Where do these roles come from?" They come from our development, as Dreikurs elaborates:

We all play the role that we unknowingly decided to play in our formative years; it was our movement within the family constellation into which we were born. In order to function, we follow our concepts of ourselves and the world, we take on certain roles and look for people whose roles provide what is missing in us, a role that supplements ours. (p. 88)

As we mentioned previously, our life styles are created during our formative years and are difficult to change. We look for someone who has similar goals yet a different role, one that complements the role we choose. That is, if a man considers himself the breadwinner, he may desire someone who wants to be taken care of. If a woman considers herself to be a (potential) wonderful mother, wouldn't she want a man who wants not only children (a common goal) but also a woman who would take care of them (and perhaps him)?

How couples perceive each other determines the cohesion of the marriage. The interpretation of stressors can bring a couple closer together or drive them apart. As Dreikurs observes:

Economic stress can either intensify the cohesiveness of the family or disrupt it. If it is a problem for both to face and to solve, they probably will come closer. But if the wife blames her husband for not earning enough, or he his wife for spending too much, then the problem becomes unsolvable. (p. 96)

Essentially, the unity of a marriage comes down to choosing what to focus on. Often couples decide to dissolve their marriages because they have shifted their focus so that their spouse's virtues become faults.

Usually couples are not aware of the refocusing, although they may occasionally say, "I never noticed it until now, but . . . " Couples may also not be aware that it is within their power to turn a negative into a positive, that is, to focus on the positive things more often and make the most of those qualities. For example, their differences could be a beautiful variety or change of pace.

Therefore, life style matching from ERs can be used prior to marriage to help couples become aware of each person's assets and interfering ideas in an effort to make each person more sensitive to what will keep the marriage harmonious. In addition, life style matching can be used with couples who are having marital difficulties in an attempt to refocus their attention on the positive things each spouse contributes to the marriage (Mosak & Maniacci, 1998), and onto their own interfering ideas that cause difficulty. Essentially, life style matching can help reveal which behaviors should change, which need to increase, and which should decrease.

Therapy or Counseling

How might the use of the term "therapy" with marital treatment be inappropriate? "Therapy" refers to changes in the life style. Those changes typically involve enhancing the flexibility of the individual's behavior — that is, changing his or her views and behavior, not necessarily in that order. Counseling refers more to guiding the individual by employing strategies. Clinicians offering marital counseling are skilled at assessing the style of each spouse as well as their style of interacting.

Suppose, for example, that upon gathering and interpreting the ERs of a couple, you learn that the husband feels that for him to be "a real man," he should not show any emotion. You also find out that the wife is withdrawing from her husband because she feels as though she "cannot reach him because he is too distant." Being a very sharp clinician, you quickly recognize the problem. The husband has to realize that his definition of "a real man" has to change. His wife has to realize that her husband thinks differently from her and that she did nothing to drive him away.

Another example: Suppose a couple comes into your office, and, after gathering their ERs, you find out that the wife is "a baby" who requires constant attention and, for lack of a better word, babying. The husband is "a pleaser" and attends to his wife all of the time. "A perfect match!" you say.

Not so fast.

It appears as though the husband is having trouble at work, and his position has been threatened because he is often late and leaves early to attend to his wife. As a result, he has been given a pay cut and is very anxious about his career and his ability to support the family. Now his wife feels as though her needs are not being met in two ways. First, he is attending more to business than to her, as he is worried about the stability of his career. Second, his reduced income translates into fewer gifts, less travel, and fewer romantic dinners at nice restaurants. She may start thinking about another man who can baby her.

That is why it is so important in marital therapy to treat both parties. The Adlerian holistic approach recognizes that the marital pair is greater than the combined separate personalities. Occasionally, the maladaptive interaction requires basic changes in the marital life style. This would call for an application of therapy rather than counseling. We treat systems, no matter how small the system is.

Attraction and Conflict

The question of why people are attracted to each other and why they separate, fight, or create interpersonal tension has been the object of much speculation among laypersons as well as those in the professional field. Laypeople ask, "Why do people fall in love?" and some of their conclusions are "It's chemistry," or "Likes attract," or "Opposites attract." The problem is that those people are thinking in terms of physical magnetism, math, philosophy, chemistry, and clichés rather than psychology.

It's funny when you think about it. There is a cliché to cover everything in human behavior. People just pick the right one at the right time to prove their point. Anything from "an eye for an eye" to "turn the other cheek" can be found in our rationalizations. Two of our favorites are the equally popular yet totally contradictory adages "Absence makes the heart grow fonder" and "Out of sight, out of mind."

We need to relinquish that type of thinking when we discuss working with couples. We're supposed to be clinicians, not cliché-ians. We want to investigate how each spouse views the world and everything in it. There must be an examination of long-term goals and methods to achieve those goals. Early recollections are a very powerful tool in comprehending those aspects in clients coming in for marital counseling.

Pew (1978) defines the concept of "number one priority" as "a set of convictions that a person gives precedence to; it is a value established by order of importance or urgency, that takes precedence over other values" (p. 1). Different people may choose among four different "number one" priorities: comfort, pleasing, control, and superiority. Those who seek comfort keep away from things that cause stress. Those who want to please others steer clear of situations with the probability of rejection. Those who desire control avoid humiliation. Those who wish to be superior try to evade meaninglessness in their lives.

Pew writes about how marital therapy benefits from finding each person's number one priority because people choose their mates based on their number one priority. In other words, a person whose number one priority is comfort will find someone whose number one priority is pleasing. This provides a balance for each person as the person who wants to please has someone to please, and the spouse who wants to be comfortable has someone who wants to comfort. Each spouse may find a certain reciprocity in the relationship.

Another common combination is the person who wants to be superior and the person who wants control. This match works well because both find themselves competent and value what is right. But there are different combinations of people, including spouses who hold the same number one priority, but in different areas. Pew writes that one way to identify the priority : "is to ask for two or three early recollections. The interpretation of these often provides a ready identification of the number one priority" (p. 16).

Yes, we are circling back to ERs and their use in marital therapy. So you may be saying to yourself, "What about other variables, such as growing up in the same region or some such thing?" Those variables are the subject of our next section.

Sociological Considerations

Some people speculate that couples get together and stay together because they're from the same neighborhood or church. Essentially, this amounts to saying that all people from a certain location or of a certain type are the same (or at least have a much higher likelihood of marital endurance).

We say, "Nonsense!"

Think about all of the people you grew up with in your neighborhood who were of the same or similar socioeconomic status, perhaps the same religion. Are all of you the same? Did you get along with everyone from your neighborhood or even your own house?

Sociological explanations that consider demographic data — age, religion, education, occupation, socioeconomic status, common and disparate interests (see Burgess & Cottrell, 1939) — would have little appeal in Adlerian theory. Adlerian theory emphasizes use rather than possession. In other words, personality factors are critical in understanding people and how they act interpersonally. The demographic variables are merely objective factors. How the couple chooses to use these factors determines the nature of their relationship.

How individuals choose to act within their environments is much more important than the environments they're from. Think about it. These choices have been a recurrent theme in literature for centuries, and Disney has made a fortune off of such tales as the rich prince falling for the poor handmaiden, or some such dynamic. It is not the demographic factors that determine a marriage, but the personalities and goals that are most influential, and these personalities and goals can be assessed through ERs.

Psychoanalytic Views

Psychoanalytic theory makes for some interesting theater. It appears as though its construction is ripe for Hollywood's picking (no offense to either psychoanalytic theory or Hollywood). However, we feel as though it can be paradoxical at times, particularly when it comes to marital therapy.

Psychoanalytic theory will sometimes see attraction, and especially discord, as based upon mutual or complementary psychopathology, not needs. An exponent of this view, Ravich (1966) writes, "Clinical experience repeatedly indicated that psychopathology rarely occurs in one member of a marital pair without an accompanying and comparable degree of psychopathology in the other" (p. 42).

Adlerians would strenuously object to Ravich's observation, and Ravich himself adds a qualification: "I have observed patients with severe emotional illness whose marriages are not discordant. On the other hand, severe discord is sometimes seen in cases where the individual psychopathologies are much less severe" (p. 42). In other words, happy marriages can exist even if one or both people have emotional illnesses.

Adlerian Approaches

Though there is no specifically Adlerian marital counseling or group therapy (Corsini, 1964), there are many forms of marital therapy practiced by those who identify with the Adlerian philosophy, theory, and principles. Marital work has assumed many forms in the work of those practicing within Adlerian principles.

Dreikurs (1935) wrote in "The Choice of a Mate" that partners regard each other as equivalent parts of one (albeit small) social community. Each person plays a role in a social interaction. So you may be asking, "Aren't you guys making marriage a bit too impersonal? Just social interaction? Isn't that a bit sterile? Where has the love gone?" Dreikurs anticipated your response. "Like all feelings," he wrote, "love seems to take possession of us without our seeking or even asking." We put forth the notion that feelings provide the energy to move in relation to our goals. Love provides the energy to move toward others and to marry. Love is a human concept. Dreikurs separates humans from animals with the distinction between a physical reaction and mentally determined action. That is, people have and foster love, and this love is uniquely human and is based on our conceptions of ourselves, men and women, and the world, and on our ethical convictions. All these things we can assess from ERs.

Dreikurs wrote: "Only within the framework of the whole personality can we understand the role played by a feeling. That is the reason why 'love' is so varied in different individuals" (p. 101).

He suggested that the kind of people we like or the feelings that we have are not accidental; they reflect our picture of the world. Accordingly, Dreikurs urges us to consider the extent to which some earlier experiences are in accord with our attitude toward life. Does a man who was pampered during childhood look for women who will pamper him? Does a woman who had a controlling father during childhood and absolutely hated it search for a laissez-faire husband? Dreikurs proposes that we formulate a role and preference during childhood. Therefore, the ideal figures we seek for marriage are dependent on social factors (our social interaction during our formative years, e.g., role models) rather than a strict biological (animalistic) urge.

The changes in our taste of a partner depend on our present attitude. That is, if we feel like we are on top of the world, only the most successful and attractive partner would be worthy of us. If we are in a pit of despair, we might be happy with someone we might ordinarily consider below our station. A rather crude example might be "last call" at a bar. When individuals have a goal of meeting someone while out at a bar, and they have not met anyone throughout the whole night, they may lower their qualifications for acceptable partners when the bartender shouts, "Last call." The goal remains the same, but their taste, and apperception, changes as to meet that goal.

We often see children change the rules and their perceptions, and retain the same goal on the playground. If they are in a race to win, but come in second, you'll likely here them proclaim: "First is the worst. Second is the best. Third is the one with the treasure chest!" In this way, the rules are changed. Being the best was the goal all along, so the rules had to change to meet reality.

Dreikurs put forth that sexual fidelity presumes total acceptance of the other person. We would like to add one element: the fear of consequences. People may remain faithful because they fear the social, financial, or other consequences that often accompany infidelity. Infidelity, he wrote, happens when one or both persons in the partnership long to avoid the other or cut ties with the partner. They seek companionship elsewhere.

We must remember that there are many reasons for infidelity. Take a moment to think about why people cheat on their significant others. What comes to mind? How about taking revenge against the other for some real or perceived transgression? Often people will get back at their significant others by cheating on them if they were once cheated on. It may be their way of evening the score. "What's good for the goose is good for the gander," they say. Another reason for infidelity is that sometimes men want to prove their masculinity. The female side of this argument may be heard as, "I need to prove to myself that I am still attractive (or desirable)." Other reasons for unfaithfulness exist; these are just a few.

Sometimes individuals avoid marriage because they feel inferior and anticipate defeat in the union. In other words, they feel as though they don't have what it takes to be a good spouse, so they remove themselves from the challenge of marriage because they fear failure. They may fear having their inferiorities revealed through the closeness of marriage, so they keep others at a safe distance by remaining single.

Dreikurs elaborated on methods that people use to distance others or safeguard against having their inferiorities uncovered. For example, a very successful woman may marry an unsuitable man in an attempt to keep her superior position and to have his faults rather than her faults be the center of attention. He could then never threaten her place of superiority, and she could blame him if the marriage does fail.

Dreikurs tells us of another distancing technique: dating someone who is married. As long as at least one person is married, there is very little chance that the cheating pair will develop close contact or be together for a period of time in which any flaws can be noticed. As a result, there will not be any opportunity for anyone to see any major flaws in the other as each person is at a safe distance where the wrinkles of the person's personality are blurred into a smoothed image.

Dreikurs describes another scenario, one in which people complain that no one who is good enough for them is available, which is amusing because around them are thousands of people of the other sex with the same complaint! Dreikurs stated, "The lack of a partner never is anything but the flight from one; and to quiet one's conscience in this respect the greatest variety of excuses are called upon" (p. 111). In other words, all of the excuses do not hide their goal of wanting to be alone. We suggest that no one is born wanting to be alone; however, through a series of real, or anticipated, socially awkward interactions, some people may prefer to be alone because there is no risk of being rejected or being made to feel inferior to others.

Dreikurs also discussed how initial attractions could turn out to be the characteristic that separates unions. For example, if a man marries a woman for her intelligence, he may want to get a divorce because "she is so smart, I feel like an idiot." Or a woman who chooses a determined, self-confident man may find herself irritated if he does not listen to her suggestions or is domineering.

An example of Adlerian marital therapy is demonstrated by Corsini (1964), who developed a "first-aid kit" for marriage that offers a method for guiding discussions with those who present with marital problems. This technique was designed for those in the general practice of medicine, and it assesses each partner's current coping with each of the life tasks. A contract is negotiated following the assessment. The contract establishes a modus operandi wherein each of the partners learns a new method of relating to the other. If the method proves successful in the immediate postcounseling period, the partners are asked to continue individually. Otherwise a referral is made to someone who specializes in marital work.

Pew and Pew (1972) developed a similar technique, "taking the temperature of the marriage," in that they focus upon the life tasks and interpersonal perceptions and ratings. This husband and wife therapy team advocated obtaining ERs among other life style information in conjunction with marital history, self-ratings, and other ratings. With the information gathered, they urge that attention be given to four areas delineated by Dreikurs (1970). The areas are: (1) mutual respect —no fighting or giving in; (2) pinpointing the problem (the underlying issue); (3) reaching a new agreement; and (4) decision-making and responsibility.

Pew and Pew stated that marriage is something that measures social interest and cooperation. Both partners are invited to accept their responsibility and solve their own conflicts. The use of ERs, along with self ratings and other ratings, promotes growth in these areas.

The approach to be presented in this Chapter derives from the analysis of life style, primarily from life style information that ERs provide. We explain attraction and discord as a result of the interaction of the life styles. The life styles of the two partners create a complex interactional system in which each person's line of movement interleaves with that of the partner's. The life styles, not the pathologies as Ravich understands it, mesh.

Some people will tell us that they want to delay marriage until they straighten themselves out psychologically. But as we have discussed, psychological disorders do not preclude long-term, harmonious marriage. The test lies instead in the interweaving of the individual life styles. Hence, it is possible that a good match can be made between one with masochistic traits and one with sadistic traits. Each of these individuals would be considered individually as maladjusted. Yet together they might make "beautiful music."

It is not a marriage made in heaven; but they are made for each other by virtue of their harmonious life styles.

A Case Example

The following case may illustrate some of the above assumptions and exhibit how counseling generates some hypotheses. Adler (1931/1969) in *The Case of Mrs. A*, developed a method for generating hypotheses that he referred to as guessing (see also, Dailey, 1966). (As we said, the Adlerians like to keep the terminology as simple as possible.) Guesses are made about the interaction of the couple.

A couple sought counseling after five months of marriage. It was the second marriage for each of them. His complaints focused on how demanding his wife was. She required much attention, and he couldn't provide it because he worked 13 hours a day. She was dominant, and he felt like a prisoner. She countered with "He only considers me after *his* needs are met."

Her story centered on his selfishness. He considered everything and everyone else before her. He didn't have time or energy left for her because she was a secondary priority. He countered with "She's not only selfish; she's spoiled." She felt that he was hot-tempered and wanted his own way.

So what are your guesses about the couple? What does each person believe? Where are they heading? What are their individual goals? How do they see their roles in the marriage? It is important to make guesses to gather pertinent information and form impressions. It is also a good way to expand your thinking about the couple.

Granted we have given you little information, but what are your impressions? Do you believe that each partner engages in finger pointing? If so, for what purpose? If one blames the other (perhaps rightly so), what might the other spouse do? Might the spouse beg for one more chance? Could the spouse say, "Put an egg in your shoe, and beat it! I don't need you"? Might the other spouse say, "I realize what I did was wrong, and I will do as you ask?" Do you believe that each person casts the spouse as the villain so to make the therapist believe that he or she has been wronged and is a victim? What guesses might you make about this couple given the information they present? You have been invited into their game; what role are you going to play?

"Games Married Couples Play"

Mozdzierz and Lottman (1973) described a number of "games married couples play." Their work is similar to Berne's (1964) concept of games.

Essentially, the concept that Mozdzierz and Lottman put forth is that "spouses are unconsciously engaged in a struggle for personal prestige and/or domination" (p. 182). In other words, within the social interaction of married couples there exists the one-upmanship game between husband and wife, a striving for superiority. We have truncated some of the examples that Mozdzierz and Lottman describe.

The "I'm Right; You're Wrong" game is one in which each spouse avoids being proven wrong while trying to prove that the other spouse is. Even when one partner admits to being wrong, the other partner is seen as "wronger." (One spouse may confess to doing something wrong, but quickly follow up with "But you did *that*, which is 10 times worse!") Their biased apperceptions influence their view of the other and of the situations. This leads to emphases and omissions that reveal the one who is complaining to be right, noble, and perhaps martyred. Being more right then the other spouse allows dominance and control over the relationship. By definition, no equality is ever achieved in the relationship.

This is particularly evident if one spouse had an affair. The other spouse may use this as the "ace in the hole" for the duration of the marriage. The infidelity may be seen as "the worst of all evils," and the one who was cheated on has a perpetual fountain from which to drink. For example, if a husband cheats on his wife, the wife may always go back to that affair to garner attention. "He hasn't been attentive to me since the affair!" The wife may hold his feet to the coals and say, "You need to make it up to me. Let's go on a cruise (or buy a new house, etc.)." She may continually refer to the affair to put him down in front of friends, family members, and coworkers. She may do her best to prove that he is a jerk and that she is an innocent victim who tolerates his stupidity and insensitivity.

Another game Mozdzierz and Lottman described is "I've Got a Debit; You've Got a Credit." We see this when each spouse makes a note of who did what and who is "owed" something. There is continual tally and comparison, with no room for flexibility. You may see this in a therapy session when one spouse says something like, "You chose the color of the kitchen, and therefore I get to choose what color to paint the house." Each spouse distrusts the other and fears being shortchanged.

Dreikurs (personal communication) presented another version of this "bookkeeping" transaction with couples who were looking for a "50-50" marriage. While some couples view this arrangement as equitable, Dreikurs disagreed. In this type of arrangement he found that each partner was vigilant to see that the other partner did not get 51% to his or her 49%. He countered with a proposal to relinquish "bookkeeping" for a "100-100" marriage in which each partner does whatever the marriage requires.

The "Pay Attention" game is one in which one spouse desires more attention than the other will give, and therefore the spouse feels justified in using whatever means necessary to get that attention, whether it is by nagging, yelling, being coldly silent, or even physically abusive. (Think of the neglected teenager whose hair is purple, who has numerous body piercings, and generally goes out of the way to get attention.) In other words, "I am not a person to be ignored. Don't try to dismiss me because I'll get your attention either actively or passively."

The "I Don't Want to Discuss It" game that Mozdzierz and Lottman describe is the converse of the "Pay Attention" game. Through silence and being unexcitable, a spouse may feel invulnerable, unsinkable, and the winner. It may seem like a test of wills. Each spouse will demonstrate that whoever "breaks" first wins. (It's kind of like the automobile game of "chicken": two people drive head-on toward each other with increasing speed, and the person who turns away first is labeled "chicken.")

"This is War" game is a no-holds-barred attack by each spouse with the goal of hurting the other more than being hurt. We may think of this game has having one rule: "There are no rules." We may be taken off guard by the depths that couples engaged in this game will sink to. Each one may try to outdo the other with "low blows." (Remember the Michael Douglas and Kathleen Turner movie *The War of the Roses*, in which a husband and wife attack each other in a vicious divorce battle?)

The "It's All Your Fault" game is one in which one spouse tries to absolve himself or herself from any connection to a problem by blaming the problem on the spouse's incompetence. (A milder form of this can be seen when one parent says to the other: "Do you know what *your* child did today?")

The last game detailed by Mozdzierz and Lottman is the "Where Would You Be Without Me?" game in which one spouse claims selflessness and sacrifice for the other spouse, thereby securing his or her own superiority. When couples engage in this game we often hear lines like the following: "If it wasn't for me, you'd still be _____," or "When I met you, you were_____, and now look where you are! You and your whole family should thank God you met me!"

As you can see, each game is a struggle for what Sicher (1955) called "vertical movement." Each spouse tries to become superior over the other instead of focusing on mutual goals and equality. These games can be seen in therapy and assessed through the gathering and interpretation of ERs. Matching their life styles, especially through the understanding of their ERs, allows for an exploration of the dynamics underlying the marriage.

Marital Life Style Matching

In this section we provide a number of ERs for you to read, make guesses about, and summarize. We gather ERs from the husband and wife separately. We do not want them to know what the other is talking about. However, we do review them together to highlight each spouse's life style and how that influences the marriage. Again, seeing the couple together is the preference in Adlerian practice. To see only one person is to get half of the story. If we hear only one spouse's words, we have to guess what the other spouse is like. Dreikurs (1967) has indicated his preference for treating the marital relationship as a unit by comparing it to watching a two-character play. Imagine, if you will, watching a play in which a character answers the phone and starts speaking with someone offstage. You have to infer what the offstage person is saying. Marital counseling of individuals rather than couples presents the same difficulties. In each case, the observer's or therapist's biases may be revealed more than the "offstage" person's role in the marital transaction. If we hear only one spouse's words, we have to guess what the other spouse is like. Dreikurs shows how this may reveal the observer's biases.

We'll start with the husband's ERs. Please look at the themes of the recollections. Can you determine from his ERs his role in the marriage and where he might conflict with his wife? At the end, we will provide a summary based upon all of his ERs. However, we encourage you to create your own guesses while reading the recollections.

ER 1. Age: 6

> One day my mom took me to my grandmother's house. I love going over there. She said to my mother, "Anytime you want to leave him here, I'll be glad to take him. He's my little prince!" When my mother came back to pick me up, I screamed bloody murder because I wanted to stay with my grandmother. She let me do anything I wanted.
>
> Most vivid: "My grandmother telling me that I could do whatever I wanted to do."

ER 2. Age: 5

> I remember one night I got up at about 2 A.M. and went into the living room and starting watching television and eating ice cream. I must have been watching it straight through until morning. When my parents woke up and saw me, my father was very angry. He yelled at me, and he was so loud about it, too. He sent me to

my room. I remember muttering to myself as I walked to my room that my father treats me poorly. I was just watching TV and eating some ice cream. It wasn't like I was burning down the house. I started to wonder why my mother didn't say a word in my defense. Nothing! When I got to my room, I ripped down a poster of Superman and threw my toys around.

Most vivid: "My father being enraged and me breaking up my toys."

ER 3. Age: 8

I was in the fields by my house, and I took my father's good Swiss Army Knife. I cut my arm, and I was so upset that I threw the knife into the weeds. I couldn't find it afterward. I stayed out as long as I could because I knew my father would be mad with me and that he would yell at my mother for letting me take the knife.

Most vivid: "Cutting my arm and losing the knife in the weeds."

ER 4. Age: 8

I remember this one time when I was rollerblading in the park with my friends. A bunch of other guys called us names for using our rollerblades. I was really upset, and I told my friends, "Hey, we shouldn't stand for this. We can beat up those guys and then make them eat their words." Well, we got our butts kicked. We ended up rollerblading home as fast as we could. My friends did not want to fight.

Most vivid: "Getting beat to a pulp!"

ER 5. Age: 7

My cousin used to tease and taunt me. He thought he knew everything and I knew nothing. Everything he had was good, and everything I had was worthless. [This part is a report.] So one day we were playing soccer in the front yard and started arguing over whether or not a kick was in bounds or not. We argued about who was wrong and who was right. The argument turned to pushing, then shoving, then hitting. It went on for a long time. All of a sudden we both stopped throwing punches. The following day we played together again.

Most vivid: "He was wrong, and he wouldn't admit it."

Have you written a summary of this man's ERs?

If you have, compare it to ours:

"Women should let me do what I want, and when they don't, I'll scream my head off. When women make me do things, I hate it. When men don't let me do what I want (no matter how innocuous it is), I'll curse them and beat myself up. I'll also lose faith in the women who don't support me when I'm in trouble. Women will let me get wrongly punished. I fight for truth and justice but that fails because people do not see my point of view. I should have what other men have, even though I'll hurt myself. I have a tendency to beat myself up and make matters worse (out of the frying pan and into the fire) when the going gets rough. And it does get rough, because I believe that it is a violent world and that when push comes to shove, I'll lose. Furthermore, I can't rely on men to back me up as they run and will not stick their necks out for me. I argue with others about who is right and get into fights over it. However, disagreements (at least with men) escalate and then evaporate."

His growth-impeding convictions are:

1. He does not see the possibility of social cooperation and of good human relationships.
2. He believes people are inherently warlike. They are designed to fight with one another.
3. He believes that he is right, and anyone who disagrees with him is wrong. Even when he is indeed wrong, others are even further off the mark.
4. He believes that he is able to admit his faults and errors. And the ability to do so, allows him to elevate himself above others morally.
5. He thinks that women are there to let him have his way. Any woman who refuses him is wrong. If a woman makes any demands on him, she had better be prepared for a fight.
6. He believes that if he can't play it good, he can play it loud, and the one who screams louder wins the argument.
7. He believes that men will abuse him and run out on him when he needs support.

You might speculate that with this type of life style he would marry a woman who would not put any demands on him. Then, in theory, they would get along very, very well. Well, we would have one point, but not two. That is, what do you make out of his perception of the world as a warring place? We have to satisfy another point of his life style that we are cognizant of. If he married a undemanding woman, how would he confirm his belief that people cannot get along? This is a conviction that he constantly tests. He wants to always come out right in his understanding of the universe.

For that reason, a demanding woman makes the ideal choice in terms of his life style, even if not at the behavioral level. Since he demands to do that which he likes to do, those choices become automatically right. When she disagrees or demands from him, she is automatically wrong. Then, because he is right and she is wrong, they must fight so he can prove to her and others just how wrong she is. Furthermore, he chooses a woman to fight with instead of a man (such as a coworker or boss) because when he fights men, he loses. Therefore, he must fight with women, for the fear that fighting with men will end with him getting beaten to a pulp and having to run away.

What predictions would we make if the therapist was a man? A woman?

This man chooses a woman who fights with him because it reinforces his understanding that the world is a violent place, and as long as she fights him he can feel outraged at her temerity and noble for being righter than she. He may demonstrate that he is "the bigger person" by admitting guilt. The admission allows him the elevated status of being noble about his "wrongness" and at the same time lowering her status because she wasn't "big enough to admit when she was wrong."

So why would this man want to perpetuate such a condition?

If he admits responsibility for his "sins," he gets to elevate himself on the grounds of moral superiority ("At least I have the decency to admit when I'm wrong!"). Continuing skirmishes throughout the marriage reinforce his perspective that people are hostile and intolerant. In a strange way, he may feel that "all is right with the world" when people fight because it is what he expects. In addition, it may challenge the belief that positive social interactions and cooperation are possible. Believing that people can get along would shatter his understanding of the world and make for a very uncomfortable existence. He may feel as though he were watching an episode of *The Twilight Zone.* As mentioned previously, that would create a large amount of cognitive dissonance.

Now that we have a handle on his line of thinking, we can guess how he might behave. That is to say, we can expect him to look for and engage in relationships that ensure that his expectations come true. Once somebody does something wrong, he can immediately go into the familiar territory of claiming that he told them so because he knew all along that something bad might happen. In other words, he's engaged in a type of self-fulfilling prophecy. Consciously or unconsciously, he will do only those things that reinforce his Weltbild. He will shy away from relationships in which there is a high probability of smooth sailing. (We can see the same thing in a racist who watches the news and makes negative comments on people of a particular race when they get arrested or are suspected of law breaking. "See another one of those _____ is arrested again! What did I tell you? Probably as guilty as sin. You can't trust them, as far as you can throw them left-handed." But he makes no acknowledgment when people of that race make positive contributions to society.)

For our purpose in this section we are focusing on the areas that might be troublesome for a marriage. (So if you were asking, "Hey, where is all the positive stuff in ERs that you have been talking about?" don't worry — they are there.) In the above recollections we do not see any conflict resolution or positive interactions. When good things do occur, he does not know why. Therefore, it is preferable to holler when things are not going his way rather than to seek conflict resolution. The hollering is in accord with his life style. It's a theme that we see in the recollection: "Give me what I want, right now, or I'll scream my head off and make you regret even the idea of denying me anything. And screaming doesn't bother me because I came here for a fight anyway, especially if you're a woman."

His ERs are only half of the story. What do you expect to see in his wife's ERs? Look at her recollections and see how her life style allows a certain complementary (albeit difficult) role with her husband.

ER 1. Age: 4

> My brother was chasing me down the hallway. He took a hockey stick and tripped me. I broke one of my front teeth. I picked up the tooth and showed my mother. She punished him. I saved the tooth in a jar on my dresser. I despised him when he did that.

> Most vivid: "Him tripping me."

ER 2. Age: 5

> My older sister had some of her friends over even though our mother told her not to have anyone over. They were watching music videos, and one of them spilled soda pop on one of my books. My sister picked up my book and put it in the trash and then covered it over with paper.

> Most vivid: "My sister putting my book in the trash."

ER 3. Age: 9

I was in Chicago, and my family decided to go into the Wrigley Building. My sisters and I challenged each other as to who could walk up the stairs. My mother and father were too lazy to join us, and they took the elevator. I remember my sisters couldn't go any farther and stopped at a floor and took the elevator. I was able to go the distance, and I got there before anyone.

Most vivid: "Reaching the top."

ER 4. Age: 8

I was invited to go to a birthday party for the girl down the street. I said that I would go, and my mother bought her a present. Well, I thought the present was cool, and I wanted it, so I pretended I was sick, all doubled over and moaning, and did not go to the party. My mother left the house, and I unwrapped the present and started playing with it. She came back into the house and saw me dancing around having a great time with the present, and she slapped me across the face, and it hurt. I detested her very being. I ran into the bathroom and slammed the door as hard as I could.

Most vivid: "Being slapped."

What are your guesses as to the meaning of this woman's ERs? Here is our summary:

"Men harm me, causing me to lose face. I have to criticize a man to other women for them to be punished. I hold on to the memory of the damage that men do to me. Women do not listen to other women, and they surreptitiously cause me harm or loss. I pay a price for other women's fun. I am in competition with other women. Other women don't have the tenacity or strength that I do. When I want something, I'll lie to get it, but other women see through my act and act violently against me. When that happens, I isolate myself. While I may do wrong, others act even more wrongly than I."

Her growth-impeding convictions were summarized as follows:

1. She (like her husband) cannot rely on people getting along. This is especially true for the relationship between men and women. Though other women may be able to get along with each other, the client is still an outside who has to pay a price for other women's fun.

2. She just can't win with a man. She can, at best, try to run away, and lose face in the process. Then she may have to criticize a man to other women in order to get some justice.
3. She does not take action to solve her problems. She is a victim or her brother, mother, and sister. She is also an observer. She did not speak up when she saw her sister throw the book into the trash. This suggests that she does not give herself enough credit to be able to solve situations or cope with adversity.
4. Though she does display tenacity, it is in competition with others.
5. The only time she gets a gift is through feigning illness. A woman who finds her out victimizes her eventually.

So there we have two summaries of ERs from a husband and wife. We have the ingredients, but what is the recipe? Why might each of them have picked the other? We suspect that it is because both believe that good social interactions, especially with the other sex, are not possible. In addition, she gets some superiority through being a victim, because for her it is better to be a victim than a victimizer, which is what men and other women are. Both the husband and wife can count on the other to make for interesting times. And as such, they play a complementary role in the marriage. In addition, each spouse invites the other to play the game Berne (1964) called "Uproar." Each sees the other as a wrongdoer, and consequently each sees the other as wrong. No matter how wrong each person is, the spouse is more wrong! If he does wrong, he says, she makes a federal case of it. If she does wrong, she says, he is a complete jerk about it. She may tell all of her friends "what a jerk he really is."

Both looked for, and married, someone who reinforces their *Weltbild* that people, especially men and women, are continually warring. She believes that she cannot win with men and must run away from them and demonstrate how morally superior she is to men and other women. The husband will not cave in to his wife's demands and will holler and point out her wrongs whenever he can and feel morally superior to her. Nor does he look for problem resolution in the marriage because there is an investment in keeping things at odds.

At the same time, there are a number of positive items within their recollections that are the building blocks of therapy. For example, he is not afraid to air his grievances. He knows what he likes in life. He has a sense of right and wrong. He considers how men might act unfairly to women. He does not act cowardly when there is a confrontation and will stand his ground. He can act independently. He can bounce back from an argument. She is tenacious. She knows where to go for justice. She knows well enough not to get bit twice by the same dog, so to speak. She can be a winner (especially among women). She knows what is fair, especially in terms of punishment (from a woman).

Through counseling, couples can see that their expectations of social interactions and the things they think and do can perpetuate marital discord. Through therapy, they can create goals that they both agree on, and they can broaden their cognitive and behavioral repertoire to gain the skills necessary to maintain a healthy marriage.

Summary

Divorces are common. When possible, both partners should be involved in therapy, not just one. Psychological disorders do not necessarily doom a marriage; it is the conflict between life styles that cause difficulty. That is why it is so important in marital therapy to treat both parties. The Adlerian holistic approach recognizes that the marital pair is greater than the combined separate personalities. It is not demographic factors that determine a marriage, but the personalities and goals of the individuals in the marriage. It is our contention that personal adjustment is not a necessary condition for the survival of a marriage, and that personal maladjustment does not necessarily hurt the endurance of a marriage. The test lies instead in the interweaving of the individual life styles and the valences attached to the life style convictions. Within the social interaction of married couples there exists one-upmanship games between husband and wife in which each may try to be superior to the other. Marriage is not necessarily a good in itself. People do marry for various reasons, some good and some not so good. Some people don't marry at all. However, if people decide to marry, it would be beneficial to have compatible life styles.

12
ERs and Vocation

The interpretation of ERs may be very useful in career guidance and counseling. In this Chapter, we will show you how ERs can assist in helping clients find careers that mesh well with their personalities and goals.

If you were to ask 10 adults to describe themselves, most descriptions would not only contain their job position, but would probably *start* with what they do for a living. Work, for most of us, is an inherent part of who we are. It is one of the ways we contribute to society. Those who are happy doing their jobs will often say that they would do it for free. (Just don't tell their bosses.) These people truly enjoy their work because what they do at work reflects their life style. For other people, their work is just a job. They are in it for the paycheck and little or nothing else. If they won the lottery during their lunch break, they would leave that job in midshift.

So we have a clear distinction with which to start this Chapter — those who like their jobs and those who hate their jobs. The difference, as we see it, is how well the personality matches the job requirement. To some people being on stage is horrifying, yet others love to be the center of attention. Life style differences can be seen in the different types of work. Accordingly, we can use ERs to comprehend our clients' life styles and use that information for career guidance. It is important to remember that not only life style influences vocational choice. Other things such as salary, job location, opportunity, and education guide job selection.

Life Style and Vocation

We are going to look at ERs in part and in whole for clues that we can use as clinicians to help guide our clients.

Orgler (1939/1963) underscored the importance of using the first childhood memories for vocational guidance. She stated that for a good vocational match to life style, clinicians must look at elements of their clients' recollections that are in harmony with the requirements of the profession. Certain clues, such as sound and movement, may reveal occupational inclinations. For example, she describes a young man who remembers an engine whistle in a recollection. She then tells us he is an "acoustic type" (one of Adler's learning types) who is "probably suited to an occupation in which he can use his ears — perhaps a profession connected with music" (p. 42). Though we advise against making a recommendation from one recollection, we can speculate from material and ask our clients to consider, verify, or refute our speculations.

Our goal is to find one or, better yet, a number of occupations that may mesh well with one's life style. This may also be of use when working with those clients in transition. For example, Alfred Adler's daughter Alexandra Adler (1959) wrote about how individuals may fulfill the work task in an environment that does not conflict with their life style. "For instance, a borderline schizophrenic may finally be able to manage comparatively well as a clerk if a screen is placed between the customers and himself such as is possible in a post office" (p. 187).

Spoilt Son

Orgler asks that we also look for movement in our clients' recollections. Why? She believes that if clients are the "motor type" (another one of Adler's types), they may not like those jobs in which they have to sit all day. She believes that one's immobility or resistance to engaging in work can be observed in ERs. She illustrates with the first recollection of "A thirty-two-year-old man, the eldest, spoilt son of a widow." By this description alone might you guess what his recollection is about?

The recollection is:

> I was about four years old and was sitting at the window while my mother knitted socks, and watched the workers across the way [positional detail] building a house. (p. 87–88)

Here it is quite clear that the boy is watching other people at work; work is at a distance. Fast-forward 28 years, and he is a spoilt son who is content to watch other people work.

As Orgler indicates, movement, or lack of it, can be seen in ERs. If the ERs are filled with stories of action and movement, perhaps it is best that a person find employment that mirrors that kinetic frame of mind.

It is very important to query your clients' about their feelings at the time of the events in their recollections. For example, if they are pleased with the action, perhaps through achieving something, then it may be best to place them in a like environment. If they dislike movement, then a job with less activity may be better suited for them. The interpretation of each variable presented may be translated this way. It is necessary to look at the major variables (such as sight, sound, movement, etc.) and ascertain whether clients were pleased with what happened in the recollection as indicated by a feeling associated with it or the most vivid part or overall theme.

Orgler believes that individuals choose the ER because there was some interest there. In regard to the previous recollection it can be stated that, "The action of his memory, led by his life-style, seizes upon an incident which reveals his peculiarity [sic]" (p. 88). From this we can assume that the "spoilt son" chose a memory that clearly illustrates a preference to watch other people working. He can also be a different type, for example, an observer (aka a "people watcher").

In continuing with this example from Orgler's book, we must remember that in our work as clinicians or vocational counselors, we must think about how we can take such persons and help place them in jobs that make the most of the "onlooker" tendency. If we were to focus on his immobility and state that he is a lazy or "spoilt" man, we only discourage the person and paint ourselves into a career-guidance corner. Furthermore, any attempt to change "the symptom" would fall on deaf ears, as it is part of his life style. As therapists, we have to sometimes play matchmaker. We have to match the life style to the work.

According to Orgler, it turns out that the spoilt man "entered a firm of art dealers" (p. 88). He found a job in which he can still overlook other people's work!

Second, we see that it is necessary to determine our clients' feelings about their recollections in order to choose the direction of the placement. Are they getting what they want, or are they discouraged from a goal in the recollection? This should give you some comprehension of the recollection as having a "traffic cop" function (Mosak, 1992). That is, does the recollection show that the person should move toward or away from a certain variable? For example, do clients move toward excitement in their recollections? Do clients move away from social interaction in their recollections? From these lines of movement, plus the feelings associated with the recollections, clinicians may be able to gauge whether or not clients should pursue that line of work.

Third, we must not be discouraged when we meet clients who prefer to be onlookers or who present challenging recollections. There are occupations for all life styles, and it is the duty of the career counselor to help those people discover a corresponding vocation. If you thought that people who give such ERs are just plain lazy, then you give up too easily. There is something that can always be done with the material found in ERs in regard to career guidance. That is, if we believe that there is no job that would be a good match for the individual, then we may not be looking hard enough to find a position that fits the person and is on the useful side of life. Early recollections may help guide you and your clients.

Incurable Burglar

Orgler continues with a story about an "incurable" burglar who was cured by Alfred Adler.

> My first memory goes back to the time when I was two and a half years old. My younger brother and I were sitting on the floor in front of the drawer that had fallen out of the kitchen table and were picking up the breadcrumbs. It was winter and bitterly cold [modifying detail]. It was at a time when father had left us again and had wandered off on his own. (p. 241)

Orgler continues (this part is an early report rather than an ER):

> Mother had to depend entirely on herself — that is to say, on what some kind farmer would give her, where she had been working during the summer. I was my father's favorite, and yet I hated him, especially so when he beat my mother. When at home, he used to work in a quarry and earned quite a bit. But he brought little or nothing home. On Sundays he used to come home drunk and then beat mother, and only I was permitted to stay in the flat with him. He threw his clothes down in a corner and immediately fell asleep. On these occasions I always used to go through his pockets, and I always took out some money, sometimes even a "Gulden," which I would radiantly take to my mother. I do not think I was aware of having committed theft. I did it more out of compassion for my mother with the subconscious wish to help her. This performance was repeated regularly, became accepted as a matter of course, and this was often for weeks the only money which mother got indirectly from Father. (p. 241)

In this recollection do you believe that the child achieves his goal? Is he happy with the outcome? The answer to both is "yes." So you may be saying, "How am I going to find a job for an apparent thief?" Therein lies the challenge. Looking at this recollection, what occupation might you find for people who apparently would rather take the wealth of others than make their own?

First, look at the key points in the recollection (and report), and remember to reframe his actions in the positive. Does he help others? Yes. In the report, the client is helping an abused mother. Does he consider it thievery or consider himself a thief? No, and you shouldn't either! Is the client wise in how he carries out his pilfering? Yes, because he does his "work" when the chances for being caught (and perhaps beaten) are low. Third, is he reliable? Yes, because he did his "work" regularly.

So there are some positive things with which you may work. And focusing on the positive aspects of your clients' behavior always helps in reaching a goal. Remember that there is a job for every life style that exists. Though it may not be your task to find it for clients, you can encourage them in their search. Finally, never give up, because if you do, then it's likely that your clients will, too.

What are some job possibilities for someone who gave you the above recollection? Here are our suggestions: working in a woman's shelter, raising money for charities (legally, that is), working for casinos to catch thieves who steal from the gambling tables. All these appear to match, to some degree, the client's ER. (Some police departments consult with people of this sort on how to protect people against burglary.)

Research on ERs and Vocational Guidance

A number of studies support using ERs in career counseling. In addition, it has been demonstrated that the interpretations of people's recollections often parallel their work. For example, Holmes and Watson's (1965) article illustrated how the manifest content in the recollections of nurses and teachers was related to their vocational choice. Early recollections were seen as supportive of people's life styles and ultimately their choice of occupations. (It was also suggested that the higher the degree of interest in others and the community, the higher the rate of productivity generally.) In terms of vocational guidance, therefore, ERs undoubtedly can be very helpful. They can indicate possible occupational pursuits and, conversely, which vocations one ought to avoid. And because one of the main life tasks according to Alfred Adler is work/occupation, its helpfulness in vocational guidance should not be minimized or overlooked. With that in mind we present a number of studies in this Chapter. Most of which are correlational, but are presented to show the potential of using ERs in career guidance.

Attarian (1978) looked at the connection between ERs and education preferences using Holland's Self-Directed Search with undergraduate students. He found that Adlerian-trained individuals were largely able to find the students' vocational and education interests from the ERs alone. Early recollections give a clue as to what the person may be interested in. However, people may pursue vocations for reasons other than interest. For example, people may enter medical school because their parents want them to. Or people may become dentists to earn more money than they would pursuing an interest in working with the homeless.

Hafner and Fakouri (1984a) also compared the manifest content of students using the Manaster-Perryman Manifest Content Early Recollections Scoring Manual (Manaster & Perryman, 1974). They found that accounting students showed much internal control, a paucity of visual detail, and did not mention animals or people as often as other students. Furthermore, they found that psychology students had more anxiety-provoking or fearful themes. Psychology and education students made more references than the accounting students did to people who were not kin to them and to visual details. In addition, education students had a higher number of school references. It seems obvious, at least after the telling, that psychology students would be more in touch with emotional recollections as they should be attuned to the feelings of others. Accounting students may be more interested in control and order and being away from others. It is probably no surprise that education majors would reference school more frequently.

There is a disadvantage in approaching the studies in this way. It can give us a false sense of security. Surely, psychology students had more recollections with threatening and negative affect. Of course, the accounting students showed more internal control, and the education students had a higher number of school references. But that does not mean that if you have clients with recollections wrought with threatening and negative affect that they should be psychology majors. Nor does it mean that recollections of internal control should prompt you to guide those clients to becoming accountants. What it means is that these are correlational studies. And just because we have findings in correlational studies, we cannot look at the findings backward to imply causation. The reverse is not always true. Think about it. It would be like arguing that if all criminals drink water, than all water drinkers are criminals. That is obviously wrong; although the premise is certainly true, the conclusion isn't. We must view the findings of these studies only as suggestions, not guaranteed career paths. Nevertheless, these correlational studies indicate the power of ERs to categorize like groups. We'll continue with this in mind.

Hafner and Fakouri (1984b) also contrasted the ERs of 90 male students in clinical psychology, dentistry, and law. Similar to the previous study, the psychology students displayed a significantly higher number of threatening situations and had more themes with negative affect. Similar to the education majors in the previous study, law students mentioned school a significant number of times more than did the other two groups. The incidence of "active dimension" was highest in law students and lower in dentistry students. Maybe lawyers are more active than dentists?

Hafner, Fakouri, and Etzler (1986), in yet another study, examined the manifest content of ERs of three types of engineering students: chemical, electrical, and mechanical. They found that the ERs of chemical engineering students exhibited more external control and more ambiguity regarding the setting than either of the other two groups. Electrical engineering students spoke about a few things much more often than the other two groups. These students related stories of a group, or groups of people, illness and/or injury to self and others or to animals much more often than the other two groups. Those students who studied mechanical engineering mentioned home and family members more often. Furthermore, their ERs had themes of mastery, unfamiliar situations, and hostility significantly more than the other groups.

Fakouri, Fakouri, and Hafner (1986) solicited ERs from nursing students and students in other disciplines and found that the nursing students had memories that indicated more mastery and energetic physical movement. Furthermore, the nursing students had recollections that indicated that their actions were often the result of their decisions. Now what this has to do with nursing, we are not really sure. However, it does indicate that ERs have an ability to group like individuals.

Elliot, Amerikaner, and Swank (1987) compared information gathered from ERs to the results of the Vocational Preference Inventory, Sixth Revision, in predicting college students' vocational choices and found that ERs can be suitably used to gain knowledge of a person's vocational preference. Now this is the type of study we prefer! Early recollections may be more useful than a standardized test in determining vocational preference. More studies of this type are needed to provide information in one direction or another as to the usefulness of ERs in vocational guidance.

Coram and Shields (1987) compared the recollections of criminal justice majors and other majors with the Manifest Content of Early Recollections Scoring Manual (discussed in Chapter 23) that was developed by Manaster and Perryman (1974). Their findings show that criminal justice majors have more concern for detail and more illness and injury themes and that their recollections are more often set in homes of people who are not family members. All of these factors may play an important role in the careers of lawyers, police officers, and others associated with criminal justice. In addition, illness and death themes are commonly found in the ERs of those in the health professions (see Adler, 1929/1964; Lashever, 1990).

Elliot, Amerikaner, and Swank (1987) studied the ERs of 80 students from six different majors (mechanical technology, biology, special education, studio art, restaurant management, and accounting) using a system that allowed the interpretations of ERs to be comprehended in relation to Holland's Vocational Preference Inventory (VPI). Specifically, the authors investigated whether ERs can be used to predict vocational interest with accuracy similar to an established measure. This study created a rating system to allow ERs to be comprehended within the framework of Holland's typology. Early recollections were gathered by questionnaire, and responses were coded with appropriate adjectives that described the themes of the recollections. The adjectives were summed and then compared with the VPI results, as each assessment now provided scores for six career interests (realistic, investigative, artistic, social, enterprising, and conventional) based on Holland's typology. Subjects were ranked on each of these interests for each assessment, and the themes within the ERs were compared with the scores on the VPI.

The authors found that by using ERs, "judges were also able to reliably select the vocational interest of the subjects to the same moderate level of accuracy as the VPI" (p. 358), suggesting that "the results do indicate that ERs may provide a valuable tool for career-related issues in counseling" (p. 358).

McFarland (1988) reviewed the ERs of female registered nurses and female medical technologists. A discriminate functional analysis showed that 64 of the 70 subjects were correctly classified in their occupational groups. That is a correlation of more than 91 percent, suggesting a better match than what is possible with most career assessments.

Carson (1994) examined the ERs of psychologists, mathematicians, and physicists in an effort to identify "categories of early memory content [e.g., curiosity, skepticism of received views from authority figures, and independence of thought] for particular focus in future investigations of the early development of scientists" (p. 157). However, his focus on and suppositions about ERs are different from ours. Carson believes that particular life experiences, as evidenced in early memories, create a scientifically minded individual. This reflects deterministic (or causalistic) thinking.

The Adlerian perspective is that individuals have choice and that people choose their paths in life. Though people do have influential moments in their development, they are active members of society rather than passive recipients who are molded by external events. Nevertheless, we present Carson's work as an example of a correlational study of ERs of scientists.

Carson's study is based on recollections from 19 individuals (five physicists, six mathematicians, and eight psychologists) written on a questionnaire. He found differences among the groups. For example, the interpretation of female psychologists' ERs indicated a sense of being bright, observant, and avoiding confrontation. The male psychologists' ERs "suggest an optimistic, positive, and relatively anxiety-free solution to many of the problems of life" (p. 156). The mathematicians' ERs showed that they see the world as unstable and dangerous; therefore one must master the means necessary to "see through others' tricks . . . and keep one's eyes peeled of potential threats" (p. 155). The common threads of interpretation of ERs from physicists indicated that they feel they are clever enough to overcome life's threats and to see through those who try to trick them.

We present this brief summary of Carson's article for a few reasons. His intent was to provide some evidence of the differences among ERs of particular scientists. His correlation study does in fact do that; however, there are a few caveats. First, his sample size ($n = 19$) is too small to make generalizations to the population at large; thus the study is better understood as an example of a concept rather than a correlation with high reliability, validity, and generalizability. Second, he was the sole interpreter of the recollections. Third, like psychohistories completed from ERs, this study may fall prey to the possibility that Carson projected his knowledge of the individuals' career onto the recollections. Fourth, the recollections were written on a questionnaire rather than gathered face to face, which has a major drawback: Questionnaires do not allow for immediate follow-up questions.

Vettor and Kosinski (2000) hypothesized the potential for ERs as a burnout screening device for emergency medical technicians (EMTs). They used the life style typology of Mosak (1958, 1968) to differentiate personality types that may be more prone or more resistant to burnout. They speculated that those EMTs who have ERs that indicate life styles of controllers, pleasers, martyrs/victims, aginners, and feeling avoiders are more susceptible to burnout than other personality types.

They predicted that controllers would not do well as EMTs because they could not keep things in control. Pleasers would not do well because they are unable to keep everyone alive. Martyrs and victims may overextend themselves and burn out quickly. Aginners are unwilling to cooperate with others, and EMTs must have teamwork skills when working in the life-or-death situations that are common in their profession. Finally, feeling avoiders may be deficient in their self-awareness and blind to the symptoms of burnout, thereby inviting a precipitous fall into exhaustion.

Vettor and Kosinski also suggest that some life styles would be resistant to burnout, specifically the getter, driver, and excitement seeker. Getters may be more focused on the paycheck or on being a hero than on the human suffering involved. They are not likely to be emotionally tied to the situation or to the people. Drivers are extremely motivated and may be so goal focused that they can see the overall realities of the work. Finally, the excitement seeker may be resistant to burnoutbecause the EMT profession is rife with excitement and change.

Matching ERs and Work

Now is your chance to play career matchmaker. Below are five ERs from the same person and, farther below, a variety of professions. See if you can match ERs to one of the professions listed as the most likely option.

ER 1. Age: 5

> I remember there was this kid in my kindergarten class who was walking with his head down. It was recess, and I noticed that he was not playing like the other kids. He sat down, and I asked him what was wrong. He said, "Nothing," but I wasn't buying it. So I said, "Why are you walking with your head down?" He looked at me and told me he got a C. I asked him what he usually got, and he said, A's and B's. So I said, "It sounds to me like you are an 'A' student that got a 'C,' which is much better than a 'C' student who gets an 'A.'" He looked at me and smiled.

> Most vivid: "Thinking that he was really more of an A student than a C student."

The recollection displays "reframing." That is, the client helped the other kindergartener to look at his situation from another perspective.

ER 2. Age: 9

> There was this girl I knew from school who was smoking along a building. I asked her why she smoked; she said it was the cool thing to do. I asked her what her parents thought about it. She said, "What do they care?"

> Most vivid: "Thinking that it's bad enough that her parents don't care, but she doesn't need to add insult to injury."

ER 3. Age: 5

I remember watching Bambi and crying when Bambi's mother was shot. I thought that Bambi was all alone, and I wanted to take care of Bambi or at least show Bambi how she could make it in the wild.

Most vivid: "Feeling sad for Bambi."

ER 4. Age: 6

I remember these kids building a snow fort in front of my school. Even though it was wintertime, I could feel the warmth of the sun. I went over and helped them build their fort. It felt good to help them build what they wanted. They were not from my school, and I never saw them afterward.

Most vivid: "Helping them get their fort built before the buses came."

ER 5. Age: 7

My mother and I used to watch a lot of movies and TV shows together. Mostly they were old mysteries — Charlie Chan, Sherlock Holmes, *The Thin Man, Murder She Wrote*, even an occasional *Scooby Doo*. [This part is a report.] Well, I remember one time my mother and I were watching Charlie Chan, and she was guiding me through what to look for, like facial reactions, why someone might be the murderer, and so forth. I had a great time trying to piece the clues together to unravel the mystery.

Most vivid: "Watching the characters and guessing their motives. It was pure joy!"

Career options:

1. Carpenter
2. Teacher
3. Forest ranger
4. Medical doctor
5. Movie director
6. Mystery writer
7. Therapist

Please think about the clues given in the ERs and choose a possible career that might best fit them. We made this series a bit easier than real life as you (most likely) have not had the training to discover more veiled clues that are usually presented in ERs.

In the first recollection we see that a sensitivity to others. More important, there is the ability to look on the positive side of things and make someone feel better. In the second recollection, the person is telling us that he is sensitive to others and comprehends psychodynamics. In the third recollection, we see an ability to empathize as well as a desire to help those in need, to give the skills necessary to cope with life's adversities. In the fourth recollection, we see a desire to help people reach their goals and no reported difficulties in letting go after they have reached them. In the final recollection we see an enjoyment of piecing clues together from nonverbal cues, lines of movement, and motives, as well as a receptiveness to accepting guidance on what to look for in people's actions.

We made this example particularly easy for you, especially if you are in the field of psychology. This is also an example of positive ERs. This person demonstrates social interest, a willingness to learn, and receptivity to feedback.

In reviewing the summary of the ERs, we select therapist as the best fit. The second option, teacher, is a close second, though.

As this Chapter demonstrates, the use of ERs in career guidance is very promising as it may provide a quick and accurate method to assess individuals, understand their goals and movement, and then find occupations that match the interests shown in the ERs.

Summary

Life style differences can be seen in the different types of work. Accordingly, we can use ERs to comprehend our clients' life styles and use that information for career guidance. A number of different studies support using ERs in career counseling. In addition, it has been demonstrated that the interpretations of people's recollections often parallel their work. However, we must view ERs as career suggestions, not guaranteed career paths.

13

Pre- and Postintervention ERs

Early recollections are often used to understand a client prior to the initiation of therapy. We believe that therapy can be more efficient (quicker) and effective (successful) when we use ERs because they allow us to see the world and the client as the client sees them. However, ERs are just as useful when we use them at the end of therapeutic intervention. When we gather ERs at the both the preintervention and postintervention phases of therapy (and sometimes in between), we can better assess if any change has occurred and, if so, in what direction. Changes in ERs frequently occur in therapy, and these changes appear to be in accord with our clients' changed perceptions of life (Dreikurs, 1954; Eckstein, 1976; Mosak, 1958).

Let's look at the preintervention ERs of a 70-year-old man. We'll interpret each ER by parsing it and looking at its overarching concept or concepts. Afterward, we'll recap the main points of the preintervention ERs, then review the postintervention ERs and note what changed and what remained the same. Along the way, we'll point out some important features that exist in ERs, their relevance to this client, and their relevance to the process of gathering and interpreting ERs in general.

Early recollections from one client cannot be generalized to other clients. In keeping with the tenets of Individual Psychology, we think that each person is unique, and, consequently, so are his or her ERs. Therefore, what is presented with this case may overlap with other people but is not representative of the ERs of all people. For that reason, we devote two Chapters to pre- and postintervention ERs. The next Chapter focuses on the ERs of a female client. Though these two sets of ERs will broaden our understanding of the usefulness of ERs in evaluating the success of therapy, they are hardly all-inclusive. Because every person is unique, you'll undoubtedly encounter situations not covered here; that's why you must always remember to tailor your interpretation and questioning to your particular client.

In examining pre- and postintervention recollections, you need to cover at least four areas; we'll call this the COAT method. We look for what has *changed* in the postintervention recollection. We see what has been *omitted* in the postintervention recollection. We look for what has been *added* in the postintervention recollection. And we want to *test the limits*. That is, when clients give us information in the preintervention recollection, and it is not there in the postintervention recollection, we query them to see if they remember (without cues from us); then we prompt them (for example, "Previously you gave a recollection about Christmas and a sled. Can you tell me that one again, please?"). Then we see if something is forgotten ("Gee, that doesn't ring a bell at all."). If it is forgotten, then it is not important to them anymore. As a matter of fact, when you tell some clients their preintervention recollections after therapy, they may tell you, "You must be reading someone else's memories. I don't remember such an event!" This demonstrates the power of human memory and how ERs are about current events. We remember those episodes that are relevant and forget those that are irrelevant to our current posture in life.

Preintervention ERs of a 70-Year-Old Man

ER 1. Age: 4

I hit my chin with the see-saw. I see a cloth with blood on it.

Feeling: "Amazement at so much blood."

Most vivid: "Cloth, color red."

OK, so what do we make of this? The client does not speak about anyone else in this recollection. The recollection begins with "I hit my chin," and we can speculate that this client creates his own misery. (He may take things "on the chin.") The second part of the recollection contains the phrase "with the see-saw." We already know that most, if not all, ERs have a metaphor. Could this be the metaphor for the client? That is, does this client have his ups and downs, or does his life go up and down? This is something we may want to consider as we look at the subsequent recollections. Will those recollections indicate movement from being down to being elevated, and back again? We'll find out.

Though it may appear at first that the person has included a texture response in the inclusion of the cloth in both the ER and the most vivid portion, we do not know if it was a terry-cloth towel, a flat rag, or anything in between. So before we state that the client is needy or wants affection, we need to look at what is presented in the recollection and not what we project onto the recollection.

Also, look at the attention given to the color of the blood. The client tells us that the color red is part of the most vivid portion of the recollection. As we discussed earlier, the inclusion of color details in ERs suggests that the person has an aesthetic sense. We'll look for this in subsequent ERs to see if our hunch plays out.

From this ER, we begin to think tentatively that this client may feel as though he cannot handle life by himself, that he may create his own troubles, and that he has an aesthetic eye or is creative. Another interpretation is that life bloodies him. Remember, we cannot generalize from one recollection. So with the ideas from the first recollection as a starting point, let's look at the following ERs to provide a more comprehensive picture of the individual.

ER 2. Age: 6

> I remember I was very ill and lying in bed. My parents were leaving on a short vacation with their friends. I remember it was the first time that they had left us, me and my siblings. I remember being sad because they were about to leave.

Most vivid: "Myself alone, sick in bed."

Here the client sees himself as ill. And while we have all been sick during childhood, why might the client bring this up in this recollection? He may perceive himself as sickly. Or he might think that people abandon those who are ill. Or illness may be a major concern in his life. In addition, he is sad that his parents are leaving. He is, in a way, losing his parents, though it may be for a short time. And though he has his siblings around him in his home, he feels sad losing his parents. We may want to think about whether this client is a getter, as he is losing his parents, or whether he is a victim of his parents' abandonment or is a dependent personality. In looking at the entire recollection, it can be seen that the client feels sick at the time when people abandon him. Is the client telling us that people kick him when he is down or that people leave him in his time of need or just that people don't care? We get the impression that the client is isolated in bed with no family members to console him. The client indirectly tells us what he does to overcome the predicament presented in the ER. He feels sad and perhaps sorry for himself, as well as sick and isolated, but he does nothing other than that to address his crisis.

In examining the first two recollections we see that others abandon the client in time of need, and, perhaps more important, that it appears as though this person is a "victim." In the first recollection he victimizes himself, and in the second recollection others victimize him through abandonment. Furthermore, when he is left to his own devices, things turn into a bloody mess. Though life may have its ups and downs, so far we have seen only the downside to life. And don't forget the aesthetic quality that the inclusion of color may indicate. With each recollection we learn a little more about this client, even though we have never seen this person. By the last recollection we should have a fairly clear understanding of what might bring him into therapy. We should also have some insight into what strengths he has and what kind of client goals would be clinically useful in his case.

ER 3. Age: 5

> This happened before I started school. My father took me to his work. His boss was a nice man dressed in a blue suit and looked at me and said that he was impressed that I was able to get up so early and added that I could sit at his desk. He brought me a doughnut and some color markers and a bunch of paper on which to draw.

> Feeling: "Very happy and really cool."

> Most vivid: "The desk and the boss's blue suit."

This is an interesting recollection as it shows us life on the upswing. Here the client tells us that he is very happy and that "the early bird gets the worm." It is because he is there early that he gets to sit at the boss's desk. But there is another important part to that happiness: It takes a man to give him special attention so that he can make his world colorful. The client is elevated to the highest position possible, the boss's desk. We also see the reemergence of the getter type. The client likes to get, at least from men, as we have not seen any women in his ERs thus far. This client's ERs may have multiple themes, some appropriate to a victim and others to a getter.

If you are using the Typological Approach, it is important not to halt the interpretation of the recollections when you discover a type since there may be more than one type represented (Mosak, 1979b). We also receive more information about the client's aesthetic eye in the presentation of more color details ("color markers") and in the most vivid part ("the boss's blue suit"). Two aspects of the client's second ER reinforce hypotheses we made earlier. First, he is getting something and is happy about it. Second, he includes color. The additions that are important are that there are happy times or colorful times, particularly when men elevate him.

ER 4. Age: 5

> I remember the first day of school. We were sitting at our desks, and there was this boy in front of me who was wearing overalls. One of his shoulder straps fell off his shoulder. I thought, "That poor kid. He has no support." I put his shoulder strap back on for him. I'm still in contact with him." [The last sentence is a report.]

> Feeling: "Poor kid. By himself. Let me help him."

> Most vivid: "Pulling shoulder strap up."

Again, no women are present. We might guess that for this client, it's a man's world. But what is the metaphor presented by the client? Might he be informing us that men hold each other up, like a shoulder strap holds up a pair of pants? In a way, he is supporting his (now lifelong) friend. Social support appears to be important for him. We see that he cares for others, but there is no indication that others care for him. We also get the impression that the client believes that it doesn't take much to make friends with men (just give them a little attention and support). He is caring and empathetic as he helps a less fortunate person.

ER 5. Age: 4

> I remember I was at my aunt's house. She and I were in the kitchen, and I thought I pooped my pants. I asked my aunt to get my brother who was playing down the street, and she said "No." I kept asking her to get my brother, and eventually she did. I whispered in his ear that I thought I pooped my pants, and it turns out that I had just passed gas.

> Feeling: "Petrified and embarrassed."

> Most vivid: "Not wanting to tell my aunt. My brother and I standing there talking in the hall."

Finally he introduces a woman. So what is happening in this ER? First, the client is telling us that he creates his own troubles. This is in accord with the first recollection in which he hits himself with the see-saw. Again, he shows us that he is a victim as he victimizes himself. Second, we see that he wants a man to help him in that he calls for his brother, and a woman rejects his plea for assistance. We may speculate that women refuse to help him, at least when he creates his own troubles. However, women do eventually cave in and get a man to help. We also get the impression that the client overdramatizes events; he did not poop his pants but "just passed gas." Perhaps he's just "a little stinker"? Essentially, the client is telling us that through a lack of control he creates his own chaos. Furthermore, he may overdramatize problems. In addition, he feels that women are nonsupportive, noncaring, and obstructive. In contrast, he believes that he needs a man because men are helpful to other men who are helpless, as he was helpful to the child in the previous recollection with the fallen shoulder strap.

ER 6. Age: 9

> I remember being at school one day, and I wanted a particular book that was not in the library. I asked a teacher [male] who took me to the top floor into the private faculty library. No other student had ever been allowed in that library. It was beautiful. It had cherry wood walls, leather chairs, and high bookshelves. It was dark in there, but it was distinguished and overwhelming. I thought I was in the area where deep thinking took place.
>
> Feeling: "I thought I was lucky and honored to be there. A place of deep thought."
>
> Most vivid: "The cherry wood, leather chairs, and high bookshelves."

Again, we do not see any women in the recollection. This lends support for our guess that the client believes it's a man's world and that he's looking for a place in it. We are starting to see some redundancy in the recollections; that is, certain themes are appearing recurrently. Again, the client is telling us that men can elevate him in two ways, in position (top floor), and in the realm of knowledge and recreation (library). The client believes that he has access to a place where no other student had been permitted. Here the client is telling us that if you are privileged enough to know the right person (particularly a man), you can view the good things in life. The client is a getter here as well. He receives a ticket (gets in) to the forbidden area, and not through his own effort but through whom he knows. It's great to get but even better when you don't have to do anything for it. We also see how the pursuit of knowledge is highly regarded, as the client is looking for a book and is overwhelmed by the library. There is an aesthetic bent as the client tells us that "It was beautiful," and he includes the details of cherry wood, leather, and so on.

ER 7. Age: 5

> It was Hanukkah time [a Jewish holiday in which parents present gifts to children], and I remember I wanted a doctor's bag. We weren't that well off, and the kids in my family usually didn't get too many toys. We were sitting for Hanukkah dinner, and there on my seat was the doctor's bag.
>
> Feeling: "So excited."
>
> Most vivid: "The doctor's bag on the chair."

Hanukkah recollections, along with recollections about birthdays, Christmases, and so on, are usually a telltale indication that a client is a getter. We clearly have a client with more than one theme in the ERs: the getter and the victim. Once again the client is getting something for doing nothing, and isn't he excited? It's rare to get what you want, so it's a big deal when you do. We do not see any interactions with other people or client contribution. As a matter of fact, most of the ERs given by this client have little or no social interaction. We may want to consider this as an area of concern about the client's life that might warrant investigation. The inclusion of the detail "doctor's bag" may suggest that this client is interested in sickness (perhaps education as well). Why else might that detail be recalled? The client's recollections are consonant with those of physicians — injury (ER 1), illness (ER 2), and doctor's bag (ER 7).

ER 8. Age: 5

> I remember it was Halloween. My brother had carved up this scary-looking pumpkin that looked really frightening. It was a real piece of art, a great-looking pumpkin. Anyway, I got really upset with my brother and smashed the pumpkin on the street. I completely destroyed it.
>
> Feeling: "Livid and very sad because I'd smashed what I liked."
>
> Most vivid: "Picking up the pumpkin and throwing it down on the street. I also remember yelling my head off."

We consider this a "warning ER" because it warns the client that anger is a dangerous thing. He is telling us that he hurts himself when he gets angry. Therefore, he should not get angry because he may lose something dear to him. This is also an interesting recollection in that it demonstrates the converse of the getter. To the getter, it is wonderful to get. But in this recollection, the client does not get something but loses something, and it's "very bad." Mosak (1971) points out that what is catastrophic for the getter is when life takes something away. This is similar to the ER in which the client is losing his parents temporarily and feels sad. Our money is on this client's being a getter. Not only is he a getter, but he will cut off his nose to spite his face. He wanted to hurt his brother by smashing his pumpkin, but in the process of hurting his brother, he hurt himself. Again the client has an aesthetic eye, and the destruction of a work of art, the face of the "great-looking pumpkin," is especially painful for him. Again, no women are present in the recollection, only strengthening our original assumption that this client believes it's a man's world.

ER 9. Age: 6

> It was Hanukkah, and I wanted this really interesting wind-up toy bank that had a hand that you would put the money in and it would get the coin and deposit it in the box. I'd gone with my father to all of the stores, and no one had it in stock. I was distraught. I remember seeing this box in the living room. It turned out that my father was able to get the bank for me.

> Feeling: "Surprise, excitement."

> Most vivid: "Opening up the present and seeing it was what I wanted."

Once again we see evidence that this client is the getting type. There are some details to consider. First, the toy is a bank. So the client may value getting and saving money or being wealthy. The bank actually "get(s)" money. Second, when we look at the most vivid part (the gist) of the recollection, we see that it is getting what the client wants. Third, we see that a man is able to surprise him and give him something that he wants.

We think we have enough ERs to construct a brief summary for this client's outlook. Read it and review the recollections for evidence to support the statements made.

Summary of Preintervention ERs

The summary of ERs is most often written in the first person, singular form because it is how clients see themselves in the here and now.

> Life has its ups and downs. I create my own troubles and cannot be left to my own devices. That is the downside. I feel that others may abandon me when I am at my lowest, and that is another downside to life. I have a tendency to overdramatize my difficulties in life. I am a victim of others and myself. However, I believe that I need other men to support and elevate me. When they elevate me, I believe that my life is on the upswing. I realize that men are helpful and helpless. I empathize with and support the helpless ones and rely on the helpful ones to help me. I do not focus too much upon women. They get in my way, deny me assistance, and prolong my embarrassment.
>
> I have to be careful of my anger. When I get angry, I lose control and destroy those things that I value, and cut off my nose to spite my face.
>
> In order for me to have a place in life, I should get and be treated specially. I should have privileges, not because I earn them, but just for being me. I want to receive my heart's desire, but, in my pessimism, I anticipate I may not get it. When I do get it, the surprise makes it even better. Because I'm a getter, I need people to give to me. The worst is to stand alone, unsupported, because then life can be a bloody mess. I am a beneficiary of what life and people (particularly men) have to offer. If I get (material things, special privileges, elevated, etc.), I feel great. If I don't get or life takes from me, I feel terrible. I'm not perfect because I do things I shouldn't, and I'm afraid that the world will discover that I'm a "stinker."
>
> I have an aesthetic eye, an artistic inclination.

From the ERs we can see some beliefs that the client may have that may cause him difficultly. For example, he may feel that he is special, entitled, and that life should bestow gifts and privileges on him without his having to do anything for them. This client clearly focuses more on getting in these ERs than on doing anything. He is a passive recipient. He is so passive in these recollections that it appears as though he does not need to solve problems, but only to depend on others to solve his problems for him. In the same vein, he doesn't believe that he can stand alone and without support, and he is fearful that other people may find out what a stinker he really is. Furthermore, his anger is something that can get out of control and cause him trouble.

On the other side of the coin lie the positive attributes that this client demonstrates in his ERs. For example, he is compassionate and empathizes with his fellow man. He has aesthetic interests and knows how to enjoy himself. Furthermore, he knows how to get others involved in his life, even if they provide a service to him. He is a pessimistic optimist. That is, he may think that he will not get or that he will have to go through "devastation" before he can receive something. He may also believe that if you expect nothing, you'll never be disappointed.

We also get an idea of what career might be interesting for him. After reading the ERs and receiving clues along the way, what might you say is a good career path for him? If you said, "artist," you might be right. The client tells us repeatedly that he has an aesthetic eye and felt very bad when he destroyed a work of art. He might be interested in one of the helping professions, but then he'd have to do something. He could combine both interests and consider a career in medical illustration.

Now that you have read his preintervention ERs, let us fast-forward approximately one year in this client's treatment. What follows is his set of postintervention ERs. Look for the subtle changes.

Pre- and Postintervention ERs Compared

Preintervention ER:

ER 1. Age: 4

I hit my chin with the see-saw. I see a cloth with blood on it.

Feeling: "Amazement at so much blood."

Most vivid: "Cloth, color red."

Postintervention ER:

ER 1. Age: 4

I was hit by a see-saw. I remember the school nurse [female] holding a warm towel on my head to stop the bleeding.

Feeling: "Surprise of what happened."

Most vivid: "The amount of red."

In the preintervention ER, the client creates his own troubles. In the postintervention recollection, he does not. (The change from "I hit my . . ." to "I was hit . . . " suggests that perhaps he does not cause his own misery.) In the preintervention recollection, the client is alone in the world. In the postintervention recollection, somebody is there for him. Perhaps more interesting, it is a female who is comforting him. He is telling us that life is still dangerous, but when life knocks him down, he can count on people (especially female) to be there. In his preintervention recollections, women were not seen as supportive. The inclusion of "a warm towel" suggests a need for affection (perhaps from women) that is not stated in the preintervention recollections. It is also interesting to note that the color red remains in both recollections. His artistic eye remains through the course of the therapy and is a defining part of the client.

Isn't it interesting that there is no reference made to pain in the preintervention or postintervention recollections? Can it be said that he does not feel the pain of the dangerous world?

Preintervention ER:

ER 2. Age: 6

> I remember I was very ill and lying in bed. My parents were leaving on a short vacation with their friends. I remember it was the first time that they had left us, me and my siblings. I remember being sad because they were about to leave.

Most vivid: "Myself alone, sick in bed."

Postintervention ER:

ER 2. Age: 4

> I was sick, and my parents were about to go on a short vacation with their friends. They left us in care of our maternal and paternal grandparents. I was pretty sick. I remember my mother sitting bedside and telling me that they were only going for a short time and that she and my father would be thinking of us kids. I remember feeling sad that they were leaving soon.

Feeling: "I was sad that they were going, but I knew they would be back soon."

Most vivid: "My mom by my side."

In the preintervention recollection, the client is alone and abandoned. In the postintervention recollection, the tone is much softer and more social. He mentions his mother comforting him, and she is in the most vivid part of the recollection. This suggests that he can see women as comforting and helpful. When he is sick, women are by his side. This is in contradiction to his image of women in the preintervention recollections. In the postintervention recollection, we see that he is able to self-soothe ("but I knew they would be back soon"). However, he gets attention from a woman in the postintervention recollection and is much more focused. The client gives rationale and foresight as to why things are happening, as in his anticipation that both his parents are "leaving soon" and will quickly return.

Postintervention ER:

ER 3. Age: 7

> It was wintertime. My parents gave me the key to our house, and I forgot it in my room. I was locked out. Temple was a few blocks down the street from my house. So I walked to temple figuring that would be a warm place to stay until my parents got home from work. I walked there, and a couple of people took care of me. I walked home and met my parents as they were getting off the bus.

> Feeling: "First I was concerned that I would freeze, and then I felt relief when I figured out what to do."

> Most vivid: "Seeing my parents and thinking, 'Perfect timing!'"

Here we have a recollection that was not among those given in the preintervention phase. We see this new recollection because of the change that has occurred in therapy. The recollection, like ones from the preintervention phase, tells of being alone and a victim of his own neglectfulness. However, it is different from previous recollections because here the client engages in problem solving. He is an active problem solver rather than a passive recipient. He may fear being left out in the cold because he forgot his key, but he does not make a big deal out of his error. He figures out how to keep safe and warm. In the postintervention recollection, the client is more social and sticks with others who care for him and overcome life's challenges. The client has developed better coping skills.

Postintervention ER:

ER 4. Age: 7

> My next-door neighbor, Betty, and I were playing in a vacant lot. There were a ton of rocks in the lot, and we were climbing on

them and around them. We imagined that we were exploring the surface of Mars. We got into an argument, and it lasted a little while until I said, "We are here to play and have fun together." She looked at me and smiled. We went back to playing.

Feeling: "I was happy."

Most vivid: "Thinking that we should be having fun together. Focusing on the imagination we had."

This is a new recollection in two ways. First, it was not given in the pre-intervention phase. Second, it displays the client's creativity. Here the client demonstrates his imagination and the joy that he takes in it. He is a creative soul who enjoys the company of others (in this case a female). Also, we see that the client has been engaging in social interaction in the past few postintervention recollections. This is a change from the preintervention recollections. In terms of metaphor, the client demonstrates that when things get "rocky" with a woman, he has the resources to be assertive, to smooth things over, and to have fun. In addition, is he telling us that when he has fun with a woman, it is "out of this world"? (Remember they imagined that they were on Mars.)

Postintervention ER:

ER 5. Age: 6

Across the road from our school was a field with a creek and trees and wild flowers. A couple of teachers brought us across the street for most of the day. I was fascinated by the exploration of the wooded area.

Feeling: "Fascinated."

Most vivid: "I felt like I was an explorer."

This is yet another new recollection. Though we see some similar threads of others elevating him and making his exploration into a whole different world possible, we see guided active exploration that suggests that he is receptive to therapy. Moreover, the client gives us the idea that getting "back to nature" may be interesting to him. The simple pleasures in life are to be treasured. He is willing to explore with others in the lead.

When clients do not give you the same recollections that they gave prior to intervention, you may prompt them to retell the ERs that they gave prior to intervention and look for the changes. However, it is important to remember that whenever we must prompt a client for ERs, we have to discount some of their value because they are not freely emerging from the client.

Prompted ERs from the Preintervention Set

Preintervention ER:

> ER 3. Age: 5
>
>> This happened before I started school. My father took me to his work. His boss was a nice man dressed in a blue suit and looked at me and said that he was impressed that I was able to get up so early and added that I could sit at his desk. He brought me a doughnut and some color markers and a bunch of paper on which to draw.
>>
>> Feeling: "Very happy and really cool."
>>
>> Most vivid: "The desk and the boss's blue suit."

Prompted postintervention ER:

> Age: 5
>
>> My father took me to his work early one morning when my mom couldn't watch me. I had a nice time drawing with color markers. I ate a doughnut or two. I met some of his coworkers. It was fun.
>>
>> Feeling: "Enjoyable time drawing."
>>
>> Most vivid: "Drawing with the color markers."

The dissimilarity between the pre- and postintervention ERs is interesting here. This ER is not as detailed as the preintervention recollection, and the client puts more emphasis on drawing than on being the center of attention or being elevated by a man. In the preintervention ER, he gets ("He brought me a doughnut"); in the postintervention ER, he merely "ate a doughnut or two." In addition, we see some cooperation between men and women as his father is helping out his mother when she could not watch the client. Color continues to be an interest of his; therefore we'll maintain the belief that he has an aesthetic eye.

Preintervention ER:

ER 4. Age: 5

> I remember the first day of school. We were sitting at our desks, and there was this boy in front of me who was wearing overalls. One of his shoulder straps fell off his shoulder. I thought, "That poor kid, he has no support." I put his shoulder strap back on for him. I'm still in contact with him. [That part is a report.]

> Feeling: "Poor kid. By himself. Let me help him."

> Most vivid: "Pulling shoulder strap up."

Prompted postintervention ER:

Age: 5

> It was the first day of school, and this kid was wearing overalls that didn't fit him and the shoulder strap fell off. Nobody was talking with him, and I got his attention and told him to fix the shoulder strap. He did.

> Feeling: "Somebody should talk to that kid."

> Most vivid: "Thinking that he was kind of neglected and needed some attention."

Again, he shows kindness to a stranger. In addition, we see that the client is having the child help himself, instead of pulling up his shoulder strap for him. The clinician may want to learn whether the client still associates with this friend or the particulars of their lifelong friendship. Preintervention ER:

ER 5. Age: 4

> I remember I was at my aunt's house. She and I were in the kitchen, and I thought I pooped my pants. I asked my aunt to get my brother who was playing down the street, and she said "No." I kept asking her to get my brother, and eventually she did. I whispered in his ear that I thought I pooped my pants, and it turns out that I had just passed gas.

> Feeling: "Petrified and embarrassed."

> Most vivid: "Not wanting to tell my aunt. My brother and I standing there talking in the hall."

Prompted postintervention ER:

Age: 4

> I was at my aunt's house. I thought I crapped my drawers. I just passed gas [laughs].

Feeling: "Embarrassed."

Most vivid: "My brother and I laughing in the hallway after he told me I cut the cheese [laughs again]."

What changes do you see in the postintervention prompted recollection? In the preintervention recollection, the client seems more panicked. In the prompted postintervention recollection, the client is less desperate and has a sense of humor about the incident and is able to laugh off life's little embarrassments. The client no longer pesters his aunt to get his brother (who doesn't even enter the recollection until he is questioned about the most vivid part of the recollection.) Women (his aunt) are no longer seen as resistant to his pleadings. In the postintervention recollection, he is coping more appropriately.

Preintervention ER:

ER 6. Age: 9

> I remember being at school one day, and I wanted a particular book that was not in the library. I asked a teacher [male] who took me to the top floor into the private faculty library. No other student had ever been allowed in that library. It was beautiful. It had cherry wood walls, leather chairs, and high bookshelves. It was dark in there, but it was distinguished and overwhelming. I thought I was in the area where deep thinking took place.

Feeling: "I thought I was lucky and honored to be there. A place of deep thought."

Most vivid: "The cherry wood, leather chairs, and high bookshelves."

Prompted postintervention ER:

Age: 7–8

> My teacher let me get a book from the teachers' library.

Feeling: "I don't remember any."

Most vivid: "The teacher was helpful."

Here we have an excellent example of how clients omit details in their recollections. He does not give as much detail about the setting as he does in the preintervention recollection. Could this mean that he no longer values those things? Nor does he state that the faculty library was forbidden ground in the postintervention recollection. And note that he no longer sees himself as special, "lucky and honored." So what does this all mean?

The postintervention recollection is shorter, and the focus shifts from extravagance to human helpfulness. In addition, no importance is attached to the gender of the teacher in the postintervention recollection. Does this mean that men and women are equally helpful, in contrast to the preintervention recollection in which men are held in higher regard?

Preintervention ER:

ER 7. Age: 5

> It was Hanukkah time, and I remember I wanted a doctor's bag. We weren't that well off, and the kids in my family usually didn't get too many toys. We were sitting for Hanukkah dinner, and there on my seat was the doctor's bag.

Feeling: "So excited."

Most vivid: "The doctor's bag on the chair."

Prompted postintervention ER:

Age: 5

> My family was having Hanukkah dinner, and we were gathered around the table, and I was given a doctor's bag. It was something that I wanted. I really cherished it because we didn't get many gifts growing up. I thought it was really nice for my parents to get it for me.

Feeling: "I was thrilled and grateful."

Most vivid: "My family around the table eating and talking."

In both the preintervention and postintervention recollection, the client tells us that the toy was a doctor's bag, but in the postintervention ER, he places less emphasis on the bag and more on the family gathering. Is the client telling us that he no longer places importance on illness or sees himself as sickly? Keep in mind that the getter type is still presented, but we haven't seen much of the victim type ERs in the postintervention set. Apparently he does not see himself as much of a victim anymore.

Overall, there is more focus on social functioning in at least two areas. First, he refers to family dinner, and the most vivid part focuses more on family interaction. Second, he is grateful for his parents' thoughtfulness. This suggests a better appreciation and consideration of others.

Preintervention ER:

ER 8. Age: 5

> I remember it was Halloween. My brother had carved up this scary-looking pumpkin that looked really frightening. It was a real piece of art, a great-looking pumpkin. Anyway, I got really upset with my brother and smashed the pumpkin on the street. I completely destroyed it.

> Feeling: "Livid and very sad because I'd smashed what I liked."

> Most vivid: "Picking up the pumpkin and throwing it down on the street. I also remember yelling my head off."

Prompted postintervention ER:

Age: 5

> Halloween time and mad for some reason at my brother, and I threw his pumpkin on the road. I was mad at myself for ruining what I thought was a real work of art. I apologized afterward.

> Feeling: "At first I was enraged at my brother, and then I felt terrible for wrecking something that he had spent so much time on."

> Most vivid: "Feeling bad about his pumpkin. I knew I shouldn't have done it."

This recollection is somewhat similar to the preintervention recollection in that the client still cuts off his nose to spite his face. His recollections suggest that we shouldn't expect him to control himself when he is angry, and that he will hurt others and himself, not necessarily physically, but through the destruction of property or some such thing. However, he is more repentant after his misdeed in the postintervention recollection. In addition, he takes into account others' effort. He retains an appreciation of art.

Preintervention ER:

ER 9. Age: 6

It was Hanukkah, and I wanted this really interesting wind up toy bank that had a hand that you would put the money in and it would get the coin and deposit it in the box. I'd gone with my father to all of the stores and no one had it in stock. I was distraught. I remember seeing this box in the living room. It turned out that my father was able to get the bank for me.

Feeling: "Surprise, excitement."

Most vivid: "Opening up the present and seeing it was what I wanted."

Prompted postintervention ER:

Age: 6

I remember getting a toy bank at Hanukkah. It was very creative with this hand that would deposit money into a little bank vault. It was very nice. I was glad my parents got it for me.

Feeling: "Interest (in the detail of the bank)."

Most vivid: "Seeing the details painted on the bank."

This postintervention recollection demonstrates yet again that he likes to get things. We no longer see the victim recollections that were gathered in the preintervention phase. In both pre- and post-therapy sets he receives a toy bank. However, in the postintervention recollection, we see more interest in the artistic aspect of the bank and his appreciation of his parents' effort. There are no feelings of being distraught. Women are taken into account more often in the post-therapeutic intervention recollections as evidenced by the use of the word "parents" rather than "father."

Summary of Postintervention ERs

I am someone who is creative and appreciates artistic things. I enjoy social interactions, and I have a need for affection. I feel that even when it's a cold world, I can find a warm place. I can solve whatever problems life gives me. I can look on the bright side of things. That is, when times are tough, I can anticipate resolutions to problems and may be assertive enough to initiate whatever measures are necessary to make times less "rocky." I can laugh at my mistakes. I find that women are supportive and comfort me. I can have fun with women. They are even by my side when I'm not feeling well. I take interest in what others do. I believe men and women help me in life, and I appreciate their efforts.

However, when I do get angry, I have a tendency to lose control of my emotions and hurt others and myself. I am apologetic afterward.

I am willing to have a guided discovery of unexplored areas.

Can you see the differences between the pre- and postintervention recollection sets? The differences are evident and indicate therapeutic movement in distance and direction.

We hope this exercise has demonstrated the usefulness of gathering postintervention recollections. As promised, the next Chapter provides more examples of pre- and postintervention ERs.

Summary

When we gather ERs at the both the preintervention and postintervention phases of therapy, we can better assess if any change has occurred and in what direction. Changes in ERs communicate the adjustment in our clients' perceptions. In examining pre- and postintervention recollections it is advisable to cover at least four areas using the COAT method. We look for what has *changed* in the postintervention recollection, what has been *omitted*, and what has been *added*, and then we *test the limits*. That is, when a client gives us information in the preintervention recollection that is not in the postintervention recollection, we question him or her (without cues) to see if the details are remembered, and then we prompt (with specific cues, e.g., "Do you remember the time when . . . ?"). If the client does remember the event and tells it again, we see if something is forgotten. If it is forgotten, then that detail is not important to the client anymore. The summary of ERs is written in the first person, singular form because it represents how clients see themselves in the here and now.

14
Pre- and Postintervention ERs: Part II

This Chapter, a continuance of work begun in the last Chapter, explores the preintervention and postintervention ERs of a female client. We want you to think about what presenting issues this client may have come to therapy with when you read the preintervention recollections and then speculate, by examining her postintervention recollections, on the changes she has undergone in therapy.

Preintervention ERs of a Woman

ER 1. Age: 6

> I'm outside on a hot summer afternoon. I see the blue sky with white fluffy clouds, and I feel a gentle breeze on my face. I'm walking on pavement, and I feel the heat and stones on my bare feet. I'm wearing light green shorts and white T-shirt with picture of a plane taking off from a runway. I like the heat of the sun beating down on me because I just came from my basement, where it had been too cool. The road got too hot, and I start running on the cool wet grass. It felt good. I see the green of the trees and hear the birds singing as they sit on the branches. It's a beautiful area.

> Most vivid: "The warmth and the cool."

The first thing that makes an impression is the sheer number of sense responses. She relates visual, tactile, temperature, and auditory stimuli. So we might guess that this is a type of person who has her antennae out. That is, she is sensitive and sensual. Almost every sense is given, and she is extremely detailed. She may be hypersensitive to things other people say and do inside or outside of therapy.

In examining the entire recollection, we get the impression that the world runs hot and cold. She moves from a cool house to warm sunny outdoors, then onto pavement that is too hot for her, and finally onto the cool grass. Is she telling us that life can change on her? Sometimes life can get too hot or too cool for her. However, it is interesting to note that she handles the situation very well. She is able to take action when life gets too hot or too cool. The client is telling us that she is capable of making change. She demonstrates an ability to adapt to the situation, and, no matter what, she feels good.

The inclusion of a texture response suggests that there is a need for affection, but not necessarily a pathological need. Texture responses on the Rorschach indicate a need for affection, and we believe that the inclusion of texture responses in ERs has a similar implication. And what do you make out of the modifying detail of "T-shirt with picture of a plane taking off from a runway"? Would you say that she is ready to move from one location to another? Is she always (or frequently) on the move?

So from the first recollection, we are given many clues about this woman. We have to keep these ideas in the back of our minds as we investigate the clues given in the other recollections.

ER 2. Age: 6

> It was sometime after Christmas, and my father and I are outside one evening. It is cold and crisp. We are dragging a sled behind us. We were a bit cold, and so we decided to run to warm up. My father had these nice boots on with a good sole that allowed him to get good traction. I could hear the snow crush underneath him. I could not keep up with him, and I looked at him kinda hinting that I wanted him to pull me on the sled. He picked me up and put me on the sled and ran as fast as he could. It was very peaceful and beautiful.

> Feeling: "Warm and well cared for."

> Most vivid: "Father pulling me."

This recollection allows us to see how she perceives herself in relation to a man. She is telling us that even though it may be a cold world, she can feel warm and cozy when she is with a man. So how do we know this? It's "sometime after Christmas," a modifying detail, along with the fact that she is running with a man, and her feeling is warm and well cared for. However, we had better not stop interpreting there because this client has given us a richly detailed ER that is bursting with clues.

Upon further examination, we see that she can't keep up with a man because she is deficient in some way (she doesn't have the tools he has — the "nice boots"). She may consider herself deficient or that the role of a woman is to try to keep up with a man and not be able to keep up. She may feel as though she does not have the tools a man has and is deficient in some way. She may feel as though her father is a "good soul (sole)" who is willing to take care of her. However, she also shows us again that she can cope with difficulties. That is, when she can't keep up, she gets on the sled and goes along for the ride with a man. However, she indicates that she takes control of the situation and her father by giving him a look that prompts action on his part.

When she is with a man, the world is beautiful. It's a poetic presentation of a Norman Rockwell-esqe scene. She demonstrates how sensual she is with the rich detail. Her senses are turned on and sharp.

ER 3. Age: 4

> It was a beautiful spring day, and I'm outside with my mother. My grandfather's black car pulls up very quickly, and he drives off of the driveway and into a row of pine trees that lined the driveway. My mother jumps up and screams as she runs to the car. I ran after her. My grandfather was slumped over the wheel and breathing heavily. I could hear him wheezing. I was panicked. I didn't know what to do. My mother put him in our car, and we drove to the hospital. I felt a chill come over me as I heard him gurgling in the backseat. He died on the way to the hospital.

> Feeling: "Helpless, startled, and concerned."

> Most vivid: "My grandfather being unable to control his breathing."

The first two recollections paint a picture as only Norman Rockwell could. However, in this recollection the client is telling us that there is something wrong with this picture. Similar to what the client said in the first recollection, life runs hot and cold. This ER starts very pleasantly with the hope of a new spring but ends in death. Things are transient in life and do not turn out the way she expects.

There is more evidence, as shown in the number of colors given, that she has an artistic eye. Furthermore, the amount of detail in the ER suggests that she is detail oriented. In addition, the inclusion of illness suggests that this person may be involved in the health profession. Illness and death recollections are commonly found with those in the health professions (see Adler, 1929/1964; Lashever, 1990). In this recollection, we see that when something goes wrong (e.g., in illness or death threatened), she is startled and helpless. She believes that the world should be good and sunny, but is concerned when it is not. It is a shock to her when things change from good to bad.

ER 4. Age: 6

> It was cool outside, and I was with my two cousins [both female] in their house. It was warmer in there. It was this beautiful tan house with white trim. We were in their living room on a brown plush carpet eating some salty popcorn and playing foosball, but I couldn't do it well. I kept trying to control the players, but I couldn't get the men to turn the way I wanted them to, and I kept losing. I could hear them laughing at my attempts. They won every game. I stomped my feet all the way home.

> Feeling: "Irritated."

> Most vivid: "Not being able to control the men, and my cousins could."

Remember that almost all, if not all, ERs have a metaphor. She is telling us that when she can't turn men the way she wants, she loses to other women. And when she loses to other women, she shows disappointment, anger, and resentment. She continues to show us that all of her senses are operational and responsive to all types of stimuli.

ER 5. Age: 4

> My father and I are in a big department store. We were in the men's section, and my father was looking for a pair of brown pants. I remember walking on the carpeting in my white shoes and hearing the sound of the carpet underneath my shoes. All of a sudden I really had to go to bathroom. I could feel the intense pressure on my bladder, and I turn around, and I couldn't find my father to take me to the bathroom. I thought I saw him in the

far corner of the store, and I start running to him, but I trip over my own feet and end up going all over my blue dress. I was so embarrassed as all of these men looked at me after I went all over myself.

Feeling: "Panic and embarrassment."

Most vivid: "Losing control of my bladder."

Again we see that the client is very sensual. However, the theme of this recollection is one of control. She is telling us that when she gets too wrapped up in the details of life and runs after a distant man, she trips herself up, loses control, and embarrasses herself in front of men.

ER 6. Age: 7

I'm in my bed in my room. I feel the heat and pressure of the many blankets and comforters on top of me. I feel the smooth glass thermometer on my tongue as my mother pulls it from my mouth. I start to fidget, and my mother tells me to rest because I am ill, but I don't feel sick. I can't move my arms or legs under the weight of the blanket. It is intolerable. I want out.

Feeling: "Suffocated and trapped."

Most vivid: "My mother telling me I'm sick, and I'm thinking that she's wrong."

In this recollection, the client is telling us what she likes by telling us what she *hates*. She does not like feeling trapped. Here she is indoors and is uncomfortable. Furthermore, she clearly does not accept the notion of being sick. She has difficulty monitoring her own illness and needs outside feedback. Also, the inclusion of blankets suggests another texture response that indicates a need for affection. Might others have referred her to therapy because she could not properly assess her functioning?

ER 7. Age: 5

It's a beautiful day, and I'm with my family at the beach. I feel the hot sand under my toes. You could have fried an egg on it. I feel my father put suntan lotion on me as we walk. My family puts down a big red blanket down the waves of brown sand. I start walking around, and the next thing I know, I'm on my back with two men looking over me. My dad's upset. I'm really OK.

One side of my face burns. They told me that I walked into a lit charcoal grill. My parents take me to the hospital, but I know I'm OK.

Feeling: "What happened? Feeling badly, I created such a commotion."

Most vivid: "My face burning."

The client is telling us that life runs hot and cold again, figuratively. In the transient picture she paints of the world, she moves from a plus day into a minus day. (Perhaps out of the frying pan and into the fire?) All starts out bright and sunny with a man trying to protect her from a harsh world (applying suntan lotion), but ends with commotion and a trip to the hospital. Again, we see that others think something is wrong with her, but she does not see it. She is telling us that she is not on the same wavelength as others. Might this be a problem that needs therapeutic intervention?

To her, life is unpredictable. She does not know how bad things happen; they just happen ("and the next thing I know, I'm on my back"). She does not see her responsibility for the problem. In addition, her mishaps bring men to tend to her. While she tries to show people she is OK, they don't believe her. Might this client be looking at the world through rose-colored glasses? Does she need to appear fine to others or herself? How important is it for this woman to keep up appearances? Does she "lose face" or "get burned" when she acts on her own?

ER 8. Age: 8

There was this girl in the house next door. They didn't have a lot of money. She had a golden retriever with long, silky fur. A car hit her dog, and I saw her crying on her back step. I thought that I would make her feel better, so I went through a bunch of old magazines and cut out pictures of dogs and glued them onto a piece of brown cardboard. I showed it to her, and she started crying. I told her that there were a bunch of different types of dogs that she could choose. I was trying to cheer her up, but I only made her feel worse. My mother sticks her neck out of the window and yells at me for making the neighbor cry.

Feeling: "I'm sorry I've upset her, but I wish she and my mother understood."

Most vivid: "Cutting pictures out of the magazines thinking that it would make my neighbor feel better."

For this client, life is unpredictable and dangerous (dog gets run over). She recognizes pain in others ("I saw her crying"). She exhibits empathy and compassion as she tries to lift her neighbor's spirits. Nobody understands her good intentions in life. She and others are not on the same wavelength. Her neighbor cries, and her mother yells at her even though she had good intentions. Here the client portrays that she both is, and supports, the "underdog." In addition, she gives us another death recollection. Death, the one element in life we cannot control. How might someone who wants to control things think about the (somewhat) uncontrollable? People who want to control things give (1) ERs in which they control things in life or life is in control, (2) ERs in which control is "good" or (3) ERs showing the danger when they or life are not in control.

What follows is our summary of the preintervention ERs. Read them and consider what interpersonal problems might bring this woman to counseling.

Summary of the Preintervention ERs

I am a sensual person. My antennae are up and active. I have an artistic eye. I can sense when I am uncomfortable. If I have my antennae out, it may be so that I can sense when things are about to go out of control and act quickly to restore control. I keep a close watch on others, but I may not be able to perceive my own illness. I am particularly stunned and concerned when illness and death are near, and I like to deny them. I like to keep up appearances and don't like to lose face through my own actions. I don't see my responsibility when bad things happen to me. I hate losing control, especially in front of men. I am a compassionate person who can perceive when others are in pain, and I try to help them feel better. When I get everything right, I feel the warmth of the world; I see it in all of its beauty and splendor.

Mishaps bring men to me. Bad things may just happen, and I don't always see my contribution to my own downfall. When it is a cold world out there, I can feel warm and cozy when I am with a man, but I have trouble keeping up with a man because I may not have the resources men have. Men may be kinder souls than I am. I try to control men and have them pull me through life. If I can't turn men the way I want, I lose to other women, and I sulk about it. When I get too wrapped up in the details of life and run after a distant man, I trip myself up, lose control, and embarrass myself in front of other men. Women don't understand my good intentions, and treat me harshly, especially when I try to make other women happy. I am an underdog.

I believe that life runs hot and cold and that it can change at any minute. Life is unpredictable and dangerous. When I can solve life's problems, life is good and warm, and I feel good. When life is out of kilter, I feel helpless, stunned, and overwhelmed. Life is a problem to be solved, and even when I solve it, I always have my apprehensions.

I try to convince people that I am OK, but they don't believe me and insist that I need help.

Pre- and Postintervention ERs Compared

Preintervention ER:

ER 1. Age: 6

I'm outside on a hot summer afternoon. I see the blue sky with white fluffy clouds, and I feel a gentle breeze on my face. I'm walking on pavement, and I feel the heat and stones on my bare feet. I'm wearing light green shorts and white T-shirt with picture of a plane taking off from a runway. I like the heat of the sun beating down on me because I just came from my basement, where it had been too cool. The road got too hot, and I start running on the cool wet grass. It felt good. I see the green of the trees and hear the birds singing as they sit on the branches. It's a beautiful area.

Most vivid: "The warmth and the cool."

Postintervention ER:

ER 1. Age: 6

It's a beautiful summer day. There is a gentle wind, and I'm walking under the warm sun. I see green trees and lush cool grass. It is a beautiful day!

Most vivid: "The warmth and the cool."

In the postintervention recollection, we see much less detail, but a more positive ER overall. As a matter of fact, this conjures up a very pleasant image, doesn't it? So what is different, and what does it mean?

Note that there are fewer extremes here — for example, there is less hot and cold. Perhaps her world isn't as extreme as it was in the preintervention recollections. There is less tactile detail given, which suggests that she may no longer be longing for affection to the degree she was during the preintervention period. Less detail in her recollections suggests that her antennae are not out as much as they were in the previous set of recollections. It seems that she does not feel the need to be as sensitive.

Preintervention ER:

ER 2. Age: 6

> I remember it was sometime after Christmas, and my father and I are outside one evening. It is cold and crisp. We are dragging a sled behind us. We were a bit cold, and so we decided to run to warm up. My father had these nice boots on with a good sole that allowed him to get good traction. I could hear the snow crush underneath him. I could not keep up with him, and I looked at him kinda hinting that I wanted him to pull me on the sled. He picked me up and put me on the sled and ran as fast as he could. It was very peaceful and beautiful.

> Feeling: "Warm and well cared for."

> Most vivid: "Father pulling me."

Postintervention ER:

ER 2. Age: 6

> One evening in winter, my father and I were out walking. It was a beautiful night. I could see the stars on a cloudless night. We were going to go sledding under the full moon. I remember running on the snow with my father. We are dragging a sled behind us. We went sledding. Sometimes my father would steer, and sometimes I would. It was very enjoyable.

> Feeling: "Peaceful, yet exciting."

> Most vivid: "Being on the sled with my father."

In the postintervention recollection, she is more comfortable with her position relative to a man. For example, she is not deficient compared to a man. In the preintervention recollection she is not able to keep up with her father because she is ill equipped. In the postintervention recollection, she is able to run with her father and does not need to control him or have him pull her along. There is more equality with a man. Sometimes he is in control, sometimes she is. In a cold world, she can enjoy running with a man and going for a ride with him. Similar to the previous recollection, we see less detail, suggesting less need to keep sensing the environment. She is telling us that there is no need for continual surveillance and recording.

The following is a new recollection not given in the preintervention gathering of ERs. What things in this recollection indicate that change has occurred?

ER 3. Age: 9

> My cousins [both female] and I were playing tennis. We were just volleying the ball back and forth over the net. We weren't keeping score. We taught each other how to hit the ball and hold the racket. We had lunch on the court. Remember one of them brought a baguette but forgot to bring a knife. We ended up pulling it apart, and I think the bread tasted better doing that.
>
> Feeling: "It was harmonious."
>
> Most vivid: "The ball going back and forth."

In contrast to the interpretation of the preintervention recollections, we see here that the client enjoys "breaking bread" with other females. She is no longer the underdog who does not get along with women. She is informing us that she can participate in "back and forth" with other women. Furthermore, she doesn't keep score in this recollection as she did in the preintervention recollections. For her, life tastes better when she is able to play with other women, break bread with them, learn from them as well as teach them, and not keep score against them.

This recollection is an entirely plus situation. Furthermore, the presence of women can increase the pleasantness of this woman's life. Again, we do see the incredible amount of detail or need for control that we saw in the preintervention ERs.

The following is a new recollection not given in the preintervention ERs.

ER 4. Age: 9

> I remember being on my father's boat out on a lake. I was driving the boat. I remember the feel of the steering wheel in my hands and the resistance as I steered the boat to the right and to the left. I felt the power of the engine and I had that feeling that I could do whatever I wanted. I could steer it into the rocks or go straight ahead at full throttle or I could go slowly around the lake along the shore. The sun was shining, and there wasn't a cloud in the sky.

> Feeling: "I felt great."

> Most vivid: "The feel of the steering wheel in my hand and the wind through my hair."

We see here that the client retains her desire to be in control and her sensitivity to sensory information. This is a good thing, as we don't want her to totally avoid control in her life. It is good that she is able to take control. Being able to take the helm suggests that when the situation permits, she feels confident to take charge. In this case she suggests that she even has control over life and death ("steer it into the rocks").

When we do not get the recollections that we gathered in the preintervention session, we prompt for those recollections and look for changes. However, we must reduce the significance we attach to the information we glean from those ERs to some extent, as the client does not give it freely.

Prompted ERs from the Preintervention Set

Preintervention ER:

ER 3. Age: 4

> I remember it was a beautiful spring day, and I'm outside with my mother. My grandfather's black car pulls up very quickly, and he drives off of the driveway and into a row of pine trees that lined the driveway. My mother jumps up and screams as she runs to the car. I ran after her. My grandfather was slumped over the wheel and breathing heavily. I could hear him wheezing. I was panicked. I didn't know what to do. My mother put him in our car and we drove to the hospital. I felt a chill come over me as I heard him gurgling in the backseat. He died on the way to the hospital.

Feeling: "Helpless, startled, and concerned."

Most vivid: "My grandfather being unable to control his breathing."

Postintervention ER:

Age: 4

It was the day my grandfather died. I remember he drove up the driveway and into our trees when my mother and I were out in the front yard. We ran over to see what was going on. He was ill. My mother and I took him to the hospital. We drove as fast as possible to the hospital, but I guess it was his time to go.

Feeling: "Surprised (as he drove into the trees), and sad when he passed."

Most vivid: "Him driving into our trees."

So what differences do you see? She is clearly less scared by death, and there is less focus on control. Death is not as frightening as it was previously; she sees death as part of the life cycle in the postintervention recollection. We see in this recollection and others from the postintervention set that there are fewer (if any) extremes, no hot to cold and back again; she handles things in stride.
Preintervention ER:

ER 4. Age: 6

It was cool outside, and I was with my two cousins [both female] in their house. It was warmer in there. It was this beautiful tan house with white trim. We were in their living room on a brown plush carpet eating some salty popcorn and playing a foosball, but I couldn't do it well. I kept trying to control the players, but I couldn't get the men to turn the way I wanted them to, and I kept losing. I could hear them laughing at my attempts. They won every game. I stomped my feet all the way home.

Feeling: "Irritated."

Most vivid: "Not being able to control the men, and my cousins could."

Postintervention ER:

> I remember they had a foosball table, but I don't remember that day at all.

This is an example of just how flexible (or unreliable) our memories are. Clients may forget recollections that they gave earlier in the therapeutic process. If a memory is forgotten and is replaced by one or more memories with similar themes, then no therapeutic change has occurred. On the other hand, if a recollection is forgotten upon a second (or later) gathering of recollections, this suggests therapeutic change. In other words, the clients' current perspectives are different than those held earlier.
Preintervention ER:

ER 5. Age: 4

> My father and I are in a big department store. We were in the men's section and my father was looking for a pair of brown pants. I remember walking on the carpeting in my white shoes and hearing the sound of the carpet underneath my shoes. All of a sudden I really had to go to bathroom. I could feel the intense pressure on my bladder, and I turn around, and I couldn't find my father to take me to the bathroom. I thought I saw him in the far corner of the store and I start running to him, but I trip over my own feet and end up going all over my blue dress. I was so embarrassed as all of these men looked at me after I went all over myself.

Feeling: "Panic and embarrassment."

Most vivid: "Losing control of my bladder."

Postintervention ER:

Age: 4

> I remember being in a department store with my father and wetting my dress. He bought me a new outfit and brought me to the restroom, where he gave me the set of clothes to wear so I didn't have to go home in what I was wearing.

Feeling: "I don't recall."

Most vivid: "My father giving me a set of dry clothes."

Here we see the client not chase after a distant man, trip over herself, lose control, or embarrass herself in front of others. Though she still wets her dress, her father is there to assist her, and a situation in which she originally panicked and embarrassed herself turns into a bonding moment with her thoughtful father. As a matter of fact, there is no emotion ascribed to the event, suggesting that it is no big deal for the client.

Preintervention ER:

ER 6. Age: 7

I'm in my bed in my room. I feel the heat and pressure of the many blankets and comforters on top of me. I feel the smooth glass thermometer on my tongue as my mother pulls it from my mouth. I start to fidget, and my mother tells me to rest because I am ill, but I don't feel sick. I can't move my arms or legs under the weight of the blanket. It is intolerable. I want out.

Feeling: "Suffocated and trapped."

Most vivid: "My mother telling me I'm sick, and I'm thinking that she's wrong."

Postintervention ER:

Age: 7

I remember being under the covers in the bedroom with my mom taking care of me. I was real sick, and I must have been running a fever because I remember being really hot. I hated being under those covers. I had about a million blankets on me. I remember the glass thermometer in my mouth.

Feeling: "Uncomfortable, hot."

Most vivid: "The heavy blankets on top of me."

This recollection focuses more on her mother's taking care of her rather than her mother's telling her she is sick. As a matter of fact, she acknowledges that she was "real sick," so it appears as though she is better able to accept the idea of illness.

Preintervention ER:

ER 7. Age: 5

It's a beautiful day, and I'm with my family at the beach. I feel the hot sand under my toes. You could have fried an egg on it. I feel my father put suntan lotion on me as we walk. My family puts down a big red blanket down the waves of brown sand. I start walking around, and the next thing I know, I'm on my back with two men looking over me. My dad's upset. I'm really OK. One side of my face burns. They told me that I walked into a lit charcoal grill. My parents take me to the hospital, but I know I'm OK.

Feeling: "What happened? Feeling badly, I created such a commotion."

Most vivid: "My face burning."

Postintervention ER:

Age: 5

I'm at the beach with my family, and I'm walking around, not looking where I am going, and I turn right into a lit grill. Ouch! I fell backwards and started screaming. My mom and dad and a couple of other people come over to help. My folks quickly took me to the hospital.

Feeling: "Pain."

Most vivid: "My parents taking me to the hospital."

The major changes we see between the pre- and postintervention recollections are seen in a few areas. First, the client assumes responsibility for her actions ("not looking where I'm going"). Second, she includes her mother in the recollection, which suggests that women can be caregivers as well as men. Third, she is able to recognize when she needs help and does not reject the idea that she needs help from others. Finally, while in the preintervention recollection the client goes from the frying pan into the fire (so to speak), she told us that even when things are "a day at the beach," she may burn herself. In the postintervention recollection, we see there are still a number of people around to promptly help her, and the most vivid portion of the recollection is not the consequences of her actions as it was in the preintervention recollection, but is the support of others. Preintervention ER:

ER 8. Age: 8

> There was this girl in the house next door. They didn't have a lot of money. She had a golden retriever with long, silky fur. A car hit her dog, and I saw her crying on her back step. I thought that I would make her feel better, so I went through a bunch of old magazines and cut out pictures of dogs and glued them onto a piece of brown cardboard. I showed it to her, and she started crying. I told her that there were a bunch of different types of dogs that she could choose. I was trying to cheer her up, but I only made her feel worse. My mother sticks her neck out of the window and yells at me for making the neighbor cry.

> Feeling: "I'm sorry I've upset her, but I wish she and my mother understood."

> Most vivid: "Cutting pictures out of the magazines thinking that it would make my neighbor feel better."

Postintervention ER:

Age: 8

> The neighbor girl's dog died, and she was crying in her backyard. I noticed that she was crying, and I felt sorry for her. I went over there to cheer her up. I don't remember much after that.

> Feeling: "I felt sorry for her. She was close to that dog."

> Most vivid: "Sitting on her back step and telling her I was sorry to hear about her dog."

There are some striking changes between the pre- and postintervention ERs. In the preintervention ER she indicates that although she does have sensitivity to others (we should expect that, considering how her antennae were always out), she seems to make matters worse when she tries to console her neighbor. In the postintervention recollection we see that there is less emphasis on detail, and there is no memory of making matters worse. The client is telling us that she has a big heart and will take action to soothe others. She is also saying that she does not consider herself someone who makes matters worse. In addition, there are no women kicking her around.

Summary of the Postintervention ERs

I am concerned about what happens to others. I am a compassionate person who is able to take a big step toward helping others. I believe that life does have its sudden changes, but even when things get out of control I am able to handle them in stride. That is, I can take charge when I want or need to. I am able to face illness and possible death and get on with my life. I can take responsibility for my actions when I do something wrong. I find that I am on the same wavelength as others.

I am comfortable with my position relative to men. I believe that men are caring and empathetic. I can run with a man and have fun. I believe that men and women are equal. I believe women are caring and enjoy give-and-take with other women. I do not keep score against other women.

We have presented a brief example of some of the differences between pre- and postintervention ERs to impress upon you the importance of gathering ERs at different times in intervention. As you can see from the examples given here and in the last Chapter, the changes that occur (presumably) because of therapeutic intervention can be seen in the ERs' change of content and themes.

Summary

Sense details suggest that the client is sensual and detail oriented. This has client-therapist implications, as people who give many detail responses with a variety of senses may be overly sensitive to what is said in therapy or, more generally, have a hypersensitivity to what other people say. There are a number of things that we look for when we compare the pre- and postintervention sets of ERs. The COAT method instructs us to look for things that have *changed*, been *omitted* and/or *added*, and to *test the limits* of what is presented. In addition, we want to look for changes in social interest, more flexibility of thought and action, more appropriate emotional responses, clearer or better-defined thoughts processes, a lessening in interfering ideas, and more appropriate goals.

15
Common Response Themes

An individual's ERs tend to evidence recurrent responses to certain topics, and these provide an indication of how the person responds to various life situations. This Chapter is devoted to illustrating some of the more common types of responses. The topic that the response is a response *to* (the subject of the next Chapter) can indicate what issues the client currently faces. This and the previous Chapter should help you to be able to identify the issues a client faces and what his or her responses to those issues are.

Common responses are not provided to categorize and pigeonhole individuals; instead we have included these response themes to illustrate how you might identify responses within and among ERs. While we may be categorizing responses, we are not using them to categorize and pigeonhole individuals, etc., heuristically. For example, if you see the response theme of rebellion among several recollections, you may find that the client feels as though rebelling is a part of life, and that client may actually seek out something to rebel against. The responses given here are adapted from Shulman and Mosak's (1988) *Manual for Life Style Assessment.*

ER Response Themes
Let's look at the following ER.

> My family was around the kitchen table talking about sports. I stayed in the living room and watched them.

The client is a passive spectator of the action. Recollections of this kind are an *observing response.* They may just look at those enjoying life. They may be the type who watch from the stands, too fearful of getting hurt, or who drive by a car accident without stopping. They may prefer to let others risk in life, while they prefer to be safe. They may not want to be the focus of attention or be too discouraged to try. Vocationally or avocationally, they may be attracted to astronomy, bird watching, or other relatively safe activities in which they can observe. They may be people who don't want to miss anything.

Throughout life we have challenges. Sometimes we meet them, at other times we try to avoid them. If a client gave you the following ER, how would you think he or she perceives life's challenges?

> Somebody unspooled the film canisters. People were trying to put the film back on the reel by feeding the film round and round. It was taking forever. I got a pencil and put it through the center of the reel and just spun it. The film went right back on in no time.

This is an excellent example of a *problem-solving* response. These types of responses indicate that the person engages in active problem-solving behavior. Sometimes the behavior is very creative.

Early recollections that demonstrate a range of action from compliance to defiance suggest compliance, rebellion, and revenge response themes. Clients who give recollections with compliance themes are telling us that they may submit or knuckle under to others. Themes of revenge indicate that clients may get even with others, and if they think it is necessary they may cut off their noses to spite their faces. They may even do so in a self-destructive way. An example follows.

> My mother told me that I had to eat all of my vegetables and that I could only have candy on special occasions. Even then, it could only be one piece. She said it would rot my teeth. One Halloween I hit all of the neighborhood houses twice and shoved as much candy down my throat as I could. I didn't even brush my teeth that night.

Clearly, this is an example of a *rebellion* response. It may indicate to the clinician how clients who give these types of recollections react to being pressured or forced into doing something they don't want to.

What do you make out of the following ER?

> I remember the teacher telling my class to sit down and be *quiet.* I was the first to listen and do as she said.

That is an example of a *compliance* recollection.

A revenge recollection may look something like this:

> I remember my father telling me I could not sleep over my friend's house. Later that night when he was sleeping I went to his money clip that he kept in the kitchen and took out $10.

What might you infer from the following man's ER?

> I was in gym class and I told the gym teacher that another student was bugging me.

If your first answer is "snitch," you may be more correct than you thought. These types of responses are known as *call for help* responses. In this example, the client is overtly asking for others to come to his assistance. An example of a similar call for help, but in a covert manner, can be seen in the following recollection.

> I was sharpening my jack knife and I accidentally cut myself. I did not want to tell my parents that I cut myself, but when they saw the blood I left on the bathroom wall, they called me in and saw that I was bleeding. They bandaged me up and told me not to sharpen the knife again.

Here the call for help is covert, yet still arrives at the goal of receiving assistance. What might this imply for therapy?

Moving to the next example, let's see how you might categorize the following recollection? What does it tell you about the person?

> My father came to pick me up from school. He drove up in a rusty car that did not turn off. It kept chugging even after he turned it off and got out of it. He told one of the teachers that he was my father and was there to pick me up. I felt so ashamed.

These types of ERs express unhappiness, or other forms of distress such as impotent anger as the sole response to a difficult situation.

For example,

> I remember when my father said that I could not go on a class trip. I *sat* in my room the entire day sulking.

These types of recollections are categorized as *suffering*, because that is what the client is expressing.

People who demand special attention and service from others by charm, cunning, intimidation, or force are trying to manipulate them to get what they want. Look at the following recollection and see why it falls in the *manipulation* category.

> My brother was hogging the video game. I cried and screamed to my mother until she got sick of it and told my brother to give me the controller.

Some people like to create some excitement. They seek tension and unrest. In Berne's (1964) terms, they may play "Uproar." So what might their ERs look like? They may be similar to the following.

> I remember getting a couple of matches and a can of lighter fluid. I got some paper burning, and then a few sticks, but I kept adding lighter fluid to see how high I could get the flames. It was fascinating.

Recollections like these are labeled as *seeking excitement* for obvious reasons.

Some people feel as though they have defects of some kind that they wish to hide. In an effort to enhance their status or conceal their imperfections, they pretend to be someone they are not. This recollection, from a transvestite, may fall under the category of *pretense*.

> I had big ears as a kid, and this one time I put on my mother's wig and makeup to cover those ears. I pretended I was a beautiful woman! It was my moment in the sun.

Some people have a very difficult time focusing on bad situations. They may choose to direct their attention to innocuous material or events. Read the following recollection and note what gets your attention. While you're at it, detect the response theme.

> I remember being at my mother's funeral and studying the detail in the handles on her coffin.

Recollections like this one are labeled *denial.* You have probably already figured out that the client is choosing to focus attention on the handles of the casket rather than on the mother's death. Do you think this person is trying to get a handle on emotions or on this situation?

Some people are quick to make a pact with themselves to never engage in particular behavior (e.g., eat five doughnuts at a time or ride a bike on a busy road). The pact is to augment the clients' security or self-esteem. For example, in the following recollection you see an example of *resolve*.

> All of the neighborhood kids were playing baseball, and somebody hit the ball into Old Man Peabody's yard. Old Man Peabody came out and took the ball. I was so angry; I promised that I would never do that to a bunch of kids. I mean, who would be so low as to take away a baseball so kids couldn't play on a beautiful summer day?

In this recollection, the client makes a vow to be a good person by never taking away children's fun.

Children and adults like a sense of accomplishment and purpose. Recollections that demonstrate competence, like the following, show how clients are competent or incompetent at a skill.

> I remember the first time I rode my bike with no hands.

> I went skating only once, and during that time I fell on my butt about a million times.

Either example can be categorized as competence through the client's display of a skill or lack of accomplishment.

Recollections that show prosocial behavior can be labeled *social interest*. Social interest may be understood as a feeling of belonging along with a concern for others, and community participation. Here is an example.

> We were walking home, and this kid dropped his books, and all of these papers were being carried away by the wind. He and I ran after them as fast as we could.

Is the client active or passive in response to a situation? A response that indicates either reaction is called an *activity* response. For example,

> I remember I wanted this girl to kiss me, but I was too shy, so I just stood there and made her come to me.

> This bully starting pushing me on the playground, so after he pushed me down I grabbed a fistful of sand and threw it at his eyes. Then I pummeled him!

Early recollections that contain a faked illness to get out of some obligation may indicate *distance keeping*. Here is an example:

> I told the gym teacher that I sprained my ankle so that I didn't have to run outside in the cold.

A recollection that has collaboration for a purpose, be it for good or evil, is an example of the category of *cooperation*. The absence of collaboration falls under this category as well. Here are two examples:

> My father and I were playing catch in the yard.

> All of the boys in the class joined together to defeat the girls in a chess tournament.

Any recollection that clients give that show how they overextend themselves and then get hurt is an example of the *overconfidence* type of response. For example:

> I remember riding my skateboard down this steep hill, thinking that I was the best skateboarder in the world! I'd be able to do it with my eyes closed! I started going too fast and couldn't slow down. I ended up running into a tree. It wasn't pretty.

Some people make statements that indicate delusions of grandeur. Look at the following recollection and see an excellent example of just that.

> I climbed to the top of the rope in gym class. I was invincible. I had no concerns whatsoever. I believed that I was the best student athlete in the world.

When clients offer ERs like this one, making themselves more important than they are, this response can be categorized as *self-aggrandizement*.

Some people like to find fault with others and ideas and places, you name it. It is their way of avoiding responsibility. The recollection that follows can be placed in the *criticism* category of responses.

> I was in a bicycle race with the other kids. I came in fourth out of five. I was certain I would have come in first if my bike wasn't old and rusty.

> I remember my first grade teacher gave me detention for talking in class. I remember thinking that this old bag is a real witch.

Clients who offer excuse-making memories like the previous one are quick to criticize and often the last to provide solutions and assistance.

As a last example in this nonexhaustive list of common responses, we suggest the category of *feeling avoidance.* People who avoid feeling may avoid movement. If they are indifferent about something, then they are not motivated to move toward or away from it. Feeling avoiders also try to suppress or ignore affect. For example, when you ask clients for a feeling of their ERs and they state,

> I didn't have a feeling. I just thought it was interesting.

They may be telling you that they do not focus on their emotions and do not wish to do so.

Each response theme illustrated in this Chapter should give you some indication of how that person may approach life's challenges, including therapy.

Summary

Common response themes are not provided to categorize and pigeonhole individuals. We have included some common response themes to illustrate how you might identify clients' responses within and among ERs so you can be sensitive to, and question, how clients perceive themselves.

Several examples of common types of responses of ERs have been presented. The list presented is not exhaustive, and we encourage you to explore other themes that are not illustrated here.

16
Common Thematic Topics

This Chapter explores the topics commonly found in ERs. As we said in the last Chapter, the *topic* of a recollection indicates the issues that the client currently faces, and *response* refers to the client's typical actions or reactions in relation to those issues. A familiarity with common topics will help you to identify themes within and among ERs so that you can detect areas that may be important for your clients. If, for example, you see the topic of "obstacles" among several recollections, you may find that this is an area that you should concentrate on in therapy. What follows is adapted from Shulman and Mosak's (1988) *Manual for Life Style Assessment.*

Common Thematic Topics in ERs

In this section, we will present some of the common themes found in ERs, then will provide a number of recollections and ask you to categorize their themes.

> I remember mom coming home from the hospital for the first time with my baby brother. Everyone was looking at him, and I was in the corner by myself.

How might you classify the theme? Here you have the birth of a younger sibling (or the entry onto the scene of another person) who takes center stage. We will consider this recollection as having a *dethronement* theme.

Here is another one. Review it and name its theme.

> I was lying on the couch, and my dad came home with a bag full of candy. It was so unexpected.

This one is easy. ERs like this have unanticipated events. Mark this as an example of a *surprises* theme.

This one may present more of a hurdle to identifying its theme.

> I remember seeing a glass of milk in the kitchen, and I was really thirsty. However, I had to go through our living room that was being renovated. I could not make it to the kitchen because all of these workmen were in the way, and they had their tools on the floor along with some lumber. It was a real mess. I never got that glass of milk.

This is an interesting recollection because there are many places in it to get hung up on. That should give you a clue to its theme. Here obstructions and the actions of others block the client's way. Simply, it is a theme of *obstacles.*

Next we have two examples of a similar theme.

> I remember being at day care and being by myself. I hated it.

> We had a big family, and this one Sunday we had a lunch that started at 2 o'clock and lasted until 9. Everyone was there telling stories and jokes, and having a great time.

Both recollections have something in common. What do you think it is? It is the relationship with others. Early recollections of pleasant interactions with others or a distance between the client and others can be categorized under the theme of *affiliation.*

The next theme is often found accompanying themes of affiliation. But that is as much as a clue as you are going to get from us. Here are two recollections that illustrate the next theme.

> I was lying on the couch watching TV. My mother was in the kitchen cooking, and we were waiting for my father to come home from work. Everything was right in the world. I felt warm and safe.

> I was in my room during a thunderstorm. I was frightened.

What is related to affiliation and relevant in these examples?

Both recollections center on feelings of security or insecurity. Affiliation is related to these feelings, as it is the most important basis for security in early childhood. These ERs can be categorized under the theme of *security*.

Finding the theme of each ER is interesting and can tell you much about a client. In the next section we present a list of recollections. Take a piece of paper and write down one or two words to describe the theme of each recollection. The purpose of this exercise is to get you in the habit of identifying topics. Check to see if your guesses are comparable to our answers provided at the end. Good luck.

1. I remember trying to put this puzzle together. I finally completed it. I felt great.
2. I was stuck in a barrel. I went to sit on its edge, and I fell in. I couldn't get out. I was panicked. Luckily my brother came by and pulled me out.
3. My father and I were in the garage. He went inside the house to get a phone call from my aunt. I took off my training wheels and took my bike out on the driveway all by myself. I was so happy!
4. My mother told me that I had to change out of my school clothes when I came home and before I went out to play. This one time I didn't. She found out, and I was grounded for a week.
5. I remember my family and I in line at the movie theater. I had to go to the bathroom really bad, but I wanted to see the movie, and I didn't know where the bathroom was anyway. I thought I could hold it until after the movie, but I ended up peeing my pants in front of everyone.
6. My family and I were on a roller-coaster. It was my first time. I made a promise not to scream out of fear. As I went through the ride, I was completely terrified, but I never screamed. I kept my cool on the outside.
7. I remember coming home with an A paper and my parents taking down my brother's picture from the refrigerator and putting my paper up in its spot.
8. My younger sister took my Boston Red Sox pencil sharpener. I was angry. I ran after her and slugged her in the back of her head and got my pencil sharpener back.
9. The other kids in my class started cheating on a test when the teacher left the room for a minute. I didn't cheat. I'm not a cheater. I thought it is best to be honest, even if I didn't do well on the test. Later, one of the kids got caught, and he got an "F." They were a bunch of losers for cheating.

10. In second grade we had a smorgasbord where all of the kids participated and brought something in from home. We all talked with each other, and it was very interesting how we pitched in and created something. It was good clean fun.
11. It was the first day of school. Everything seemed new and different. I was not used to how people were supposed to act.
12. I remember this one time being on the little roller-coaster at the amusement park. It went up and down and side to side. Lights flashed, music played, kids were screaming. It was great.
13. My family was in our trailer in Hurricane Alley, and there was this huge storm. The trailer rocked back and forth. I was scared shitless.
14. I was in my neighbor's house, and she was getting into her bathing suit. I remember peeking in and seeing her naked. Later, we played spin the bottle.
15. I was playing football with the other guys in the neighborhood. And I just couldn't throw the ball that far. They called me "girlie" and "faggot" for the rest of the day.
16. I was on my bike in front of the house and fell on a bunch of rocks. My mom came out and carried me in. She kissed me on the forehead and put some bandages on and had me lie down on the couch as she and dad brought me food and orange juice.
17. I was keeping score for the baseball team at the local park. I was not sure what was going on or if someone had scored a run. I was confused and felt out of sync with everyone else.
18. I was riding my older brother's bike that was way too big for me. I couldn't sit on the seat, and I lost control and ended up on our neighbor's grass that was wet. I was heading for the fire hydrant, and I knew I was going to hit it, most likely with my head. I started to fall and then, by chance, all of a sudden, the bike righted itself, and I kept on going. Eventually I made it back home.
19. Once I was sick as a dog. My parents were very concerned. I was in my bed, and everyone came in to see how I was doing.
20. There was this one time when I was lying by the pool taking the sun while we were on vacation. The weather was perfect, and the wait staff kept coming by to see if there was anything I needed. There was a cute girl who sat next to me, and we talked for hours. It was great.

Now that you have your guesses written down, compare them to our answers. Give yourself 5 points for each correct answer. We give the theme first, then a description.

1. Skill tasks — These types of ERs have situations that require some competence from the client.
2. Dependency — There are two types of recollections that fall into this category. This recollection has the client being dependent on others. The next recollection is different yet falls under the same category.
3. Dependency — This recollection shows the client being self-reliant.
4. External authority — Recollections like this have the client expected to comply with an imposed set of rules.
5. Self-control — In recollections like this, clients indicate an inability to control themselves.
6. Self-control — Contrary to the previous example, the client is quite able to maintain control.
7. Status — Here the client is very important in the eyes of others and becomes significant in his family (or group).
8. Power — In this recollection we notice a demonstration of the client's control and dominance. This theme centers on who is dominant and controlling, the client or someone else.
9. Morality — This memory shows just how moral and right the client is and how immorality doesn't pay. The client is more righteous than the other students. Recollections with a theme of morality illustrate the use of a moral attitude to elevate the client's status. It may be more important to the client to be morally superior to others. It may be a way of finding status.
10. Human interaction — In the recollection given, there is a strong focus on social interactions. Memories with this theme show the client's picture of the social interactions.
11. New situations — The theme presented in these types of recollections may show the prototype of how the client perceives and reacts to new situations. New situations ERs may be linked to competence and security issues. Clients may, or may not, develop competence and security based on their perception of the outcome.
12. Excitement — These types of ERs emphasize the excitement of the situation and the feelings associated with that excitement. In this case it is pleasant.
13. Excitement — In contrast to the previous ER, the excitement is the main subject of the recollection, and it is very unpleasant for the client.
14. Sexuality — The example given here revolves around sexuality. Even though sex is not directly mentioned, sex games, sexual interactions with adults, or observations of sexual activity all fall into this thematic category.

15. Gender — This ER focuses on masculinity and femininity. These types of memories may be combined with themes of sexuality.

16. Nurturance — In this example, the client is receiving affection, nurturance, attention, and service from others.

17. Confusion — This type of recollection concerns itself with ambiguity and poor comprehension of situations.

18. Luck — These types of ERs exhibit just how lucky or unlucky the client is. Does the client see himself or herself as immune from danger, or a target for it? Such a client sees fate as in control and either on a person's side or not.

19. Sickness and health — This memory shows the effect of illness and how it shapes the behavior of others.

20. Garden of Eden — Life should be so good! The ER given is of the Garden of Eden variety. For the client, this is how life should be, not how it is. Heavenly bliss just exudes from these types of recollections.

Now tally up your score. If your total is from 0 to 50, keep trying. From 51 to 70, you're getting warm. A few more practice sessions and you'll be doing great. From 71 to 95, you must be an Adlerian familiar with this work. And if you have a perfect score of 100, congratulations!

Summary

We have included these common topic or "issue" themes to illustrate how to identify themes within and among ERs so you can infer areas that may be important for your clients. Common themes are not provided to categorize and pigeonhole individuals.

17
Reliability and Validity

In order to be useful measurements, psychological assessments must meet two basic criteria. Assessment instruments must be valid, and they must be reliable (American Psychological Association, 2002). So what does this require of ERs to be a reliable and valid projective technique?

Before we consider using ERs as a projective technique, we must clarify the importance of reliability and validity. Whenever we use tests of any kind, we would like to have these two measures. Reliability is the ability of the test to come up with the same, or very similar, results repeatedly. We can use our bathroom scale as a good example of this. Provided we have not lost or gained weight, our scale should give us approximately the same reading over and over again. If we weighed 150 pounds yesterday, we should weigh approximately 150 pounds today. As for validity, there are several different kinds to be considered relevant to the use of ERs. We'll start by considering concurrent validity. This type of validity is the correlation in results of two measures, one standardized. An example of this might be our bathroom scale results versus the reading from a scale at the Department of Weights and Measures. As we will detail later, results from the interpretations of ERs do positively correlate with other standardized measures. Validity in this case is the accuracy of the result. Are we actually 150 pounds, or are we 170 or 135? In addition, we cannot have validity without reliability. Sure, the scale may read 150 pounds day after day, but if we are actually 195 pounds the scale is not giving valid results (no matter how much we want to believe it). That's reliability without validity.

Though there are many types of validity, we would like to briefly focus on one: face validity. This type of validity is not a true form of validity, and it is actually low in the use of ERs and other projective techniques (e.g., the Rorschach Inkblot Test). And that is a good thing. Face validity is the extent to which a test *appears* to measure what it is designed to measure.

When we use ERs to assess life style, the client most often has no clue as to what is truly being measured. Some people believe it may be a memory test or something else not related to its actual purpose. Clients may believe that the memories they tell us are innocuous events or shaping milestones, but they very rarely believe that ERs are reflective of their current perspectives and functioning. This is very important because people are less likely to purposefully shape their answers and paint an image that they wish the assessor to see. Therefore, the low face validity of ERs may increase their reliability and validity.

Our goal in this Chapter is to demonstrate the reliability and validity of ERs as a projective technique. Some studies cited only examined the *earliest* childhood memory. That is, they only asked people for their oldest memory. Other studies gathered more than one memory from childhood, and not necessarily the earliest.

Reliability of ERs

Reliability is an indication of whether early childhood recollections are as consistent over time as are the attitudes that are represented in the memories. Reliability can be examined by determining if an ER solicited on two different occasions generated the same information, *provided that no therapeutic intervention has occurred.*

So you may be asking yourself, "How difficult can it be to tell the same story twice?" It is not as easy as that. Early recollections contain specific themes and are sensitive to changes in detail. Therefore, a measure of reliability would be to test people and then retest them at a later date and be sensitive to any changes. It just so happens that we have a study of that.

Winthrop (1958) collected the ERs of 69 subjects twice at eight-week intervals. He reported that 68% of the paired ERs were reliable. This is not just repeating the same story two months later; it is presenting stories with similar themes indicating parallel views of self, others, the world, and people's ethical convictions. In other words, ERs may reliably provide the same or similar results time after time.

Perhaps you are the type of person who is not so easily convinced. Well, that's good, because you should not accept things based on one study. As critical thinkers, we need to hypothesize and test and retest things to make sure we're on the right track. You may be saying to yourself, "I bet the therapist or administrator gave some clues to help the person give particular types of recollections." Though such environmental conditions may influence some tests, they don't influence the results when we gather ERs.

How do we know? We have a study for that, too.

Hedvig's (1963) study compared the stability of ERs to that of the Thematic Apperception Test (TAT). She concluded that the conditions under which a TAT are given — for example, in a friendly or unfriendly atmosphere — may affect the outcome of that projective technique but will not affect the ERs. Thus, ERs are considered to be *more* stable over time than the TAT and are unaffected by atmospheric testing conditions. This supports the notion that ERs are an excellent projective technique, reliably communicable, and helpful to clinicians in making diagnoses of psychopathology. She reported that earliest childhood recollections were relatively unaffected by experimentally induced experiences of fear and failure, while the TAT stories were influenced to a greater degree.

So what does this all mean?

The themes of ERs are stable over time. Furthermore, they are stable over different conditions. So according to the Winthrop and Hedvig studies, ERs do pretty well at satisfying the reliability requirement.

Now let us throw you a curve. How might ERs change with the introduction of mind-altering drugs? Take a minute to think about how ERs might change, and for whom they would change the most.

This isn't a far-fetched idea. Langs's (1967) study examined the ERs of a number of individuals before and after they took LSD. He concluded:

> In persons with a well integrated and relatively stable ego organization, the earliest memory is a stable structure and resists shift or break even under regressive pressures such as those brought into play by LSD-25. In contrast, persons with a poorly integrated and relatively unstable structural balance, where primary-process intrusions have access to consciousness even in the waking state, have earliest-memory structures which are particularly vulnerable to the effects of LSD-25. (p. 182)

Langs suggested that the stability of the earliest childhood recollection was related to personality factors. Therefore, though the senses may change through the use of LSD, the personality, and consequently the ERs, do not change, at least not for people with "relatively stable ego organization." Early recollections are reliable even under some mind-altering (but not personality-shifting) circumstances.

Validity of ERs

Research attempting to examine the validity of ERs falls into two basic categories: research employing a clinical model and research employing an empirical model.

Clinical Model

With regard to the clinical model, research has demonstrated that results from ERs correspond to clinical data generated from patients' psychotherapy.

Early recollections have been used as an assessment technique for quite some time. Plewa (1935) maintained that earliest childhood recollections provided more insight into the dynamics of an individual than any other psychic expression. They can be so powerful because of their perceived innocuousness (low face validity). Everyone has a childhood memory, or more, and can and almost always does readily tell it to people. Most people are not aware of their incredible power to quickly and accurately provide a wealth of information. And so people freely regale others with these memories. Yet these ERs provide the assessor with a template of the individual who is telling the recollection.

In this vein, Opedal (1935) viewed a person's earliest childhood recollection as a prototype for his or her tested style of overcoming problems. That is, how people solve problems (their coping skills) should be demonstrated in their earliest memories.

So how does the use of ERs as a projective technique compare with other measures? Lieberman (1957) used a validated test battery (Wechsler-Bellevue Intelligence Scale, Rorschach, Bender-Gestalt Test, and House-Tree-Person Projective Technique) as a criterion for determining whether information obtained from the test battery was similar to the information obtained from an earliest childhood recollection.

Her results indicate that there was statistically significant agreement between the information obtained from earliest childhood recollections and the information obtained from the test battery, although the quantity of information from the test battery was more extensive. So in comparison to other measures, ERs more often arrive at similar findings. What may be as equally impressive is that fact that these findings can be gathered much more quickly and less expensively than standard projective test batteries.

McCarter, Tomkins, and Schiffman (1961) also demonstrated that ERs are a valid method of assessing personality. They relied upon the characteristics of subjects' ERs to predict their performance on the Tomkins-Horn Picture Arrangement Test. They found the results of the interpretation of the ERs to correlate to the results of the Tomkins-Horn Picture Arrangement Test in the areas of social interest, work, and the degree of activity.

Jackson and Sechrest (1962) examined the relationship between ERs and current neurotic symptoms of patients. They found that those patients with anxiety more often had ERs characterized by themes of fear. Depressed patients had more frequent abandonment themes. They also found that those who suffered gastrointestinal problems such as ulcers and colitis had themes of gastrointestinal distress. We are not implying that a descriptive diagnosis can be made from ERs, but a functional assessment can be.

Finally, Levy and Grigg (1962) attempted to compare information from earliest childhood recollections of 21 patients with information provided by each patient's therapist. The recollections were then analyzed and coded using a classification system that Levy and Grigg developed. They found that 70% of the major themes in the therapists' statements also appeared in the earliest childhood recollection, another clinical demonstration that ERs can be a very efficient and effective means of understanding individuals.

Empirical Model

An empirical model was used as a second way of investigating the validity of earliest childhood recollections. Let's review a few representative studies.

Ansbacher (1947) collected earliest childhood recollections from 271 male college students and related structural features of these earliest recollections to scores on the Maslow Security-Insecurity Test (Maslow, Hirsh, Stein, & Honigmann, 1945). The results indicated that there were differences between the earliest childhood recollections of secure and insecure individuals (with those individuals who had high security scores having ERs that detailed them participating in group activities. Those individuals with low security scores "remember themselves as cut off from the larger group, as getting or losing prestige, as having done something bad; or harming or inflicting harm on one another" [p. 38]). This study supports the idea that using an ER assessment technique can differentiate individuals' personality features, specifically security.

Correspondingly, Pattie and Cornette (1952) demonstrated that the earliest childhood recollections of maladjusted boys were more negative than those of better-adjusted children. Again, we see that gathering and interpreting ERs can be useful in differentiating personality and behavioral differences.

In Levy's (1965) study, 103 early memories (Levy's term but equivalent to the term "early recollections") were gathered from 40 psychiatric outpatients (26 female, 14 male) and placed into one of twelve categories (divided among 3 modes [givingness, mastery, and mutuality], each memory was rated for either passive or active ego participation, and for positive or negative affect quality). These early memories, once placed in these categories and compared with psychological reports, were found to identify coping skills "On the reports . . . the modes tend to correspond to the characteristic ways of coping with emotional situations as evaluated by the testing" (p. 289).

Three empirical studies are especially relevant to the research on validity of ERs. The first of these studies (Wagenheim, 1960) used earliest childhood recollections to identify differences between boys and girls who were classified as "high" or "low" (good or poor) readers. The boys who were classified as high readers tended to remember pleasant incidents, whereas boys who were classified as low readers tended to remember events that dealt with accidents and physical aggression. For the girls, there was no statistically significant difference between earliest childhood recollections and reading ability. Wagenheim suggested that additional research should investigate differences in the earliest childhood recollections of problem readers.

A second study (Kadis, Greene, & Freedman, 1952) suggested that earliest childhood recollections could be effective aids in making information that is derived from other projective materials more meaningful. The authors obtained teachers' descriptions of 20 private high school girls with regard to pursuance of tasks and relationships to teachers. Judges matched 10 TAT stories obtained from each girl with the teacher's description of her. When earliest recollections were added to the TAT protocols, correct matchings by the judges with the teachers' descriptions of subjects significantly increased. The relevance of the Kadis, Greene, and Freedman study to this validation research derives from the fact that the descriptions by teachers were used as the independent criterion for validity.

A third study (Ferguson, 1964) obtained earliest childhood recollections from 10 people diagnosed as neurotic, 10 diagnosed as psychotic, and 10 who were labeled as "normals." On the basis of these earliest childhood recollections, three judges who were trained in Adlerian theory developed descriptive formulations for each of the 30 subjects. Seven other judges (trained in Adlerian, Eclectic, and Freudian theory) matched each descriptive formulation with each subject's earliest childhood recollection. The matchings resulted in agreement that was statistically significant. One important implication of the Ferguson study for this research was that descriptive formulations based on earliest childhood recollections (and written by judges trained in Adlerian theory) could be communicated to individuals whose orientation was non-Adlerian.

The findings of these studies further support the discriminative ability of ERs and the ease with which the findings could be expressed to therapists of different orientations. In short, they are easy to use, reliable and valid, and their results can be straightforwardly conveyed.

Early recollections have the advantage of being completely unstructured and are not influenced by environmental factors. The production is influenced only by the individual's perceptual framework, which selectively focuses upon the particular memories that he or she produces. All memories contain omissions and distortions. People color and distort, emphasize and omit, exaggerate and minimize in accordance with their inner perceptions and wants. Those wants and perceptions are shown in the ERs. Those errors in our memory demonstrate people's projection and, once comprehended through ERs, can provide enormous insight.

Errors in Memory

Human memory is wonderfully inaccurate. Though sometimes people may wish for factually perfect, computerlike memory, they have something that is much more beneficial: error. We know it sounds odd, but think about it. Do you really want to be able to instantly remember every single time you goofed up on something? Wouldn't you prefer to remember those things that allow you to make better sense of the world through shading, coloring, and grouping that enables your incredibly diverse and complex world to be more comprehensible? Though human forgetfulness, apperceptions, and memory bias may seem to be detriments, they help us to survive. In addition, this inaccuracy can be tapped for psychological assessment.

There are two memory systems that you need to understand in your comprehension of how and why ERs are a useful projective technique: the episodic memory and semantic memory systems. The first holds specific memories of events that happened previously. The second is much more of a general knowledge database. That is the difference between the remembrance of seeing a particular movie and the ability to think about movies in general. (For more information, see Tulving, 1972, 1983)

In reviewing Tulving's work, W. C. Gordon (1989) wrote that these systems, though distinctive, influence each other so that when people have an experience, that experience changes episodic memory.

Gordon continues:

> Virtually all theories of memory processing make the assumption that encoding takes place while memories are in short-term storage or while they are being actively processed. In addition, most such models assume that when a memory is retrieved from permanent storage, that memory or some copy of it re-enters awareness

or the short-term memory store. When we combine these assumptions, we are faced with a particular implication. Once a memory has been retrieved, that memory may be susceptible to being re-encoded in short-term storage. In other words, one might predict that a memory that has been retrieved is capable of being altered or modified in some way. This hypothesis raises an interesting possibility. It may be that retrieval is more than simply a process by which we activate and use stored memories. Retrieval may also be a process by which we are able to update or re-code memories that have long been in storage. (pp. 278–279)

In short, our current mind-set influences our memories of specific events. Therefore, ERs are not immune from recent situations, but are in fact *corrupted by* current perspectives. And that's why ERs can be used as a projective technique. It's also why it does not matter whether the recollection is accurate or if it ever happened at all.

Several studies have attempted to verify the accuracy of the incidents that the respondents related. In Adlerian theory, the accuracy of the recollection is not germane in interpretation or clinical usefulness. The significance of the recollection lies in the fact that it is remembered or thought to be so. Though the experience of falling and skinning one's knee is probably universal, for example, not everyone recalls such an incident, and those who remember may recall it in widely different ways. The differences can be telling.

The phrase "as plain as the nose on your face" is an interesting one because people cannot see their own noses unless they take on another perspective. The same is true when we look at ERs. It helps to have a trained assessor examine ERs and supervise our interpretations because people usually have blind spots that do not allow for accurate self-interpretation. Therefore, it is difficult for an individual to interpret his or her own ERs because it is difficult to be objective. In addition, supervision is necessary when learning to interpret ERs so that clinicians do not project their own life styles onto the interpretation.

When people recall memories from their youth, they have to fill in some details because they cannot remember everything exactly the way it was. In addition, they have to incorporate feeling into that memory. Whatever they add is a projection of their apperception. That is, they can add things only from their biased perspective. They don't so much remember as they *reconstruct* events from their current perspective. They create coherent themes that by definition are self-reflective because it is they who re-create the memories.

Perhaps you would like a couple of examples. The following recollection is from a 35-year-old woman.

> On my fifth birthday, my mother bought me a teakettle set with a baby stroller and one of those little ovens that baked with a light bulb. I really wanted one of those planes that you would wind up and it would take off.

Most vivid: "Thinking that I didn't want the baby stroller."

As it turns out, when the woman went through a photo album she discovered that she indeed got one of those planes. Perhaps more interestingly, she never received the teakettle set, the baby stroller, or the child's oven. Apparently, while this woman was in therapy, her mother had (much to the client's annoyance) urged her to get married, settle down, and raise a family, which the woman did not want to do. The woman wanted to "take off" from her hometown and live independent of her domineering mother. In the recollection we can see that the woman's mother is pushing domestication when the woman does not want it. This is a good example of how poor memory allows for ERs to be used as a projective technique.

One more example, this time from a 40-year-old man.

Age: 9

> One day there was this redheaded girl in class named Cindy who I thought was very attractive. I remember I was supposed to eat lunch with this other girl; she was more plain and predictable, and I knew that I could always eat lunch with her. Well, I ended up asking this redheaded girl to eat lunch with me, and she accepted. The girl who was ordinary was upset with me. She expected me to eat with her. I said to her, "A man's gotta do what a man's gotta do."

Most vivid: "Wanting to have lunch with the redheaded girl."

You can probably guess where we are going with this one. When he looked back at his class photo, he found that there was no redheaded girl in his class! In his present, however, a redheaded woman had been recently hired as his secretary, and he found her very attractive. The man was contemplating asking her out. As you can imagine, his wife was not very pleased when, sometime later, she was told of his plans to marry his redheaded secretary. So here we have another example of how faulty memories allow for the projection of current thoughts and behavior.

Assuming the consistency of the person as a frame of reference, the memories (because they, among other things, reflect the self-concept) should all be consistent with one another. This does not imply that each memory will convey exactly the same meaning as every other memory produced by the subject, but that all the memories produce a comprehensive and coherent image of the individual. As with other projective techniques, interpretations from recollections will supplement, complement, and elaborate upon one another. Thus, ERs may be regarded, as personality is, as theme and variations.

There is one more phenomenon to cover, the disappearance of memories. We're not talking about Alzheimer's disease, but the inability of clients to remember memories that they previously reported. This is often the case after change has occurred through therapy.

For example, imagine that a client comes in for therapy with feelings of depression and gives you the following ER (and most likely a series of similar recollections).

> When I was 7 years old, we had to do this one assignment for class. It was huge. I knew that I couldn't do it. It was just too much work and too difficult. I ended up getting an F because I never started the project.

You may see that when the client perceives a task as overwhelming, it may never be started, let alone completed.

However, let's also imagine that you have been seeing this client in therapy for some time and that the depression has lifted. You may then gather a second set of recollections and look for a different theme. Sometimes when clients are asked to give a second set of recollections, they do not give a variations on ERs from the original set but give new recollections that reveal a different perspective.

Though giving different responses may at first suggest low test-retest reliability, this may not be the case. Perhaps more interestingly, if you read back their original ERs, they may say, "You must be reading from someone else's file; those are not mine!" They don't remember the ERs they gave because they no longer see the world as they did at the start of therapeutic intervention. Therefore, reliability can be consistent even with inconsistent answers.

There is one more area we want to briefly discuss, the variability of recollections. One recollection may seem to indicate that the person is passive and depressed, and the next recollection may indicate an active go-getter. Though this variation may appear to lower the reliability and validity of ERs, we propose that it does not. Why it does not is the subject of the next section.

Variability of Responses

So how do we explain this variability of responses? There are many facets to people. Individuals each act differently on different occasions, but they do not act in ways that are contradictory to themselves as a whole. As we elaborated earlier in this book, when we encounter inconsistencies, we likely have a case of the if-then contingency. For the above client, if he is passive and doesn't get anything out of life, then he may be depressed. However, in another recollection we may find out that if he is active and receiving something, then he may be happy.

Another illustration might be that while a person is in school, there are times when he or she studies very hard for a test, and other times when this person does not study at all. Yet this individual is still moving toward the goal of graduation. The key is to look at the overarching goal rather than specific details.

In the same manner, ERs will have the same variations that individuals exhibit, but they reflect the unity of the personality, the whole of the individual.

Summary

To be clinically useful, measurements must meet two basic criteria. Assessment instruments must be valid, and they must be reliable. Early recollections as a projective technique has low face validity. That is very important as people are less likely to purposefully distort their responses as they can in other tests in which the client can tell what is being assessed and shape his or her answers to paint an image for the assessor to see. Early recollections have been found to be a reliable and valid measure or personality (life style). Furthermore, it has been demonstrated that the themes of ERs are stable over time. They are also constant over conditions. Early recollections have been demonstrated to be reliable and valid even under the influence of a mind-altering substance!

Research shows that ERs have the advantage of being completely unstructured and are not influenced by environmental factors. Their production is influenced only by the individual's conceptual framework, which selectively focuses upon the particular memories that he or she produces. All memories contain omissions and distortions. People color and distort, emphasize and omit, exaggerate and minimize in accordance with their inner perceptions and needs. Those needs and perceptions are shown in the ERs. Those errors in our memory demonstrate people's projection and, once comprehended through ERs, can provide enormous insight.

Early recollections will have the same variations that people exhibit, but these reflect the unity of the personality, the whole of the individual. In short, an individual's current mind-set influences his or her memories of specific events. Therefore, ERs are not immune from recent situations, but are in fact corrupted by current perspectives. As a result, ERs can be used as a projective technique.

18
The Quantifiers

You may be asking yourself, "If understanding ERs is so useful in understanding people, why have I heard so little about them?" Answering that calls for a bit of history.

We have divided the history of ERs into five distinct periods, and we will present these chronologically over five Chapters. In this Chapter, we'll discuss the first people to use ERs, who looked at quantifiable aspects of ERs such as how many words, how many themes, and the age of client in the recollection. The next group, discussed in Chapter 19, consists of Sigmund Freud and the Freudians. Alfred Adler and other Adlerians represent the third group, and we will discuss them in Chapter 20. Chapter 21 is devoted to the Applied Group, which can be divided into two subgroups, "the descriptors" and "the predictors." The descriptors used ERs for descriptions of people, for example, composing psychohistories of individuals. The predictors believe that specific types of people give ERs with certain themes, and that when we see those themes in other people, we can then predict their behavior. Chapter 22, which concludes our history, focuses on the New Adlerians, professionals whose work evidences a resurgence of interest in Adlerian theory.

The Quantifiers
From the 1890s to the 1940s, there was a mildly interesting group of researchers on ERs whom we'll call "the quantifiers," because that's what

they did. These people did not do any interpretative studies on ERs; they just dealt with the frequencies. Perhaps unfulfilled accountants, these quantifiers viewed ERs in terms of keeping count. They counted the number of types of feelings in ERs or they counted the number of types of themes in ERs in hopes of understanding people better. Though their method was interesting from a research point of view, it provided little clinical information.

These researchers used the nomothetic approach in attempting to understand people. That is, their goal was to discover some universal laws of human behavior. This differs from the approach of Adler, of Freud, and of this book. We take the ideographic approach, which focuses on each person's uniqueness. No two people are exactly alike, not even identical twins raised in the same house. If you were to look at your best friends, who may think and act very similarly to you, even they differ from you in many respects. And that is why we look at life style as it is constructed for each individual. We look at the whole personality and view it as unique from everyone else's.

You may want to ask yourself if the DSM diagnoses (as explained in Chapter 1) are nothing more than labels that focus on the negative characteristics of people and pigeonhole them on the basis of those maladaptive attributes. Diagnosing with DSM criteria takes quantifying as a method of understanding an individual with respect to the entire population. We believe that people are unique beings that are not easy to quantify. Each person is distinctive with both positive and negative qualities. This is a key in understanding the advantages of the ideographic perspective. Adlerian theory is holistic; it takes the whole person into account and views each person not as possessing or not possessing certain traits, but as a unique person with more variations than even the most comprehensive trait system available. And as such it is much more accurate in its ability to understand the individual.

Let us return to our history of the quantifiers. Counting and surveying are usually the primary methods of understanding in most sciences. We record what we see, and from that we can generate hypotheses (guesses) about what is going on. True to form, the first approach to early memories was in the form of a questionnaire by Miles (1893), and it ignited an interest in ERs. His work was an exercise in quantification of variables.

Victor Henri and Catherine Henri (1898/1935) followed Miles's work by publishing the literature on ERs. Their work represented one of the first investigations concerning ERs. They observed that in general, the first recollections occurred between the ages of two and four years, and that in the majority of cases, ERs are represented visually.

Please take a moment to think of an ER. Do you have one? Most likely it too occurred during this time period. And if it didn't, what can we make of that clinically? Again, we see the problem with the work of the quantifiers. Quantification does little to understand the person. If you were to tell someone that your earliest memory is of an event that occurred when you were between the ages of two and four, this information would not give that person any additional evidence of your personality, and perhaps he or she would look at you a little quizzically.

Included in the quantification of ERs are frequency measures of the themes or content of the memories. As we will see later, Freud believed that early memories screened out material that was too harsh for the ego. K. Gordon (1928) published an article that disproved the then-current theory that there was a general tendency to forget the "disagreeable." She wished to counter the Freudian theory that held that experiences that are disagreeable tend to be forgotten or repressed. From her studies she concluded:

> There is no general tendency to write down early recollections which are more pleasant than unpleasant. . . . If human beings are in quest of the pleasant, it would seem to be just as important to remember what to avoid, as to what to pursue. (p. 132)

That is one of the positions we take in this book. Mosak (1992) suggested that memories and dreams could urge a person to move toward, away from, or remain motionless in regard to some event or situation.

In looking at the content of ERs, some of the quantifiers counted themes of ERs. First are the normative findings. Dudycha and Dudycha (1933) found that the majority of childhood memories date back to the third and fourth year of life, with the mean age of recall being 3.8 years for men, and 3.6 years for women. The emotions that appeared most frequently in the childhood memories of their subjects were fear, joy, and anger. Men recalled a preponderance of fearful experiences, and women recalled a preponderance of experiences that angered them.

Dudycha and Dudycha (1941) continued their work in quantifying ERs and found that the three situations that give rise to the largest number of fears (as expressed in ERs) are animals, punishment, and strange people and/or situations. Once again, this discredited Freud's idea of memories serving a function to protect a person's ego from disagreeable events. They also concluded that "some emotion accompanies nearly every early memory" (p. 678).

We believe this is important. People use their emotions to initiate or stop movement toward their goals, whether in ERs or in reality. When we are fearful of something, we tend to back away from it. When we are happy about events or people, we tend to move toward them. Adler (1927/1998) referred to these emotions that move toward and away as conjunctive and disjunctive, respectively. Horney (1950) wrote similarly, describing movement as to, away, or against. When we are ambivalent about things, we don't move at all. These emotions and memories are important in describing who we are, our goals, and our line of movement toward those goals.

One interesting thing about quantifying ERs is that the information can be used as a point of departure for future research. If ERs are used to move people toward or away from things, what might the ERs from individuals from a perilous environment look like? Would they be more unpleasant to make the person more wary of the dangers that exist?

A study answered that question. Purcell (1952) published a study that showed that the expressions of optimism versus pessimism, and joy versus fear (in ERs) were significantly related to security feelings in people. He compared ERs of individuals from favorable and unfavorable environments and found:

> The mean percentage of memories that were unpleasant was more than twice as great in the unfavorable environment, as in the favorable one (52% versus 24%). Hence, boys coming from an environment of poverty, violence, neglect, and overall insecurity, seem to mirror that environment in their earliest memories. (p. 321)

This study and others like it demonstrate the types of contributions that quantitative analysis makes to the field. It is easy to misinterpret the data and conclude that an unfavorable environment causes unpleasant ERs. This is not the case as almost half, 48%, of the individuals from the unfavorable environment had favorable or neutral ERs. Furthermore, it does not tell us anything about the individual. Think about how this finding further rejects the idea of causality. Do bad experiences force people to repeat bad experiences (e.g., does being neglected or abuse force people to neglect or abuse others) or does free choice allow for variation? Quantitative studies of ERs are still conducted, but their findings are more congenial to research than to ideographic clinical applications.

Overall, the presence of quantified studies can promote understanding when placed in the context of movement. It is not the percentage of types or the quantification of themes that are important. These data are helpful only when presented in context of the individual's environment and his or her movement in it. The quantifiers were the first to measure early recollections and, as is usual with pathbreakers, the pioneers get all the arrows, and the settlers get the land. The quantifiers did not get people thinking seriously about ERs. Although the quantifiers were the major force in groundbreaking research in the field, they are not thriving today.

Summary

The first people to use ERs are those who looked at quantifiable aspects of early memories, such as how many words, how many themes, the age of the person in the recollection, and so forth. The quantifiers used the nomothetic approach in an effort to discover some universal laws of human behavior.

19
The Freudians

Almost concurrently with the quantifiers, Freud introduced his concept of screen memories. Freud placed emphasis on what the patient did not say in the memories. He emphasized their hidden meanings.

Freud (1899/1950c) considered a patient's early childhood memories as "internal screens" (Deckerinnerungen), the function of which was to screen out repressed traumatic events that would threaten the ego if brought into consciousness. He stated that the material that was remembered is important only in guiding the therapist toward what had been repressed.

Freud (1917/1946) wrote, "Our recollections are our own possession coming from actual visual experiences in combination with what we have heard from others" (p. 357). These screen memories are well adapted in concealing repressed material and serve a defensive function. According to Freud, it was the duty of the psychoanalyst to find the repressed event hidden behind those "screens." To Freudians, screen memories, like dreams, contain elements of repression, displacement, condensation, symbolization, and other forms of secondary elaboration.

Imagine that a client states, "as a child I remember washing my doll in a tub and putting him underwater." A psychoanalyst may extrapolate from this recollection that the sibling rivalry between the patient and her younger brother was so great that she had tremendous feelings of anger toward him that were, and are, unacceptable and need to be repressed from her consciousness. Freud (1899/1950c) considered the innocuous content of the memory to be evidence of its screening function.

Holmes (1965) supported the Freudian view. He questioned the accuracy of ERs as a projective test technique. That is, his findings showed that ERs are not as clear and accurate a measure of personality factors. "The first freely-associated early recollection was, unlike later ones, defensively distorted in terms of the affective tone" (p. 317). Holmes concluded therefore that this distortion or screen was a function of the subject's security feelings. However, Holmes failed to take into account the variation of recollections that normally occur.

We find Holmes's conclusion to be spurious for reasons that have to do with the overall theme, or themes, of ERs. One recollection may be different than the others in tone and/or content and may give the impression that an incompatibility exists. However, due to the unity of the personality, there can not be any dissonance within the person. So it is up to the therapist to determine how two seemingly contradictory points can be connected in one line. Sometimes we can use the "if-then" contingency. For example, if one recollection has a theme of getting and another of giving, (two initially opposing themes), we can see the line between these two points once we add an if-then statement that must exist to resolve the dissonance. So, the person might have a logic that can be framed in the following way: If I am alone, then I should get as much as I can, but if I am with friends, then I should give to them. Holmes' statement about differences of tone runs counter to the unity of the personality and we suggest that it does not take into account the totality of functioning of the person. It is viewing of individual components, rather than the complete gestalt. It is not advisable to make assumptions from one recollection (Ansbacher, 1953; Mosak, 1958; Purcell, 1952), just as it is not prudent to judge a movie based on one frame of film. If Holmes is going to rely on the "screening" function, he is speculating and as such requires that interpreters project their life styles onto the client's ERs. Imagine in a theater watching a play, but the curtain never rises. You have to guess what is happening behind the curtain (or screen). However, the information that you may receive (muffled sounds, footsteps, etc.) do not represent what is actually going on. Your guesses are much more likely to be a projection of your internal states, moods, and concepts than what is actually happening behind the curtain.

There is a paucity of Freudian literature on early memories. However, some work in the 1950s and 1960s elucidates the Freudian perspective on early memories. According to Kahana, Weiland, Snyder, and Rosenbaum (1953), "earliest memories are an organic part of the personality, and, as such, reflect total personality functioning" (p. 75). Our question is how the Freudians can state that early memories reflect all areas of personality functioning if they are designed to hide certain aspects of thoughts and behaviors, specifically those areas that are too traumatic to the ego?

Kahana et al. continue, "They reflect the patient's principal unconscious conflicts, and may refer to emotionally traumatic childhood experiences, the patient's main ego defenses, and at times, to transference trends" (p. 73). This again implies that the clinician has to speculate on the unconscious conflicts. In the Freudian literature, the ego is described as serving a central part in the recovery of early memories, whereby the "synthetic" function of the ego makes it possible to reorganize and restructure them.

This reformulation is capsulated by Niederland (1965), who states that through ERs,

> content and affect of memory can be dealt with in a "revised" fashion by both the ego and the superego, permitting a more realistic solution of the conflict between the archaic, instinctual, and defensive forces which made the original traumatic event, pathogenic. (p. 570)

However, as you read earlier, people do recall negative (or unpleasant) memories. And as we said above, this procedure may turn out to be more of a projective test for the analyst than for the patient. Therapists are invited to project what they think is behind the screen, and speculate about what was not said by the patient. Isn't speculating on material not presented in a recollection equivalent to a detective making a case on a lack of evidence? It's like convicting someone of a crime without any evidence, but from the proof that the detective only thinks is there. We propose that guiding therapy on the basis of this lack of evidence is dangerous to both the client and the therapist as it adulterates and misdirects the actual meaning of the manifest content and the purpose of the ER.

Another downside of the Freudian method of interpretation is that its practitioners must be familiar with all of the psychoanalytic jargon, such as repression, unconscious, libido, and so on. Those who did not adopt the Freudian premises could not understand how to interpret what the Freudians call screen memories.

Another problem with the Freudian concept of screen memories is that it's backward-focused and causalistic. This deterministic viewpoint is not shared by non-Freudians who hold a free will viewpoint. To the Freudians, people are the result of what happened to them. However, we believe that people are able to get beyond traumas and lead productive lives. People are able to interpret events, choose how to react to them, and even anticipate them. In addition, people may actually interpret and react differently to trauma and traumatic events (think back to the World Trade Center example in Chapter 1). Freud's concept states that people react in certain ways to trauma and then hide it from their consciousnesses to protect themselves. From a non-Freudian point of view, they may or may not.

What is especially poignant for our discussion is that the concept of screen memories may doom someone who is in therapy because the therapist will project onto the client's past the cause of all the client's problems!

Freudians still elicit ERs through free association, and relying on Freud's concept, continue to see them as screen memories. So although both Freud and Adler looked at ERs as an important tool of understanding the patient, they saw their purpose differently. Freud looked backward and saw people using early memories to screen out traumatic events. Adler looked forward and saw people using those memories to achieve their goals. Mosak (1958) details how an ER may be interpreted by an Adlerian and a Freudian analyst.

> ER 4 — This was in school. The teacher punished me for something by putting me in a dark closet. I guess she forgot about me, so when I got hungry, I ate her lunch. After a while I had to go to the toilet. I was frantic and didn't know what to do. So I tried the door and it was open, so I went home. On the way, I filled my pants and I thought that when I got home, my mother would be angry with the teacher for causing all this. Then three boys appeared and wanted some money from me. I didn't have any, so they got out a knife and cut three slits in my belt. I went on home but don't remember what happened when I got there. (p. 309)

Mosak gave the following interpretation from a Freudian perspective:

> A Freudian might see in ER 4 a recapitulation of the psychosexual development of the patient. The boy is put in a dark closet (the womb). Later he eats the teacher's lunch (oral stage), fills his pants (anal stage), goes towards mother (beginning of the oedipal phase), and meets three boys (three is the symbol for the male genitalia and could be representative of the father) who cut slits in his belt (since the belt is a long, pointed object, he is symbolically castrated). (p. 310)

Mosak's interpretation from an Adlerian perspective is as follows:

> This is a rather complex recollection in which the patient commits certain anti-social acts but does not accept responsibility

for his mischief making. His teacher is responsible for "causing all this." The mechanism [*sic*] of projection come to the fore here and afford us a clue to a possible paranoid process when taken together with ER 2 [not shown]. Again he is exempt from the usual roles. He has a special privilege of non-conformity, and if others do not respect this privilege, they are unfair. The masculine world is depicted as hostile and threatening. Hospital records indicate that the patient was actually diagnosed as paranoid schizophrenic. Although he is engaged in overt homosexual activities (contrary to classical Freudian theory), he did not regard himself as a homosexual, but as something special — a "bisexual." Prior to hospitalization, he had been employed as a radio announcer (confirming our guess in ER 1) (not shown) in a city known for its thrilling atmosphere. (pp. 309–310)

Now let's go through the recollection and explain our perspective of it. We'll do it in the form of the life style convictions approach.

Self-Concept:

- I don't know what I do wrong. ("The teacher punished me for something . . . ")
- I engage in anti-social acts (e.g., eating the teacher's lunch).
- When I do wrong, I pay the price. (Punished by being put in the closet, he "had to go to the toilet" after eating the teacher's lunch. This put him in a pressured situation: "I was frantic and didn't know what to do.")
- Women forget about me. ("I guess she forgot about me.")
- I am not man enough to defend myself (from the three boys who cut his belt).
- I can't control myself. ("I filled my pants . . . ")
- I fear how women may react to my losing control. ("I thought that when I got home, my mother would be angry with the teacher for causing all this.")
- I don't acknowledge the consequences of my actions. ("I went on home but don't remember what happened when I got there.")

Self-Ideal (the way the client believes life [or he] *should* be):

- I should not be punished.
- I should get women's attention.
- I should be able to get away with things.

- I should be able to stand up to men.
- I should have more money (it is the lack of money that resulted in the boys' getting out a knife and cutting "three slits in my belt").

Weltbild:

- Women punish me. (The teacher [female] puts him in a dark closet.)
- Women abandon me. ("She forgot about me . . . ")
- Men threaten and emasculate me. (The boys threaten him and then cut his belt.)
- I anticipate that women will fight my battles for me. ("I thought that when I got home, my mother would be angry with the teacher for causing all this.")
- The world is punitive. (Teacher and three boys punish him. Mother may get angry with teacher for "causing all this.")
- Men and women treat me poorly.

Ethical Convictions:

- If people wrong me, I'll wrong them back. ("So when I got hungry, I ate her lunch.")
- Women neglect me, and that is wrong.
- Men demand from me, and that is wrong.
- If I do something wrong, even if I don't know what it is, I will pay a price for it.

Summary

When Freud's conception of screen memories appeared, he emphasized the hidden meanings of the memories. A fundamental problem with this procedure is that it may turn out to be more of a projective test for the analyst than for the patient.

20
Alfred Adler and the Adlerians

In propounding his theory of memory Adler (1927/1998) wrote: "The function of memory . . . [is] dominated by the necessity of adaptation. Without memories it would be impossible to exercise any precautions for the future. They are not fortuitous phenomena but speak clearly the language of encouragement and warning. There are no indifferent or non-sensical recollections" (pp. 48–49).

Adler believed that ERs could reveal people's self-perceptions and worldviews, their life styles. Take a moment to think of all of the events that happened in your childhood, tens of thousands of hours of activity in which memories could have formed. Of those, only a minute fraction is accessible to memory now. An Adlerian would say that the fact that certain events are selected and others are let go demonstrates how you see the world and your place in it.

As mentioned in Chapter 1, Festinger (1957) demonstrated that people have a low tolerance for cognitive dissonance. That is, we have a difficult time holding two opposing ideas in our minds. We do as we think and think as we do. In other words, we hold on to, and express, stories that are in agreement with how we perceive the world. It is for this reason that incidents are remembered and retold in accord with our self-perception and worldview. Therefore, once we have the client's ERs, we have many of the clues to solve the mystery of the person. We retain those events that are consistent with our understanding of the world, and we act according to those perceptions. Why might we remember those events? What feelings do we have when we visualize those situations? How do those feelings correspond with how we move through life?

Adler (1956) believed that each memory told had a purpose and did not occur by chance. The recollections told illuminate people's core life styles that were learned early in life and as such show the rules learned in regard to what is important in life, movement toward goals, and so forth. Through the interpretation of the manifest content of these memories, the person's life style convictions can be understood. This is because people project their understanding of the world and their view of themselves and the world onto these stories.

According to cognitive dissonance theory, discord occurs when we try to do and think two opposing things. For example, if you absolutely hate watching figure skating and buy tickets to a figure skating event, it will "rub you the wrong way" and create dissonance. On the other hand, if you like watching baseball there will be no dissonance in buying tickets to a baseball game. People act in accordance with their perceptions of the world. Likewise, we keep those stories that make sense to us and that reinforce our view of the world. As a result, people tend to see and remember and retell events through the filter of their personality.

Having this knowledge helps to solve the mysteries of people's comprehension of their world and where they stand in it. Once this knowledge is attained, a therapist is afforded considerable insight to help solve people's problems, guide therapy, and be more clinically effective.

Examining a part of somebody can, to the trained eye, often tell much about the entire person. What if you were investigating a hate crime and were inspecting the room of a possible suspect. Would the finding of swastika raise a red flag and give you some insight into this person? Would the finding of this clue permit you to extrapolate an image of the whole person? What might be the personality, beliefs, and goals of this person?

The understanding within Individual Psychology is that each person's direction of movement is set in childhood prior to the development of logical judgment. It is during this time that children interpret themselves, others, and the world and act according to those apperceptions. (Think of apperceptions as perceptions with a conclusion; such as it's too hot today because of global warming. Apperceptions do not have to be factually accurate.)

There is a solidifying of goals and lines of movement prior to the onset of logical judgment. You may ask, "How can someone set goals before they can think logically?" Human beings are interesting creatures; they have to interact with individuals before they can develop language skills. When they are born, they are not well developed compared to most other animals, which are able to cope with their world soon after birth.

Humans need a much longer time for development after birth. They rely on their caretakers to feed them, clothe them, bathe them, keep them safe, teach them how to walk and talk, and so forth. As you can imagine, much learning occurs in the temporal window between birth and the development of logical thinking. Consider the development that occurs prior to language development; this is why ERs are filled with symbols and metaphors.

Human beings understand and communicate with symbols long before they can communicate through language (e.g., stove is hot). Metaphors are figures of speech or images that symbolize but do not literally represent the actual thing described (such as "He's a pig" or "She's a witch"). First, humans use symbols, and then they use more complex symbolism in metaphors. They never lose that ability.

During their early development, humans interact with their environment and learn what works and does not work to get fed, bathed, paid attention, and so on. Therefore, they must learn from their interaction with the social environment such things as what things are important (goals), what their values are, how they can reach their goals (line of movement), and how others treat them. That is exactly the reason why these things are so ingrained in people. The incorporation of this knowledge is so primary in human development that it is closely intertwined with who people are — their personalities, self-images, and self-ideals, as well as their picture of the world and ethical convictions. These conceptions are then projected onto their ERs. As Plewa (1935) stated, "The first recollections acquire a very special significance because in them can be seen the individual's whole conception of life, his apperception of life's problems, his whole psychic movement" (p. 90).

An example of this may be a man who relates an ER of not walking on a wet kitchen floor to get something to eat for fear of slipping and falling. This may be very relevant for a current situation; perhaps he is considering asking for a raise from his boss and fears losing his job. The essence of the recollection is that he finds it better to be safe than sorry. He may remember this incident currently as it serves a purpose in his current situation. Also, it is important to note that he may have never had this experience. It does not matter, as it is the symbolism of the recollection that plays an important role in keeping him safe.

If his "better safe than sorry" attitude is taken to an extreme, he may become, for example, an agoraphobic, a person who exhibits obsessive-compulsive disorder, or someone who is inhibited in any movement in his life. In examining the ERs, clinicians must be able to see areas of discouragement and their association with pathologic possibilities. It is also important that they examine the recollection, as well as the current situation, within a social context and see how the person moves, if at all, within both the recollection and the current situation.

For example, if a person is afraid of making or keeping a commitment, there are several ways in which a recollection may display that underlying movement. The patient may give a recollection of being invited to a child's party and then not going or being the only student in class forgetting to bring in a permission slip for a class trip or quitting a baseball game in the first inning. All indicate a reluctance to fulfill an obligation to others. It is important to interpret ERs, for that matter all behavior, in the social context as people approach their community in a way that is in accord with their life styles. The meaning of the recollection applies to more than just the individual; ERs indicate the relationship of the individual to society. For example, think of people you know who are spoiled. Not only do they see themselves worthy of being pampered; they probably expect you to indulge them.

Early recollections can indicate what a person values through a negative connotation. Read the following recollection:

> I was in first grade. We were standing in the lunch line, and I wet my pants. I was so embarrassed.

What is this person trying to tell you? We see how awful it is when this individual loses control in front of others. Do you think that it is important for this person to remain in control? How might that need for control cause social problems and prompt a visit to a therapist?

Continuing with history, in 1935, a student of criminology under Alfred Adler, Lawrence Opedal, concluded from his studies of delinquents that: (1) "the main activity of an earliest memory lies close to the offender's main interest in life," and (2) "the earliest memory often reveals the offender's tested style of overcoming his problems" (pp. 54–55). This coincides with the Adlerian point of view. This suggests research that would happen years later, using ERs for vocational guidance. That is, if we can identify a client's main interest in life, might the client prefer to engage in that behavior for a living? Furthermore, this study indicates that people exhibit their coping mechanisms for life's difficulties in their ERs. This information is useful for the therapist in helping the client overcome obstacles.

As mentioned previously, ERs can be used for functional assessment. According to Friedman (1950), early childhood memories of sickness are remembered differently by the neurotic and the psychotic. She concluded that ERs "can be used as a diagnostic aid, or an indicator of psychotic and neurotic features" (p. 269). This study is limited to the description of *sickness* by the neurotic and psychotic. We still believe that diagnosis cannot be made with ERs (see Chapter 9). Early recollections can be used for functional assessments, not DSM diagnoses.

This study compounds the influence of the life style on perception and behavior. If we can comprehend the patients' life styles, we can see through their subjective eyes. If we can see through their eyes, we are better able to help them therapeutically.

Orgler (1952) demonstrated this in a comparative study of two first recollections. She concluded the following:

> We see that two people can remember similar events in quite different ways. It is clearly evident that the external event is of minor importance. It is the "life-style" which molds the experience. Therefore, Adler's conception of early recollections seems most correct in that:
>
> 1. The life-style decides whether an event is experienced as a trauma or not, and,
> 2. The life-style molds the childhood memories. (p. 30)

How might you see yourself, others, and the world differently if you had a different personality? If you consider yourself a lucky person and were in a car crash, wouldn't you be likely to see yourself as lucky to be alive rather than unlucky to be in a car crash? If you are a person who is paranoid, might you see others as causing the crash and be suspicious of them? People react to events different all based on their life styles.

In addition, we can see from Orgler's work that our life styles color our memories to fit our view of the world. Therefore, we can use these ERs to see how others paint their world, whether it's rose-colored or green with envy or blue with despair or yellow with fear or red with anger or black with hatred or any variation of the spectrum. But be certain of one thing: We all have life styles through which we see the world.

Once we can see the life styles of others, we can predict their behavior on a probabilistic level. That is, no one can ever predict behavior because environmental and personal variables are in constant flux and the person must adjust to these changes. So, the best anyone can do is predict behaviors based on how probable they are for the individual. Remember, Individual Psychology being a freewill psychology, emphasizes personal choice and social context. Both of these are open to change. Consequently, we have to deal with probabilities.

For example, Kadis, Greene, and Freedman (1952) demonstrated the use of early childhood recollections for understanding adaptive and maladaptive behavior:

> ...a knowledge of ECR's [Early Childhood Recollections]
> improves one's prediction of functioning traits, specifically in
> areas of a) task/work — an "approach" category b) relating to
> others/elders — an "authority" category. They also help the
> observer to distinguish between characteristics which are func-
> tioning, and those which are latent. (p. 32)

As Saul, Snyder, and Sheppard (1956) wrote, "Early memories reveal
the central core of each person's psychodynamics, his chief motivations,
form of neurosis, and possible emotional problem" (p. 229). What better
way to begin and conduct therapy than by gleaning this information about
your client?

According to Eisenstein and Ryerson (1951), "An outstanding memory
acquires special significance emerging into awareness even in one's adult
life, for it is a 'condensed statement' of one's inner orientation which gives
way to the aphorism: that the WAY a person remembers, IS the person"
(p. 213). They further write that the formation of the memory is related to
the needs of the child's personality (at the time the incident occurs) and
that the nature of the memory (as it is recalled at some subsequent time) is
dependent upon the needs of the personality at the time of recall.

So what does that mean for us, the eternal students of human behavior?
A person's memories inform others and the person of who he or she is.
People retain, alter, or create memories to guide their thoughts and behaviors so that they can understand and survive in this world. Furthermore,
they remember things only in a way that matches their perceptions (and
their personalities) and that they believe are of functional significance. In
essence, they retain those events with which they believe they can become
more adaptive to the world as they see it.

Summary

Adler believed that ERs could reveal people's view of themselves, others,
and the world around them. Simply put, ERs reflect the life style. People
retain those events that are consistent with their understanding of the
world, and they act according to those perceptions. According to Adlerians,
memories inform others and the person who tells the memory of who that
person is. People retain, alter, or create memories to guide their thoughts
and behaviors so that they can understand and survive in this world.
Furthermore, they remember things in a way that matches their perception and personality, and that they believe are of functional significance.
In essence, they retain those events that they think can help them to be
more adaptive to the world as they see it.

21
The Applied Group

The Applied Group added another dimension to the use of ERs. People of this group incorporated ERs into psychohistories and reviewed the ERs of famous individuals. Even Freud used ERs in an attempt to better understand Leonardo da Vinci (Freud, 1910) and himself (Freud, 1897). On the whole, Applied Group adherents used ERs to explain the individual's past rather than to understand goals. Psychohistories are not therapeutic. The Applied Group used ERs to explain behavior *after it* occurred; the group attempted to give its audience some understanding of what brought people to do the things they did. Though such work is entertaining, it is not therapeutic, and it has at least one problem.

You're probably already familiar with the problem. Have you ever seen news reports in which neighbors of a person convicted of murder tell how they thought that the person was "a loner" and "too quiet"? Did you ever think what they might have said had this person achieved some medical breakthrough? They might then have described the person as someone who was "dedicated, and put his (her) work first" and frequently was "deep in thought." Both are postinterpretation descriptions, based on previous knowledge that primes the responses of the interpreter. Furthermore, the social expectation may influence what is presented to the audience. That is, if someone is completing a psychohistory on Albert Einstein, people expect to hear about something intelligent rather than something that is incongruous with their expectations. Therefore, it may be difficult for the findings of the Applied Group to find validation because ERs of famous people are biased by the knowledge of the previous behavior of the subject of the psychohistory. Furthermore, first impressions are lasting ones. Once people have a first impression of someone, they tend to hold that image, and this can and will bias their interpretations of ERs.

Rom (1965) interprets Goethe's earliest recollection given in his autobiography from Adlerian and Freudian perspectives. He provides some interesting points starting with the metaphor from the following sentence:

> A turret-like staircase led to rooms on different levels, and the unevenness of the storeys was remedied by steps. (p. 189)

Rom's interpretation? The author has no problem moving from story to story! Though this makes sense both metaphorically and logistically, we must be careful not to pick what is convenient to match what we already know about a person when completing psychohistories.

The remainder of Goethe's earliest recollection details how he pleases an "audience" of three brothers who live across the street by initially throwing his toy pots and pans onto the street for the "fine crash it made." As his three-member audience called for more of the performance, Goethe ran "backwards and forwards" through his house collecting his family's earthenware plates, which "afforded a still more lively spectacle."

Goethe concluded his recollection with a report:

> Not till later did any one appear to hinder and restrain. The mischief was done, and to compensate for much broken crockery, there was at any rate an amusing story, in which the mischievous authors took special delight to the end of their days. (p. 192)

Rom uses this report to augment his understanding of Goethe. His conclusion is that Goethe took delight in satisfying his audience in a show of sound and movement. After interpreting the same recollection from a Freudian perspective, Rom states the idea that Freud's method of interpretation is "within the framework of psychoanalytic theory, generalizing, or nomothetic" (p. 193). He puts forth that the Adlerian approach to interpreting ERs is tailored to the individual, in other words, idiographic. As such, the emphasis is put on the individual, suggesting that "when two people do the same it does not mean necessarily mean the same" (p. 193).

We present these excerpts from Rom's article for three reasons. First, it is an example of a psychohistory presented from an Adlerian perspective that highlights the importance of an idiographic approach. Second, it is also an example of the perils of psychohistory. That is, it gives in to the temptation to focus only on the material that matches what we know about the client under investigation. If we presented this recollection but told you that it was from a burglar, we could just as easily have tailored the interpretation to match our knowledge. Third, Rom does something that we do not advise: he interprets from just one recollection. We believe that many recollections need to be interpreted for a comprehensive and more accurate impression of the client.

Bruhn and Bellow (1987a) interpret the earliest memory (EM) of Dwight D. Eisenhower, the 34th president of the United States. They employed the cognitive-perceptual model of interpretation, which looks at the

> perception-memory-perception feedback loop in which the individual's perception of the world is held to be constant unless the individual is confronted with experiences having sufficient psychological impact that presuppositions, or basic axioms, which the individual has about his or her world are called into question. Once these axioms change, the perceptual process accommodates itself to the new world view. Parallel shifts in long term memory are then hypothesized to take place, consistent with the adaptive function of memory. (p. 372)

Bruhn and Bellow state that Eisenhower's EM illustrates how an issue is resolved after demanding effort. Their analysis from a cognitive-perceptual point of view focuses on how the memory shows Eisenhower's "interests, needs, perceptions, and expectations of himself and others" (p. 372). You may ask, "Isn't this awfully close to the Adlerian method of interpretation?" Our answer is, "Yes, it is similar but not the same." The cognitive-perceptual model overlaps with the Adlerian model, but it is not as comprehensive and does not focus on the same material. The cognitive-perceptual model suggests that "most EMs contain an element of 'unfinished business'" (p. 372), a view similar to the Gestalt perspective that implies that "the individual's goal has been blocked, with the result that a tension to complete the action permeates the recollection" (p. 372). The Adlerian view puts forth that ERs are a reflection of *current* functioning rather than a holdover from the past.

In Eisenhower's earliest memory, after a long train trip and horse and buggy ride to Topeka, he is in a house with "dozens or hundreds of people," to whom he was related. In this crowded house, Eisenhower stated that he "felt lonesome and lost among them" and "began to wander outside the house." He becomes fascinated with a well that his uncle warns him against approaching for fear he will fall in. Later Eisenhower, as a boy less than five years old, approaches a pair of geese and is intimidated by the gander, which pushes against him "aggressively and with hideous hissing noises." His uncle gives him a broom devoid of all straw except for a bulbous end with which to strike the aggressive gander. In the next confrontation, a frightened and trembling Eisenhower strikes the gander, which runs off. Subsequently, the gander "kept his distance and [Eisenhower] was the proud boss of the backyard" (p. 374).

Bruhn and Bellow suggest that Eisenhower's earliest memory is one of achieving the kind of mastery and control that comes through the striking of an enemy. They further state that the issue of mastery and control "was a major, ongoing concern for him" (p. 374). The Adlerian perspective maintains that it is (at the time of the telling of the memory) still a major concern for him, that Eisenhower would not have recalled it if it was not relevant at the time of remembrance.

Returning to the overlap of perspectives between the cognitive-perceptual model and the Adlerian understanding of ER, we see that both interpret his recollection as telling us that Eisenhower believes he needs to be in control and uses force to be in control. It also shows that Eisenhower has to overcome his fears and put on a brave stance against his adversaries. He sees the world as dangerous, but it can be mastered through the use of force. Help is obtained from another male, his uncle, and through that guidance he is able to achieve superiority over his "enemy."

As is taught in many literary classes, there are three themes of conflict that appear in literature: man vs. self, man vs. man, and man vs. environment. We can look for these themes in ERs as well. Eisenhower's earliest memory has two of those. Man vs. self is seen in Eisenhower's ability to overcome his anxieties about the aggressive gander. Man vs. man is evidenced in how even though Eisenhower may feel as an outsider among all of the "hundreds" of relatives, he is able to bond with and take feedback from another male. Man vs. environment is shown in his ability to master the yard that housed the confrontational waterfowl.

Ansbacher (1978) interprets an ER from former President Lyndon Johnson as presented in Kearns Goodwin's (1976) *Lyndon Johnson and the American Dream*. The recollection recounts a five-year-old Lyndon as he walked from his home to his grandfather's house. Lyndon left the dirt path that his mother told him to stay on, as she was fearful that he would fall into the nearby river. He walked by the river, tripped over the roots of a dead tree and hit his head. He could not get up, but soon his parents were there and picked him up and carried him home. Lyndon recalls his mother's voice was "not as cold as it usually was," and his father's voice "was warm, too." The recollection ends with an offer from a five-year-old Lyndon that he would have gone through that experience "a hundred times" if he could be assured that his parents would act as "nice and friendly" as they were after bringing him home.

Ansbacher interprets this recollection as a reflection of Lyndon's independence and activity. His mother is viewed as fearful, and Lyndon as courageous. Ansbacher also suggests that Lyndon was resigned to take his punishment, as he was willing to take his punishment of immobility for not listening to his mother and tripping over the tree roots. Lyndon fears only abandonment, as he might be left "forever." However, there is the display of warmth by others, Lyndon's parents, that makes Lyndon's mishap not only acceptable but worth repeating "a hundred times" if he could see his parents be warm and friendly.

Though psychobiographers willingly interpret such snippets of information, we advise against it, especially when the risk of projecting a priori knowledge onto the interpretation is great. Nevertheless, we present this sample as an example of how ERs have been used in various ways.

Pearson and Wilborn (1997) interpreted three ERs from former Democratic Texas governor, Ann Richards, who lived near an Air Force base in her youth. In the first recollection, Ann recalls a time when her mother put a pressure cooker full of beans on the stove and forgot about it. The building pressure blew the release valve off of the pressure cooker, and beans fired through the hole of the cooker and into the ceiling. Ann believed that the Japanese were attacking them. A terrified Ann hid behind a chair in their living room and wet her pants.

Pearson and Wilborn suggest that this recollection shows that Richards views the world as a fearful place. They present another of her recollections in which Ann reaches for what she thought was a wire wrapped in snakeskin, and it "crawled off." Richards ended the recollection stating that the event severely scared her.

In both recollections, Ann tells us that the world is a scary and unpredictable place. Out of nowhere, a terrifying event can happen.

In the last recollection given in the Pearson and Wilborn article, Richards recalls an Easter egg hunt in which she spotted the most coveted egg in the hunt first but didn't get it because a woman pointed the egg out to her daughter. Richards recalled the unfairness of the event; the painfulness was particularly strong because it took place at church.

Overall, Pearson and Wilborn's interpretation of Richards's ERs shows that she sees the world as unpredictable, dangerous, and unfair. In addition, other women gang up on her, take advantage of her keen vision, and seize what she thinks should be rightfully hers.

Bruhn and Bellow (1987b) interpret three ERs of the former prime minister of Israel, Golda Meir, as presented in her autobiography *My Life* (1976). In the first recollection, she recalls watching her father barricade a door with wooden planks as her family waited for a pogrom to attack her family. She knew that her family was being persecuted for being Jewish and felt as though her family was different from the Gentiles around them. In addition, she recalled the anger with her father and his ineffectual attempts at securing the family with a board nailed to the entrance.

Bruhn and Bellow interpret Meir's recollection as one that shows us that she is vulnerable, that men's attempts to protect her are inferior, and that being Jewish and different can put her in harm's way. There is an overarching feeling of fear in the recollection.

Meir's second recollection centers on her mother giving Golda's gruel to a younger sister. Meir detailed the feelings of deprivation and injustice, because food was difficult to get, and others were given what was rightfully hers. Bruhn and Bellow state that Meir's statement to herself in the second recollection is, "I need and *deserve* more than I get" (p. 77). Life is seen as difficult, a struggle in which great personal sacrifice must be made for the good of others.

In the last recollection given in the article, Meir recalls a time after the childhood deaths of five of her siblings. She recalled how a wealthy nearby family offered her mother a job as a wet nurse and how her family moved into better living quarters in which her family's health and cleanliness improved. Bruhn and Bellow interpret this recollection as one that demonstrates Meir's value of competence and how it is a matter of life and death. The authors also suggest that luck plays a role for Meir, although it does not assure existence.

We, however, interpret this recollection as Meir's understanding of how a woman giving her lifeblood in service to the wealthy improves physical and medical conditions. We'll also add that luck plays only a peripheral role in the recollection. We prefer to interpret this aspect as "The Lord giveth, and the Lord taketh away."

Summary

The Applied Group added a dimension to the use of ERs. Adherents incorporated ERs for psychohistories and reviewed the ERs of famous individuals, astronauts, and so forth. They used ERs primarily to explain the individual's past rather than his or her present. The problem with their approach is that it is based on previous knowledge that primes the responses of the interpreter, making it more indicative of the interpreter's viewpoint than the subject's because the interpreter has to project himself or herself into the analysis.

22
The New Adlerians

From an Adlerian perspective, the use of ERs is important in any field that requires comprehension of human behavior. Mosak (1958) wrote:

> It should be possible to deduce from them some clues as to how the individual perceives himself in his relationship to his perceived environment. Early Recollections have the advantage of being completely "unstructured"; the individual does not respond to some "external stimulus" as in the Rorschach or TAT, the properties of which may influence his production. (p. 303)

Here is the prime idea of ERs as a projective technique. It is the blank slate of the ER procedure that defines it as a projective device with many advantages. There are a number of factors to take into account when someone provides an ER — the duration of the story, the content, the theme, the situation, the environment, the emphasis of details, the number and kind of people, the time of year, the feeling, the most vivid part, and so forth. Each of these variables is provided by the client and by definition comes from within. Whatever is given is a projection and worthy of interpretation. And, unlike Freud's screen memories, only the material that is presented in the ERs is interpreted.

Mosak also states that "as with other projective techniques, interpretations from recollections will supplement, complement, and elaborate upon each other" (p. 304). In other words, the material that is presented in some of an individual's recollections will support the material presented in others. This demonstrates strong intratest reliability as complementary information is provided with each memory. Early recollections provide overarching themes and specific details. The themes of the ERs represent the individual's fundamental attitudes toward life, and consequently they are interpreted thematically. Once thematically understood, then the administrator attends to the specific details of the ERs to support the interpretation. For this reason, Mosak cautions us against diagnosing one's life style from a single recollection. "The recollections describe a 'modus vivendi' rather than a 'modus operandi'; although frequently behavioral response is elicited as well as basic attitudes" (pp. 305–306).

In other words, ERs depict clients' way of living, but not necessarily their way of setting about a task or operating (think of *modus vivendi* as the way a person, or group of people, lives. Think of *modus operandi* as a specific way of doing something). Early recollections may tell us that a client finds it very important to get things in life (he or she is a "getter") but cannot detail specific behaviors for each circumstance (e.g., what the client might do at next week's class reunion).

As we said earlier, it is important to obtain specific instances from the client to ensure accuracy of interpretation. Mosak stresses that recollections must be actually visualized lest they be merely reports of incidents in one's life. Visualization makes the story more specific and helps to bring out the details of the ER, providing more information to interpret.

As a projective technique, ERs are inexpensive, expedient, and have wide-range utility in psychotherapy. As Mosak stated, "They are useful in rapid psychiatric screening, differential diagnosis, vocational guidance, and in the analytic psychotherapies" (p. 310). The literature from the time of Mosak's article until the present continues to laud and support ERs as a valuable resource in the field of psychology.

Early recollections can also be useful in predicting the dynamics of the therapist-patient relationship, as Mosak (1965) suggested in regard to actual treatment by a psychotherapist:

"Knowing the attitudes of the patient and the major trends in his/her personality towards work, self, authority figures etc., may be very helpful in matching the right client to the right therapist. Thus through Early Recollections, potential relationship difficulties between the client and the therapist might be avoided" (p. 78).

This book details a number of additional areas in which ERs can be used, for example, marriage counseling, human resource management, sociological studies, and vocational guidance.

After Mosak's article appeared, Kadis, Greene, and Freedman (1952) used ERs in conjunction with another projective technique, the TAT. They concluded that the kind of ERs that people present is a very clear reflection of their current functioning. "There tends to be a lower incidence of pleasant ERs amongst neurotics in accordance with their pessimistic attitude towards life (compared to a so-called normal group)," they wrote. "More than other studied groups, the ERs of anxiety neurotics seem to be characterized by themes of fear, illness, accidents, and/or trauma" (p. 5). They also found that people who are depressed have a preponderance of ERs with abandonment themes, that people with gastrointestinal disorders have a preponderance of ERs involving gastrointestinal distress, and that people with clear obsessive-compulsive tendencies have a preponderance of ERs about sex.

So what do the findings tell you? The results support the idea that ERs show life style through the themes and content of the memories. Furthermore, ERs can show current problems through stories of the past. Also, certain themes suggest certain types of functioning. Previously cited research indicates that ERs are not able to provide nomenclature diagnosis (Ferguson, 1964; Kadis, Greene, & Freedman, 1952; Mosak, 1965). While unable to do the latter, they can do process diagnosis and provide an understanding of the individual in relation to others.

Remember that the stories have more meaning for the speaker than they do for us. That is why the interpretation can be done only on the material presented. Allow us to elaborate on why we can interpret only the information given and must not project anything onto it. We need the person who is telling the ERs to be present so that this individual can understand how he or she has structured life and given meaning to it. Ansbacher and Ansbacher (1956) stressed that ERs should be interpreted with the full cooperation of the "counselee."

> His/her memories are the reminders he carries with him regarding his own limits, and the meaning of his/her circumstances. As early recollections represent the "story of one's life," they serve to keep the client concentrated on his goal, and to prepare him/her (by past experiences) so that the future will be met with an already tested style of action. (p. 351)

Thus, it is in the client's best interest that both therapist and client engage in the cooperative interpretation of this very potent material, so that maximum benefit and accuracy can be derived.

A word of caution, however, does resound throughout the literature to therapists who wish to use ERs in their practice. In the words of Bach (1952):

> Memories, dreams, and projective drawings are quite vague and thus are easily subject to the subtle influences or "biases" which we all share in common. The therapist's own orientation and interest therefore has a suggestive influence on memory statements, such that the interpretations seem frequently to reflect the speculative talent of the psychiatrist, rather than the intrinsic meaning of the EM [Early Memories]. (p. 96)

Dawn of a New Age

As you can see from the history presented here and in preceding Chapters, ERs were for too long used by only a very small number of practitioners. Only recently have ERs gained currency as a meaningful projective technique with a broader audience of mental health professionals. The reason is simple: Psychologists, though well meaning, are sometimes slow to adopt testing, and this was the case with ERs. Most psychologists did not become interested in projective testing until World War II when testing was used in the treatment of "combat fatigue." Also, psychologists doubted that they could gather such deep meaning from a test that took just a few minutes to administer; they dismissed it as superficial. Those people who did use it did not create a format for scoring or an interpretation system. Many psychologists loathed using something with so much subjective interpretation. There were no reliability or validity studies. As a matter of fact, the Rorschach Inkblot Test had a scoring system at the time, and even that assessment technique did not have an acceptable level of reliability and validity. That is, clinical researchers could not obtain the same results twice (giving two different descriptions of the client), which essentially made the test invalid. So they speculated about how to make ERs a reliable instrument. In short, ERs had to prove their worth.

Fast-forward to the current era. We now have years of theorizing and experiments to call upon, as well as certain tests devoted to understanding ERs and the life style. The methods we present in this book follow coherent and replicable procedures for understanding ERs and their illumination of the life style.

Early recollections are capable of painting a surprisingly detailed picture of people, their desires, lines of movement, social interaction, self-perception, and so forth. They are robust assessments that can be used throughout the therapeutic process and demonstrate what areas a person needs to address in therapy and, as shown earlier in this book, when change has truly occurred.

Summary

Clinicians must look at a number of variables when reviewing ERs (e.g., duration of story, content, theme, feeling, most vivid). Early recollections have intratest reliability as each recollection provides complementary information. Early recollections describe our clients' ways of living. Early recollections must be able to be visualized because the visualization provides specific detail and augments the information given in each recollection.

Early recollections can be used for a number of purposes, but they cannot be used for DSM nomenclature diagnoses. Clinicians should interpret only the material presented in the recollection.

23
Other Methods of Gathering and Interpreting ERs

This Chapter describes different systems of collecting and assessing ERs. These systems are presented in roughly chronological order and reflect different perspectives on using ERs. What follows is not an exhaustive list of all systems; rather, we highlight some of the more prominent ways of looking at ERs.

Methods of Collection

Drawing ERs

McAbee and McAbee (1979) suggest that drawing ERs is a valid method of bringing clients to comprehend their basic attitudes. They assure the clients that their artistic ability will not be critiqued and that only their comments about the drawing and event are important. According to McAbee and McAbee, the process helps clients recall information and guides the clinician in understanding the client by allowing the clinician to witness the client's body language while drawing.

ERs and Hypnosis

There are many different levels of hypnosis, ranging from zoning out while you drive on the expressway at night to being so deeply hypnotized that you can have surgery without anesthesia or walk and cluck like a chicken as part of an outrageous audience-participation stage act in Las Vegas. The important thing to remember about hypnosis in regard to the collection of ERs is that anything that is done in a hypnotic state can be done equally well without being hypnotized.

In regard to the purpose of this book, we are interested in those instances of hypnosis in which individuals undergo age regression, a method of recall through reliving. The hypnotist asks the person to go back to when they were five years old or some such age and have them relive an event. Sometimes this too is part of a stage act, and those under hypnosis may even add a childlike voice to their presentation.

Being curious people with ERs in mind, we must ask ourselves if hypnotic age regression brings to the fore a truly "accurate" memory that can be retrieved only during a deep hypnotic trance. And if so, what are the implications for ERs? That is, does the phenomenon of projection, as understood in relation to ERs, no longer exist because the hypnotized person is actually reliving the event? Furthermore, if those under a hypnotic trance are better able to remember details of an event, what does that mean for gathering and interpreting ERs?

Olson (1979) discussed ERs and hypnosis, specifically hypermnesia (heightened memory) and age regression. Olson cautioned that age regression through hypnosis is never a complete submersion into a particular age because there must be some part of the ego that the hypnotist is able to communicate with and give direction to. And if part of the ego is in the "here and now," as demonstrated by the hypnotized person's ability to take direction, then by definition there must be some projection onto the content of the ER. However, we may not be sure if the projection is from the client or the hypnotist, who, at least to some degree, is guiding the direction of hypnosis.

As to the claims that hypnosis can uncover more accurate memories than other methods, you may be saying, "Surely, that must be a unique contribution of hypnotic age regression to gathering ERs." For that we refer back to Olson.

He believes that hypnotic age regression "can be used in ER retrieval in order to intensify and clarify feelings when clients have difficulty defining or getting in touch with feelings in a waking state" (p. 225). Individuals may have an emotional reaction under hypnosis because the event is sharply focused. That is, the ability to focus is possible, and even probable, under hypnosis, and as such this state may augment and refine those emotions connected to the ERs. On the other hand, Olson adds, "It must be noted, however, that the same effect can be achieved without hypnosis in many cases, and that hypnosis is certainly unessential to the therapeutic use of ERs" (p. 225). Therefore, whatever information is gathered from

ERs from individuals under a hypnotic trance can in many cases be collected just as well when those people are not hypnotized. This is especially true if the suggestions of the hypnotist risk altering the content of the ERs.

So what can hypnotic retrieval of ERs be used for? As Olson said, some patients do have trouble getting in touch with their feelings, and for them, hypnosis can be useful, say you have a client who is much too tense to be able to focus on the past. Hypnosis may be useful in lowering that client's level of anxiety so that ERs are more likely given. Similarly, if you are experiencing much resistance from clients, hypnosis may allow for a lessening of resistance through relaxation and a general lowering of defenses.

But in general, hypnosis may not be worthwhile in gathering ERs because of the extra time and effort required. In science the less complicated method is preferred among two or more methods that arrive at the same conclusion or provide the same, or similar, results. Also, hypnosis is not as powerful as popularly assumed. Furthermore, the power of suggestion in hypnosis (e.g., "Go back to when you were five years old . . . ") may corrupt the memory itself. All these considerations make the nonhypnotic retrieval of ERs preferable. The usual method of collecting ERs is much less directive than in hypnosis: "Tell me a memory from your childhood." Suggestion is used to try to prompt individuals who say they cannot remember any events from their childhood, for example, "Give me a memory from your first day of school." Prompted recollections gathered in or out of hypnosis are discounted to some extent because of possible clinician influence.

Lamb (1985) describes her success with clients in reconstructing memories associated with traumatic events. "Through hypnotic guided imagery or fantasy, previous memories are then replaced with newly constructed memories of neutral or positive events" (p. 57). Thus, phobic behavior can be alleviated or greatly diminished, and clients can achieve a sense of closure to formerly upsetting experiences. (Clients, of course, must be highly motivated to decrease their phobic reactions and have the ability to experience hypnotic age regression.) The client's help is actively solicited in formulating the "reconstructed" memory, so that "the client can then react emotionally to it, and therefore transform it into an important part of his/her psychic life" (p. 61).

Coram and Hafner (1988) compared the content of ERs gathered from individuals in a hypnotic state with the content of ERs from the same individuals in a nonhypnotic state. They used the Manaster-Perryman Manifest Content Early Recollections Scoring Manual in comparing recollections from the two states and found that ERs do change in content after immersion in a hypnotic state, but not in the way the authors anticipated.

Specifically, they found that the change of context as people undergo hypnosis makes them more liable to mention eight variables with a significant increase in frequency. Those eight variables are mother, misdeeds, mastery, mutuality, hostility, visual, motor, and active. Coram and Hafner conclude that "hypnotic early recollections may actually be less reliable [than those retrieved nonhypnotically] in revealing the concepts upon which individuals operate" (pp. 477–478).

Early Memory Test

In an earlier Chapter we discussed how your memories of an event may differ from those of others who were present at the same event. Each of us has a unique perspective, some more accurate than others, but each with its own bias. Getting multiple perspectives is equivalent to a taped instant replay of a football play from different angles.

Mayman and Faris (1960) used ERs from three sources (client, client's mother, and client's father) in an attempt to comprehend the client's view of himself and the parents' view of the client. This format was used to study the interpersonal environment in which the client's ego developed. The use of multiple perspectives from three sets of memories was employed to infer the childhood behavioral patterns and diagnosis of a 24-year-old man.

The method consisted of asking the client

> …for his earliest memory; his next earliest memory; his earliest and next earliest memory of his mother; earliest and next earliest memory of his father; most striking early memory; and anecdotes which were commonly told about him by the family. The parents were asked for their "most striking" early memory of the patient; the "most characteristic" early memory; and any other memories of him which "stand out." (p. 506)

This procedure generated three sets of stories that were then analyzed in a manner similar to the TAT, reviewing the memories' structure, styles, and themes. Mayman and Faris assumed that "a set of early memories can mirror for us an individual's early relationships as he may have experienced them at the time his personal identity was most open to the formative influence of others" (p. 520). Mayman and Faris felt that the style of relationships that people had in their childhood was replicated in current relationships, so that people's conception of relationships that were formed in childhood are related to their current difficulty.

This study looked further than most other investigations as it examined the meaning of the relationships for the client and his parents. However, Mayman and Faris discovered that the results of this study could have emerged from the clinical information alone.

The most interesting aspect of the Mayman and Faris study is its use of multiple perspectives of a person's childhood to provide additional evidence, supporting or conflicting, to that supplied by the client in an effort to gain an idea of the client's social situation. Nevertheless, this study has some errors that should be addressed. While multiple perspectives may offer move evidence in an attempt to better approximate the "truth," the clinician must be aware that each perspective has its own bias. Early recollections are a client's own projective test. Using parents' memories of their child introduces confounding variables, such as the incorporation of their projections. Also, in science we cannot generalize from a sample of one. As such, we cannot take this study with only one subject and extrapolate the findings to the general public.

Mayman (1963, 1968) developed the Early Memory Test (EMT), in which clients give an account of their earliest memories of themselves, their caregivers, and others. The EMT also requires that the person ascribe an overall feeling to the memories. Mayman thought that with this information, he could then understand the person's primary relationships as he or she perceived them, and how people developed their identities from those experiences. The manifest content is not just viewed as a screen to distort the latent meaning of the EM, but also as a reflection of the ability of the individual to manage the latent content. In other words, it demonstrates how the client processes and adapts the information to the conditions of an environment. According to Mayman (1968), this "adaptive" function is seen as just as important as the content of the repressed material (p. 123). So how people handle their latent content (presumably socially unacceptable material) reflects their adaptation skills.

While we're sure you know our position on latent content by now, it is interesting to note that manifest content can also be seen as a coping mechanism through its purported ability to camouflage latent content. We prefer to evaluate what we know (the clients' actual words), rather than what is not presented. One of the reasons is that the variability among people and the particularities of the individual may lead to different interpretations of the (invisible) latent content. Because it is invisible, its presence is hypothetical and we believe that any attempt to interpret latent material may be highly prone to error and misdirection. That is, how one therapist interprets an event or feeling (such as horseback riding or excitement) may be different from the interpretations of other clinicians. Therefore, we propose adhering to what is presented by clients as each person has his or her own connotation for events, people, and feelings.

Tape-Recorded and Written Recollections

Allers, Katrin, and White (1997) collected ERs from 60 Caucasian females who were separated into three groups of 20 subjects each: those who gave recollections that were tape-recorded, those who gave handwritten recollections, and those who gave both. The authors used the Manaster-Perryman Manifest Content Early Recollections Scoring Manual to evaluate the content of the ERs. Though tape-recorded ERs "contain significantly more words and self-references than ERs produced in handwriting," tape-recorded and written methods "produced approximately the same projective material" (p. 345).

An investigation of written ERs indicates, "The written form is no less reliable than the oral format" (Evans, 1980). We believe that although the main accounts may be roughly the same, written ERs may be less nuanced because the subject may omit feelings, most vivid details, and other details unless there is subsequent oral questioning.

Created Versus Actual Recollections

Mosak (1958) stated that ERs do not have to be accurate to be useful. Buchanan, Kern, and Bell-Dumas (1991) tested this premise by investigating whether created ERs would be similar to actual ERs. They conducted two studies. The Manaster-Perryman Manifest Content Early Recollection Scoring Manual was used in both studies. Buchanan, Kern, and Bell-Dumas found that in both experiments an agreement of theme between created ERs and actual ERs of approximately 44.5%. The authors suggest that created ERs may be used with clients who report that they are unable to remember any events from their childhood.

The SALSA

Watkins (1982) published a questionnaire, which he called the Self-Administered Life-Style Analysis (SALSA), that was designed to easily obtain life style information from clients. It was sparked by the idea that such an instrument would save time, stimulate the client to think about his or her worldview and its current effects, and avoid setting a client-therapist pattern in which the latter would be the initiator. The SALSA is divided into four basic sections: (1) personal views, (2) approach to life tasks, (3) description of, and relationship with, parents and siblings, (4) ERs. The author of this questionnaire states that "the views of self, others, and life, have been incorporated into the S.A.L.S.A. in hopes of grasping the fundamental picture upon which the client operates" (p. 344). The client fills out the questionnaire and brings it to the next session for joint scrutiny with the therapist.

We see potential problems in the fourth portion of the SALSA, the ERs portion. First, we believe that a questionnaire format is subject to interference by others. For example, we do not give the MMPI to clients and ask them to fill it out at home because others may be providing information for them. Second, questionnaires may be too narrow or leading in their presentation and may reduce the role of the clinician in ways that impede the client's progress. How can a clinician ask questions about ERs if the clients are home when the questionnaire is completed? Though the therapist may ask follow-up questions when the clients brings the form back, the possibility exists that the ERs may not be as fresh in their minds, and clients may not be able to answer questions that would clarify the recollections.

Methods of Interpretation

An Example of Quantification Methods

Though very few people get excited about numbers and (perhaps dry) research, quantification may help us understand a phenomenon. Quantification of ERs may provide information that spurs further research or better comprehension of past or present data.

Waldfogel (1948) states that although there have been many studies of ERs (e.g., Blonsky, 1929; Colegrove, 1899; Dudycha & Dudycha, 1933; Gordon, 1928; Henri & Henri, 1898/1935; Miles, 1893; Potwin, 1901), many approached the gathering of recollections differently from one another, making quantification difficult. Today, there are an even greater number of ways in which we can elicit and evaluate ERs. Some are general, yet others very specific, such as asking for recollections of parents or siblings, or of specific feelings such as fear, or of their first year in school.

Because of the importance of the information given in ERs, many approaches have been developed to collect these recollections, and varied scoring systems developed to assess their meaning. Waldfogel reports that some of the methods used were unreliable and misdirected. He set forth to obtain more complete information, quantitative and qualitative, and to study individual differences in recall. Waldfogel's study conducted a group administration of the assessment to 124 college-level psychology students, asking students to write down their early memories of events that happened up to their eighth birthday, and then rate each memory on a five-point scale in terms of how pleasant, neutral, or unpleasant it was.

Between 35 to 40 days later the procedure was repeated on the same students.

Waldfogel counted the number of ERs and found that there were more given in the second recall, that some people can consistently recall more childhood experiences than others, and that "the availability of specific childhood memories varies considerably from one occasion to another, even when the external circumstances are remarkably similar, and when the two occasions are separated only by a few weeks" (p. 9). Furthermore, there was no difference found in the number of recollections provided by men and women.

Waldfogel also found that there were more memories the older the child was, with the average age of first recall between three and four years of age, with females recalling events earlier on average than males. The study also showed that the two most frequent emotions connected with ERs were joy (about 30% of the recollections) and fear (about 15% of the recollections). Again, the results were similar for both men and women. The ratio of pleasant memories to unpleasant ones was approximately five to three. Less than one-fifth were neutral.

He concluded, "No significant relation was found between the number of childhood memories and the various psychological measures employed" (p. 26). Furthermore, there was no significant correlation between the number of recollections given and such measures as intelligence, memory, emotional stability, ascendance-submission, and conservatism-radicalism. Rather, he suggests any relation between personality and memory is more likely to appear in the content of the memory. In addition, Waldfogel found that the large number of childhood recollections contradicts Freud's assertion of childhood amnesia. The variation of emotion ascribed to these memories also combats Freud's idea that they were just ordinary memories.

Though we believe that quantification of ERs does not provide the detail we need to be helpful to us in session, these results may guide us toward new research and better comprehension of ERs. But until newer research comes out, it's difficult to gauge the significance of Waldfogel's findings.

Langs's Manual: Scoring Manifest Content

For those of you who long for a handbook for scoring ERs, here's the first one created. Though it may not be as popular as it once was, and is not recommended by us, it is worthy of your attention for historical knowledge if nothing else.

Langs, Rothenberg, Fishman, and Reiser published a paper in 1960 called "A Method for Clinical and Theoretical Study of the Earliest Memory." From this study, they devised a *Manual for the Scoring of the Manifest Content of First Memories*. They examined the manifest content of the first childhood memory by recording the patients' responses and asking them to draw their memories. They studied approximately 400 adult inpatients and outpatients of two groups (paranoid schizophrenic and hysterical character disorder). The *Manual for the Scoring of the Manifest Content of First Memories* was used to describe, classify, and extract the manifest content of the first memory.

Langs's understanding of earliest memories is similar to that of others. He viewed first memories "as existing on the borderline of infantile amnesia, and we have viewed them as highly selected, precisely constructed, overdetermined dynamic mental productions" (p. 525).

This is a key point in the basic understanding of early memories and their importance in assessment and therapy. If people have the ability to construct and reshape their memories, then ERs are imbued with people's perceptions of themselves, others, and the world around them. Furthermore, their examination can provide a concise understanding of their motives, lines of movement, and level of functioning, all of which are important in the therapeutic process.

The patient's drawings of the events in the ERs may provide more information in at least three ways. First, the assessor may be able to find emphasis in a drawing that is not given in the retelling of the event. Heavy shading, underlining, and other methods of communicating through drawing may emphasize certain people, feelings, areas, and events that the person cannot communicate in words. Second, it can give the person's perspective on the event. For example, is the picture drawn from a bird's-eye view or a worm's-eye view? Each perspective conveys different meaning that the therapist can explore with the client. Third, when a person draws a picture, he or can may express feelings and thoughts through body language. How the person holds the pen or pencil, the expression on his or her face, the use of movement, and other behavioral manifestations can relay much more information as the person visualizes an event and places it on paper. If a woman makes a fist while drawing her father, she may or may not be aware of it, but the therapist should be!

The scoring manual that Langs et al. devised is divided into four major sections: questions about the memory at the time it was given; who and what was referenced; the manifest themes, the patient's role and self-image, and other items that relied on the scorer's judgment; and items that imply diagnostic, interpersonal, and dynamic possibilities.

The findings of this study refute Freud's proposition that ERs are screen memories. "Only 1 of the 6 memories met all three criteria for screen memories," the researchers wrote (p. 526). For persons referenced in the ERs, the researchers found more mentions of women than men, family members than nonfamily members, adults than children, and mother than father. These results may bespeak the typical settings of childhood, with female caretakers, adult supervision, and limited social networks.

The findings showed some differences between the two groups studied. The hysterical character disorder patients "reported a greater number of clear-cut settings, tended to describe more than one setting and to include more settings that were away from home and outdoors" (p. 528). The paranoid schizophrenic patients "reported more settings that were not clear and were more likely to set their memories at home and indoors without change" (p. 528). However, as we said in Chapter 9, ERs are not appropriate as diagnostic tools because of the variability of the person's personality, setting, and purpose.

Langs et al. also introduced another method of assessing ERs, and that is through using a word count process. This quantitative method showed a difference in the number of words used by each group. Those diagnosed with paranoid schizophrenia used, on average, 22.7 words, and the patients diagnosed with hysterical character disorder used an average of 49.6 words. However, it is difficult to extrapolate the meaning, if any, in the differences, given the limited variety of respondents, the short time span of examination, the small geographic area from which participants were selected, and other factors. Too, the smallness of the sample mean that the results have limited applicability.

There was also a difference in themes between the two groups. "Themes predominant in the H-Group [hysterical character disorder] included punishment, illness, open hostility, open rejection, concern with moral issues, and travel, while themes of happy occasions and direct references to time were greater in the S-Group [paranoid schizophrenic] (p. 101).

Another difference appeared in the image-role section, with the hysterical character patients being scored as attacking more often than the paranoid schizophrenic patients; others were seen as attacking much more often in the memories of hysterical character patients. Also, those diagnosed with hysterical character disorder had memories that were primarily motoric, and those diagnosed as paranoid schizophrenic had memories that were more ideational.

However, it is perhaps more important to understand what Langs et al. have contributed in introducing the *Manual for the Scoring of the Manifest Content of First Memories*. It is the application of a systematic approach in recording, interpreting, and expounding on early memories and their place in psychology. They write:

> The results of the application of [the] Scoring Manual to the memories demonstrate that such manifest material is psychologically important and useful. It appears that first memories may reveal a wide range of data and that they are related to clinical diagnosis in a gross manner. (p. 531)

In a later study, Langs (1965a) used first-memory content to predict the personality features of 48 male actors using 62 first-memory variables and 76 personality measures. He found a significant relationship between personality and first memory by examining such variables as themes; image and role of people; view of, and reaction to, the environment; and the extent of interaction. Langs concludes that first memories are a way to express concepts formed from important early experiences and are predictive, and reflective, of current functioning and personality.

Similar to the previous study, this research has limitations because of the limited variability of its subject group, which undermines the validity and generalizability of the findings.

In his article, "First Memories and Characterologic Diagnosis," Langs (1965b) wrote that first memories of people diagnosed as obsessive reflected problems with aggression and concern with losing control over their impulses. The first memories of people diagnosed as hysterics detailed relationships with women and tended to be active; this suggested heterosexual concerns and an inclination toward action. People diagnosed as narcissists had memories that concerned separation and loss.

Though character structure seems to be revealed in all of these findings, we find the results lacking because of the correlation-based structure of the research. For example, though Langs found that early memories of those considered to be obsessives indicated problems with aggression, we cannot say that people who have problems with aggression in the themes of their ERs can be labeled "obsessive."

Ideographic Approach

Gushurst (1972) developed a manual for an ideographic approach to the interpretation of ERs. He felt that most interpretive methodologies for ERs used a nomothetic approach that forced ERs into predefined general categories that distort or eliminate unique information from them. He believed that a particular school of thought or model influences the interpretation of the recollections because the information may be subject to the biases of the interpreter. His manual was considered ideographic because it was a way of understanding each unique client without forcing the person into a particular school of thought. His research strived to preserve the ideographic meaning of ERs while providing high inter-interpreter reliability and validity of other accepted personality measures.

Clinicians may project their own biases into almost any test results. With all of the inherent subjectivity within the field and among clinicians, our personal and professional lenses influence how we see and apperceive the world. For example, consider how the recollection of striking out at a baseball game might be interpreted differently among feminist therapists, Freudians, social psychologists, and behaviorists.

Manaster-Perryman Scoring Manual

Manaster and Perryman (1974) created a scoring manual in which 42 variables could be coded from the manifest content of ERs. These 42 variables were divided into seven categories: characters, themes, concern with detail, setting, active-passive, internal-external control, and affect. The content of each recollection could be assessed for the appearance of these variables and scored accordingly.

Manaster, Berra, and Mays (2001) summarized the growth and utilization of the Manaster-Perryman Manifest Content Early Recollections Scoring Manual (MPERSM). They reviewed three types of studies: "those that compared persons with different occupations or occupational interest, those that compared persons with various psychopathologies with each other and with controls, and those that compared unlike uses and collection strategies of early recollections" (p. 415).

The found that the MPERSM has "substantial reliability and validity" and the capacity to differentiate among groups.

The Willhite Method

In 1979, Robert Willhite published "The Willhite: A Creative Extension of the ER Process." In it he described a process whereby clients give ERs and then creatively extend them so that they can resolve what they don't like about them.

Essentially, the process consists of eliciting ERs from clients, having those recollections divided into logical segments (e.g., "I was in the driveway with my sister," "We were playing hopscotch") and listed in column form. Clients are encouraged to label each segment as either "a fact" or with emotion (e.g., happy, scared, loved). The ERs are labeled *Self-Concept*.

Willhite suggests that when clients label as fact a segment that should be labeled with an emotion, this denotes a point at which they are blocking their emotions. An example of mislabeling would be when a client labels the segment "My mother gave me a big, warm hug" as a fact instead of an emotion (e.g., happiness, acceptance).

Clients are then encouraged to create an altered recollection of the same event with the same number of logical segments listed in a column, but changed to how clients would like the events to turn out. Clients are encouraged to use their creativity in coming up with these altered recollections, which represent the clients' *Self-Ideal*. The Self-Ideal column also has emotions attached to each segment. Willhite proposes that if clients suggest the ideal situation, they will be more likely to see it as a possibility, and more likely to engage in the listed emotions and behaviors, than if a therapist gives the ideal situation. This use of fantasy shows the therapist how clients would prefer things to happen, and because the suggestions came directly from the clients, they may be more willing to change in the direction they can envisage.

Willhite suggests that when clients see the two columns juxtaposed it is more evident at which point the clients have to generate different emotions to circumvent the previous pattern that was represented in the original ER (the Self-Concept column) and move toward the goal state of functioning (the Self-Ideal column).

Willhite also recommends that everything clients say be tape-recorded because people have a tendency to say irrelevant or distracting things just prior to painful parts of memories.

The next step is to list just the emotional sequence of Self-Concept, as Willhite believes that this sequence represents clients' personal interactional styles that lead them to the conclusions seen in their ERs (the Self-Concept). Willhite suggests that changing this pattern of emotions leads to movement toward the clients' Self-Ideal.

Willhite recommends that at this point in the process, therapists should have their clients elaborate their current interactional problems. He calls this section *Private-Logic-At-Work*. He states that this section is very similar to the Self-Concept as both show clients' dysfunctional pattern. (This should make perfect sense as all along we have said that ERs are projections of current functioning.)

The analysis begins with an examination of the last segment or two of the Self-Concept, which Willhite sees as indicating clients' life goals and fundamental views of life.

The Self-Concept and Private-Logic-At-Work show the clients' current perspectives and how they lead to particular goals (e.g., "I'm a failure," "I must always get what I want," "Everyone should do as I say," "I should help others every time I can"). Each segment of the ERs (Self-Concept), the Self-Ideal, and Private-Logic-At-Work are labeled as being facts or emotions. Willhite puts forward the idea that change in behavior should be focused on the emotions associated with the behaviors. The recognition of the emotions enables a change to novel behaviors that lead to desired outcomes. Willhite believes this to be the strength of his method. And because the alternative ways of thinking, feeling, and behaving are suggested by the clients, they are more likely to envision themselves engaging in those behaviors. Consequently, clients are more likely to reach their Self-Ideal states.

The objective is to interrupt the chain of behaviors that led to a particular outcome for clients in the past. Altering clients' views of how life should be accomplishes this. The use of client-generated Self-Ideals makes it is easier for therapists to gauge just how much clients are willing to change and how they are going to do it. Clients must recognize their dysfunctional patterns before they are able to change them.

Willhite believes his technique zeroes in on clients' flawed attitudes and directs them toward new ways of thinking, feeling, and acting that will lead them to their ideal states. His insistence on encouraging clients to use their creativity helps them to understand that there are different ways of looking and acting. It is up to them to choose how to see the world.

Though Willhite's theory are method are provocative, he seems not to consider that private logic and symptoms may be *purposeful* and hence less readily eradicated — and with much less salubrious results — than he anticipates. A large body of literature in psychology would in fact seem to testify that the very things Willhite is trying to displace are coping mechanisms. If we remove those crutches, then clients have nothing to use to cope. And clearly it takes more than knowledge of a behavior or perspective to change it. For example, most if not all people who smoke tobacco are familiar with its risks, yet they do nothing about it. If some clients are aware of perceiving others as untrustworthy, there may no therapeutic movement at all in getting them to see others as trustworthy if they are using that paranoia to keep people a safe distance away.

Bruhn's Cognitive-Perceptual System

Bruhn (1990) introduced a cognitive-perceptual model that views early memories as "fantasies about the past that reveal present concerns" (p. 42). As with other models, his does not stipulate that the memories presented have to be true. Bruhn stated that his cognitive-perceptual theory is more concerned with the memory process itself than with Adler's emphasis on goals, Freud's on drives, or social learning theories' on a concept of reinforcement. The person's desire, however conflicted, is to increase the range and scope of his or her adaptability or personal competence. The system attempts to scientifically predict behavior based on the person's schema. In essence, the early memories provide an idea of how the person perceives his world and adapts to it. That which conflicts with the schema is forgotten, and what remains is shown in the early memory, which more accurately stated is actually a striving for competence.

The cognitive-perceptual model seeks to glean a general impression of the individual from the perceptions given and the emotions attached to the memories. The person's fears, joys, interests, and so on constitute a frame of reference that continues through time. This perspective is shaped by the person's schema.

Bruhn states,

> Memory primarily consists of schema about the world, rather than traces or images of the world. Attitudes derived from past experiences endure in longer-term autobiographical memory rather than a heavy loading of factual information. The process of justification operates to help the individual construct events from memory so that the "factual details" mesh with the attitude that initially emerges in the recollective process. (p. 49)

Only the information that is adaptive is retained. In other words, there are two filters that the information must flow through.

Bruhn divided long-term autobiographical memory into two categories: "A. Negative affect memories that reflect the frustration of major needs; (They express fear) and B. Positive affect memories that depict the satisfaction of major needs (They express wishes)" (p. 52).

The procedure consists of asking for the earliest memory and the following four memories that are associated with it. Next, the client is asked for the clearest or most important memory in his or her lifetime including significant events after 10 years of age. Following that, the clinician asks for traumatic memories, inappropriate sexual experiences, and memories of parents using alcohol and drugs.

Bruhn described another method for working with early memories. The Early Memories Procedure allows for a written record of the memories that can be reviewed with the client (for the client's awareness and examination) and may provide a structured method for the inexperienced clinician. The clinician groups autobiographical memories into three types: those that protect the original perceptions and constructions, those that safeguard the original perceptions and include revised constructions, and those that do not preserve original constructions or perceptions.

The Early Memories Procedure has two parts; the first requires six spontaneous early memories, and the second asks for 15 directed memories. Scales are used to rate such variables as clarity, affect, and significance. The individual is requested to explain the most significant memories and his or her reasons for selecting those early memories. Next, the individual selects and interprets a memory and then is asked about the assessment experience.

The combination of spontaneous early memories and directed memories is designed to ensure it is a projective assessment and to touch upon areas that may be important but were not elicited in the spontaneous early memory section. Bruhn states that "positive" early memories represent wishes for adaptive behavior. For example, if a child remembers being praised for getting an "A" grade on a difficult subject, he or she may view hard work as productive and socially rewarding. "Negative" early memories depict fears and what the person wants to avoid. If a person remembers being bitten by a dog, he or she may avoid dogs, or animals in general. Those memories that are consistently labeled as neutral, or devoid of emotion, suggest that the person blocks feelings.

Though Bruhn does not believe his approach is similar to Adlerian theory's approach, there are some parallels and associated conceepts. First, Bruhn asserts that there is a focus on the memory process, more so than on the content of the memories. This focus appears in Adlerian theory as well. First, memories, as well as dreams, tell us what to do and what not to do (Mosak, 1992). Second, Bruhn states that people want to increase the range and scope of their competence. Adlerians agree, and they call this the striving for superiority. Third, Bruhn believes that memories provide clues to maladaptive and unresolved issues. Our question is, "Aren't unresolved issues nothing more than goals that need to be met?" And, as such, aren't they very close to the "final fictive goals" that Bruhn states are not inherent in his process? In other words, Bruhn believes that final fictive goals are not intrinsic to the process of gathering early recollections. However, it appears as though they very way may be. Fourth, the concepts of schema and life style appear to have a tremendous overlap. Fifth, Bruhn suggests that we can find out how a person derailed. Does that mean that "mental illness" is causal? And, doesn't causal imply that clients have little or no choice? Sixth, we believe that Bruhn's system may have to discount some of the responses as they may be pressured from clients. That is, Bruhn suggests that clinicians direct their clients to give one memory and then ask for an additional four memories that are related to the first. It implies that the client must have additional related memories, and it also suggests that the client may be pressured to come up with more memories. There are some parallels and some differences between Bruhn's system and the Adlerian approach.

The Adelphi Early Memory Index

Karliner, Westrich, Shedler, and Mayman (1996) introduced the Adelphi Early Memory Index (AEMI) as a scoring system for early memories. The authors acknowledge the irrelevance of whether or not the memories are of factual events and are more concerned with how people see themselves and others as projected through stories of the past. Specifically, what can be examined in the ERs is how people construct, organize, and represent their experiences, whether they are aware of it or not.

The authors proposed this system as "the first systematic, empirically derived interpretative system for assessing global psychological health and distress using the EMT [Early Memory Test]." The AEMI does not entail extensive clinical training, which expands its use to a broad audience of practitioners.

All items on the assessment are rated on a five-point scale from "not applicable" to "highly applicable." The authors wrote:

> We interpreted the first factor as a general affectively toned object representation factor that reflected the affect tone of the memories and reflected whether the self, others, and memory outcomes were depicted in a generally positive or negative light. We interpreted the second factor as a narrative style or narrative quality factor. The third factor reflects the presence or absence of traumatic experiences in the memories (e.g., physical or sexual abuse). Interestingly, these factors reflected much of the previous theoretical and empirical work on the EMT, which indicated that affect tone, object representations, narrative structure, and trauma were significant indicators of psychological health or distress. (p. 57)

The authors found that the AEMI allows reliable assessments of psychological health or distress when used by experienced clinical judges. Also, the AEMI can account for the interrater variability, and the scores from the AEMI, used in combination with standard self-report scales, can discriminate between those who are mentally healthy and those who portray mental health falsely through psychological defenses.

Summary

Quantification of ERs may provide information that spurs further research or better comprehension of past or present data. Waldfogel found that men and women vary little in terms of the number of recollections they give; that some people are better able to consistently recollect more childhood experiences than others; that memory for childhood events increases with age and mental development at the time of the event; and that the large number of childhood recollections contradicts Freud's assertion of childhood amnesia.

Langs et al. devised the *Manual for the Scoring of the Manifest Content of First Memories.* They examined the manifest content of the first childhood memory by recording the clients' response and asking them to draw the memory. The manual was used to describe, classify, and extract the manifest content of the first memory.

Mayman and Faris used ERs from three sources (the client, the client's mother, and the client's father) in an attempt to comprehend a person's view of himself and his parents and to study the interpersonal environment in which his ego had developed. Mayman and Faris felt that the style of relationships that people had in their childhood were then replicated in current relationships.

Mayman developed the EMT, in which clients gave an account of their earliest memories of themselves, their caregivers, and others. The EMT also requires that the person ascribe an overall feeling to the memories.

The "Willhite" method has the client give written recollections in addition to oral recollections, which are tape-recorded and analyzed. The client and therapist then divide these ERs into numbered frames or "thought units." The Willhite method attempts to teach clients the role of emotions and how they can enhance or detract from personal relationships. It shows clients how they see the world and asks them to think about how things should go in order to bring about change.

The SALSA method is divided into four basic sections: (1) personal views, (2) approach to life tasks, (3) description of, and relationship with, parents and siblings, (4) ERs. The client fills out a questionnaire and brings it to the next session for joint scrutiny with the therapist.

McAbee and McAbee suggest that drawing ERs is a valid method of bringing clients to comprehend their basic attitudes.

Hypnosis has been used to elicit ERs. Olson discussed how ER retrieval with hypnosis can be useful with clients who have difficulty getting in touch with their feelings while awake. Olson also suggested that hypnosis is unessential to the therapeutic use of ERs. Lamb used hypnosis with clients in reconstructing memories associated with traumatic events.

Hypnosis and guided imagery is used to replace old memories with new memories that are neutral or more positive.

Bruhn's cognitive-perceptual system attempts to scientifically predict behavior based on the person's schema. In essence, the early memories provide an idea of how the person perceives his world and adapts to it. That which conflicts with the schema is forgotten, and what remains is shown in the early memory.

Bruhn described The Early Memories Procedure, which allows for a written record of the memories that can be reviewed with the client (for the client's awareness and examination) and may provide a structured method for the inexperienced clinician.

Karliner et al. introduced the AEMI as a scoring system for early memories that examines ERs for how the person constructs, organizes, and represents their experiences, whether they are aware of it or not.

24
Dénouement

This book has been quite an exploration, hasn't it? Twenty-plus Chapters chronicling a personality assessment that has been around for approximately a century but remains largely a mystery. It almost feels like an archaeological find. As with any many discoveries, there are many layers that take time to appreciate and to have their impact made known.

Let's start with the straightforward information.

Early recollections are those stories we tell of specific events, large or small, that we believe occurred prior to our 10th birthday. These stories reflect our personality and current functioning in theme and metaphor as we retain in, and/or project onto, those memories things that are in accord with our current perspective. Early recollections can be used in individual therapy, group therapy, couples therapy, career guidance, prediction of the client-therapist relationship, and a number of other ways. We detailed a number of methods through which ERs can be interpreted, and we have presented many examples.

This, our last Chapter, is designed to be a concise summation of the essence of the book. It is to answer many questions that were raised in the text — much like the last Chapter in any good mystery novel. Though we have presented a number of ideas directly, we did cloak many other suppositions throughout the text, and it is to these that we will turn next.

Hidden Messages?

In our overview of this book you will see that it is more than a presentation of a technique; it's an exhibition of a theoretical psychological perspective. We have veiled some of the fundamental points of theoretical orientation on which this book is based.

Why? Early recollections are much like people; they do not exist in a void, and they have their own social supports. In other words, we have couched our presentation of ERs in a particular framework. Our theoretical underpinning is the structure that supports our presentation of ERs. That orientation has some ideas that may not be endorsed by mainstream psychology, insurance companies, or the pharmaceutical industry. And that is why we have interwoven clues throughout this text that hint at much more than ERs. That is, while we were conducting "detective work" with ERs, we have also provided you a perspective, one so subtly placed in our journey through the Chapters that it may have gone wholly unnoticed.

The following pages illustrate the lucrative relationship between insurance and drug companies, and how it negatively affects talk therapy, diminishes the likelihood of addressing underlying personality issues, and decreases acceptance of personal responsibility.

Survival of the Fittest

As we said earlier in this book, the days of long-term psychotherapy are over. The system has changed. Money and the medicalization of psychotherapy changed it.

Money pressures have created an age of cheap remedies and an increasing reliance on treating psychological problems medically instead of psychotherapeutically. Some people believe that every psychological condition can be treated medically. Among them are people who are highly motivated by money to believe that way.

Long-term psychotherapy isn't terribly efficient or economical according to any business model. Insurance companies are particularly economically savvy. Whatever methods can achieve results quickly and cheaply are favored because there is more money to be saved. In order to spend as little money as possible on people's care, the insurance actuaries calculate how much money on average each procedure costs, how long it takes, and so on. The amount of money spent on a health care procedure — be it surgery, therapy, or something else — is seen as a loss. Each procedure has a calculated "loss ratio." The less money spent on people, the more profit there is for the insurance company and its shareholders. Insurance companies are in business to make money, not provide health care.

Avarice and benevolence are inversely related and orbit health care, each with its unique gravitational pull on the system. Though we believe that efficiency is good for any system, being an efficient moneymaker is different from being an efficient agency of health care. The conflict between those two efficiencies means that insurance companies sometimes prioritize profits to the detriment of people's health. The bigger the financial stake, the larger the temptation to search for treatment shortcuts. So how much revenue are we talking about? With all of our talk about how insurance and pharmaceutical companies seek a profit, it's time for us to put our money where our mouth is.

The Almighty Dollar

There is gold in them thar hills (and valleys) of mental health.

In the fiscal year ending December 31, 2003, the latest for which we have figures, Blue Cross Blue Shield reported total revenues of $182.7 billion,[1] Aetna reported total revenues of $17.89 billion,[2] and Met Life reported total revenues of $35.79 billion.[3]

Hundreds of billions of dollars, and these are just three insurance companies.

It may be cheaper to medicate people than to treat them in talk therapy. Insurance companies prefer the least expensive method of treatment that is successful. However, how they define success is different from how many people define it. Psychotropic medications reduce or eliminate unwanted psychological and behavioral symptoms without ever looking at the underlying social and/or personality aspects that may be the basis of the difficulties. But because they do (temporarily) reduce symptoms, the insurance companies call this success. Drug companies profit by the insurance companies' definition of therapeutic success. And the profits are huge.

What follows is a list of just a few pharmaceutical companies with their reported revenues for the fiscal year ending December 31, 2003. It is important to note that the revenues reported come from a variety of sources in addition to what psychotropic medications are listed in parentheses:

- Abbott Laboratories (maker of Depakote for treatment of manic episodes associated with bipolar disorder) reported revenues of $19.68 billion;[4]

---

[1] Retrieved from http://biz.yahoo.com/ic/40/40067.html on February 15, 2004.
[2] Retrieved from http://finance.yahoo.com/q/pr?s=AET on February 15, 2004.
[3] Retrieved from http://finance.yahoo.com/q/pr?s=MET on February 15, 2004.
[4] Retrieved from http://finance.yahoo.com/q/pr?s=ABT on February 15, 2004.

- Bristol-Myers Squibb Company (maker of Abilify for treatment of schizophrenia, BuSpar for treatment of generalized anxiety disorder, and Serzone for treatment of depression) reported revenues of $20.67 billion;[5]
- Eli Lilly and Company (maker of Zyprexa for treatment of schizophrenia and acute bipolar mania) reported revenues of $12.58 billion;[6]
- Pfizer (maker of Zoloft for treatment of depression, social anxiety disorder, post-traumatic stress disorder, and obsessive-compulsive disorder) reported revenues of $45.19 billion.[7]

We argue against quick fixes because medications very seldom fix an underlying problem, so the problem may simply recur, or a new problem may arise to take its place, or alternatively the person must remain on the drug long term (increasing drug profits), and no one knows the long term effects of the drugs. Given the way the system is currently set up, with insurance companies looking for the quickest and cheapest fix, the psychotropic drugs and the companies that make them are the fittest, and they survive. Indeed, they thrive.

Cut Out the Middleman!

In the United States, it is allowable for drug companies to directly market drugs to consumers. We find that incredibly interesting — isn't medical school training supposed to educate doctors on what medications are best for the patients instead of having the patient tell the medical doctor what drugs to prescribe? The drug companies are free to advertise their products to people who have almost no medical knowledge and are in no position to understand their side effects and possible interactions.

Socolar and Sagar (2001) stated that in 1999, drug makers spent 32% of their budget on production and 31% on marketing and advertising. In other words, they spent almost as much money on advertising and promoting their product as they did on making it. While marketing and advertising used 31% of the budget, 11% of the budget went toward research and development. So, yes, there is a considerable amount of money spent on promotion to consumers as well as doctors. However, doctors are highly trained individuals with finely tuned scientific minds; pharmaceutical companies' advertising does not influence their prescriptions. Or does it?

---

[5] Retrieved from http://finance.yahoo.com/q/pr?s=BMY on February 15, 2004.
[6] Retrieved from http://finance.yahoo.com/q/pr?s=LLY on February 15, 2004.
[7] Retrieved from http://finance.yahoo.com/q/pr?s=PFE on February 15, 2004.

In addition to directly marketing their prescription drugs to consumers, pharmaceutical companies court doctors by paying for a number of perks that include, but are not limited to, trips, meals, clothing, sponsored teaching, and entertainment.

A study by Chren and Landefeld (1994) showed a "strong and specific" association between physician requests that drugs be added to hospital formularies and physicians who had interacted with the drug companies that produced those drugs. The interactions were categorized as accepting money to speak at an educational symposium or perform research, meeting with representatives of the pharmaceutical companies, or accepting money from those companies.

A Bitter Pill to Swallow

In the search for wealth, there is a risk of taking the priority to be profits rather than what is in people's best interest physically, psychologically, or socially. In regard to mental health, this may be seen as preferring solutions that address symptoms rather than provide comprehensive understanding and long-term solutions.

An analogy may illustrate our point. Let's say your car has a flat tire, and you want to be back on the road as soon as possible. You might use a can of Fix-A-Flat to seal the hole and inflate the tire. It solves the problem of the flat tire, and it's cheaper than buying a new one. But it's a short-term fix at best, and you don't know when the tire will go flat again. The tire is not "as good as new"; it is temporarily functional.

We are going to equate the insurance companies with this Fix-A-Flat mentality. Insurance companies would rather have a quick, cheap solution to a problem even if it does not solve the long-term underlying issue. Even if you have to put more Fix-A-Flat in that tire every month, it will still be cheaper than a new tire, the insurance company says. Your problem is solved (temporarily), and the insurance company saves money in the long run.

The psychotropic medications are the actual can of Fix-A-Flat. Now, we believe that Fix-A-Flat is a good thing to have. It can help us out of a difficult situation, it works quickly, and it can help us get on our way with little fuss or muss. Psychotropic medications can get people out of a jam, work quickly (usually), can get people up and running quickly with little fuss or muss (more often than not, just a glass of water and a quick gulp or two), and perhaps there is less stigma and time commitment with drugs than with talk therapy.

What we are saying is that we should not treat a problem with medication just because we can because it may not be the best thing for the client.

Though psychotropic medications are able to alter the functioning of the brain, they cannot tackle fundamental personality and social issues. The medications are created in the belief that how people see themselves and the world is a result of biochemical processes that are to be chemically manipulated and controlled; psychological factors are minimized or ignored. They tout what one DuPont TV commercial promoted, "Better Things for Better Living . . . Through Chemistry."

ERs and Brief Therapy

Our solution is to provide a method of personality assessment that can be used to deliver brief therapy in a way that avoids the problems of overmedication, side effects, long-term ineffectiveness, expense, and other obstacles but that satisfies the insurance companies' need for efficient methods of delivering mental health treatment. The challenge has been that therapy is still not as quick, or perhaps as inexpensive, as psychotropic medications. And that's where ERs come in.

Early recollections can be very useful in minimizing the number of therapy sessions as the procedure is quick to use and interpret, helps us find out very quickly how to proceed, keeps therapists on track, helps therapy to become "unstuck," and provides a way to recognize when change (movement) has occurred.

Personality-based talk therapy provides a three-dimensional image of the person. Everything we see and do is filtered through our personality, and the understanding of life style is primary in treating psychological disorders. Though traditional talk therapy is no longer an option with most insurance plans, there is no reason this should be the case with ER therapy. Early recollections make brief personality-based talk therapy possible.

Soft Determinism and Personality Formation

Personality is the key to understanding, and helping, people. When we know life style, we know people's strengths (as well as other things) and can use them in therapy to encourage the person to reach goals. We present life style here to help us uncover another one of those unspoken tenets we alluded to earlier.

Let's start with the family (and environment) of origin influence. Each person has individual choice, but the concept of soft determinism is crucial in understanding human development and functioning. Heredity and environment are the settings in which people make their decisions. In human development, individuals make choices within the environment of their family of origin. Those decisions that get people closer to their goals help to sculpt a personality (life style) that is maintained to a major degree throughout the course of their lives. People create and modify the environment and heredity, just as the environment and heredity guide personality development. People are not merely passive beings; they act in accord with their personalities.

People are a creative, resilient, thoughtful, caring lot who influence heredity and environment, just as heredity and environment influence thoughts, emotions, and behavior. For the most part, people maintain behaviors, consciously or unconsciously, as long as they get them closer to their goals. Psychopathology can protect people and bring them closer to what they want. However, the use of symptoms as solutions to social problems is never a perfect method. On the one hand, symptoms help people reach their goals (partly), but people pay a price for them: they suffer. We must look at people in context and see how their symptoms function in their world. Early recollections are critical in illuminating the power, and pitfalls, of symptoms for our clients.

Symptoms as Socially Purposeful

We believe that emotions and psychopathology can be both reactive and purposeful. Can being depressed spare people the soul-harrowing pressure of tackling their world? Yes, but that is not the only purpose of depression. Being depressed can be seen as being reactive. If someone close to an individual dies, that individual grieves and feels depressed. That seems natural enough. However, we should look for the purposes of emotions and behavior as well. Does being depressed put others into the depressed person's service? "Honey, I'm too tired to do _____. Can you do it for me?" Does being depressed keep us safe? "I'm too depressed to go look for a job, they'll just reject me anyway." There are many other purposes that can be served, and that's just for depression. Only those behaviors that get people closer to their goals are maintained. Each emotion, each behavior serves a purpose. Don't believe us? You may be saying, "Why in the world would someone deliberately put themselves through such torture so that they can get out of work, or have their feelings hurt, or some other such thing? That doesn't make sense!"

Earlier in the book we aired our disagreement with the DSM. It not only labels people but focuses on their negative behavior. Though the DSM is a fundamental vocabulary for psychology — and for that reason a psychologist should know it Chapter and verse — it represents a narrow view of functioning. We prefer to look at people in their environments and see how particular behaviors are maintained and for what purpose, and at what cost(s). With this in mind, people are seen not so much as victims. People learn, or mislearn, how to perceive, act, and feel within particular environments. Barring true biological influence, such as a brain injury or other biological or structural conditions, people have choice over their actions and deliberately, although not always consciously, choose how to adapt to their environment. In order to meet life's challenges, people choose which perspective to use. People select which methods and perspectives, consciously or unconsciously, to use to try to adapt to their environment. Each behavior or "symptom" may serve more than one purpose. For brevity's sake, we'll propose some conditions and some of the possible purposes of each psychopathology.

- Might alcoholism and drug use allow a person to escape from the pressures of the world?
- Could it be that anger allows a person to take control or get even?
- Does a person act bored in order to tell others that he or she doesn't like something and perhaps wants them to do something about it?
- Might not people have delusions to allow them to succeed in areas that they do not in real life?
- Can fear allow people to protect themselves?
- Does anxiety create excitement and marshal energy for tasks?
- Can eating disorders be used to maintain a particular weight, to generate attention, or to take revenge against a controlling parent? Or could it be the only way for the person to achieve perfection?
- Do dissociative disorders protect people by denying a harsh reality?
- Does post-traumatic stress disorder keep a person on guard against the same or similar situation occurring in the future?
- Do kleptomania, pyromania, pathological gambling, or other like conditions keep the excitement level high?
- Does being antisocial allow people to hurt others before they get hurt?
- Does being histrionic allow people to get attention?
- Does checking the door 20 times to see if it is locked give people a feeling of security?
- Does hand washing 100 times a day excuse people from going to work, or force other people to take care of the hand washers, or create a feeling of safety from those microscopic, yet all too dangerous, germs?
- Does paranoia enable people to keep a safe distance from those whom they believe will harm them? Or give them power because they feel they are special and that others are out to get them?

Symptoms serve a purpose in the social world. People should not be labeled (particularly based on their negative characteristics) nor should they be chronically medicated when they don't need to be. People can be better understood, and treated, with an understanding of their conceptions of themselves and others, what they value, and in what directions they move, and under what conditions they create movement or are immobile.

We emphasize the understanding of personality and are reluctant to embrace long-term drug therapy as the panacea of the millennium. We propose a time-efficient therapy with little reliance upon psychotropic medications. We favor looking at people as active social beings who have individual choice and a way of functioning that is based on their life styles. If we know people's personalities, we know them. It is as simple as that. Early recollections are very useful in understanding life style. It is up to us to use that information wisely in treatment.

Future Research

After more than 20 Chapters on ERs, you might have thought that we have exhausted the subject. On the contrary, we're just getting started.

This book is just a beginning — in many ways, a map to an ancient world. We have opened the door for your exploration. If you were already familiar with ERs, then this book may have augmented your knowledge. If you have come across this book in your studies or through your intrinsic interest, then we hope we have introduced a subject that is useful and efficient. The key word here is "introduced." Books are wonderful conveyances of information, and though we have demonstrated through examples, there is much exploring to do.

So where do we go from here?

There needs to be additional research on the situational influence, if any, on ERs. For example, it would be nice to know if people give different recollections if they pass or fail a test. The connection between situational/environmental factors and ERs has been researched, but further clarification and replication would provide additional evidence of any relation.

There are many areas that were discussed in this book that need to be examined for the scope of their impact and relevance. For example, we speculate that those people who give color details in their ER have an aesthetic interest; we want confirmation of this relationship. Furthermore, if there is a correlation, what kinds of aesthetic interest can be determined by ERs?

Though other assessments (such as the Rorschach Inkblot Test) equate texture responses with a need for affection, research is needed to provide additional substantiation that texture details in ER indeed indicate a need for affection.

In regard to sense details, we have not made any mention of olfaction details. They are in general very rare in ERs. We find this interesting, as the sense of smell is the oldest (evolutionarily) sense, and the strongest link to memory, yet they are rare in ERs. Research is needed to supply data on whether or not people maintain a memory for smell, what kinds of people give olfaction details, and what common threads they have (such as an occupation in which they use their sense of smell). This type of research should be extended to all of the senses as they are represented in ERs.

One Chapter in this book discussed the link, or lack thereof, between ERs and diagnoses. However, there has to be further research on ERs and the prediction of pathology. The research we highlighted in this book focused only on postdiagnosis correlations. Also, there should be investigations of the correlations between typologies from interpreted ERs as described in Chapter 4 and diagnoses. And do longer recollections have more significance than shorter recollections? For example, will those who are depressed give short recollections, and people who are manic give long recollections?

More studies are needed between episodic and semantic memory and their roles in the collection and interpretation of ERs. After all, the premise of this book is that ERs operate as a projective technique based on the errors inherent in memory and the retrieval process.

There has been little exploration of the predictive ability of ERs in regard to the relationship between client and therapist. We propose that ERs are applicable to a number of areas relevant to psychology, as mentioned previously in this book. Accordingly, they may be even more useful when research provides additional information about their use in marital therapy and vocational guidance. Can ERs predict events, such as career choice, divorce, and so on?

In one section of this book we detailed a number of common response themes and topics. Those were not an exhaustive list, and they are not used to pigeonhole unique individuals. They were given as examples and as a launching point for ideas and concepts relevant to ERs and how they can be viewed in relation to each person. Common themes and responses are presented to spur ideas and academic pursuit. That is, they are another area in which research could be conducted that would augment our understanding of people.

In regard to the reliability and validity of ERs, you may have noticed that the breadth of research is limited and needs to be extended. Just how reliable are ERs across conditions? Is there a universal use of ERs among all cultures? Some cross-cultural studies can provide some insight as to whether ERs are universal. Perhaps we might conduct longitudinal studies that examine how ERs change over time, with or without therapeutic intervention? How about further research on whether made-up recollections are the equivalent interpretively as actual recollections? Do therapist-forced recollections have themes that differ from those that are given under a client's own volition?

We ask that you consider all other areas of psychology that might benefit from the use of ERs. How might the industrial/organizational area of psychology use ERs? What changes might occur in ERs after a relatively nonsocial intervention, such as aversion therapy, for smoking cessation? Would primal scream therapy change ERs to more vocal, confrontive recollections? The application of ERs to all areas of psychology can allow for cross-validation of measures.

Regarding age limits of the assessment, is it valid to do children's recollections? And, if so, from what age? Furthermore, what does that mean in relation to what Dreikurs said would be nothing more than a memory test? On the other end of the age spectrum, do geriatric patients give more ERs because their remote memory is better than their recent memory? We don't know, but research might shed some light on the subject.

Last, but not least, do men and women give different recollections? What do you think? How might there be variations in the responses given?

Well, that should be enough questions to get you started. This book was written to provide information on a powerful technique of understanding personalities. It was not produced to make you an expert on the subject or to prompt you to use ERs without sufficient training.

This book was written to whet your appetite on a process that is interesting, fun, and clinically useful. To that end, we hope it has served its purpose.

References

Adler, A. (1927). Individual-psychological treatment of neuroses. In A. Adler, *Practice and theory of individual psychology* (pp. 32–50). New York; Harcourt, Brace. (Original work published 1913.)

Adler, A. (1935a). The fundamental views of Individual Psychology. *International Journal of Individual Psychology, 1* (1), 5–8.

Adler, A. (1935b). Introduction. *International Journal of Individual Psychology, 1* (1), 5–8.

Adler, A. (1937a). Significance of early recollections. *International Journal of Individual Psychology, 3,* 283–287.

Adler, A. (1937b). *Social interest: A challenge to mankind.* London: Faber & Faber.

Adler, A. (1956). *The Individual Psychology of Alfred Adler* (H. Ansbacher & R. Ansbacher, Eds.). New York: Basic Books.

Adler, A. (1958). *What life should mean to you* (A. Porter, Ed.). New York: Capricorn Books. (Original work published 1931.)

Adler, Alexandra. (1959). Problems in psychotherapy. In K. Adler & D. Deutsch (Eds.), *Essays in individual psychology* (pp. 177–199). New York: Grove Press.

Adler, A. (1964). *Problems of neurosis* (P. Mairet, Ed.). New York: Harper & Row. (Original work published 1929.)

Adler, A. (1969). *The case of Mrs. A: The diagnosis of a life-style.* Chicago: Alfred Adler Institute. (Original work published 1931.)

Adler, A. (1998). *Understanding human nature.* (C. Brett, Trans.) Center City, MN: Hazelden. (Original work published 1927.)

Allers, C. T., Katrin, S. E., & White, J. F. (1997). Comparison of tape-recorded and handwritten early recollections: Investigating the assumption of equivalence. *Individual Psychology, 53* (3), 342–346.

American Psychiatric Association (2000). *Diagnostic and statistical manual of mental disorders* (4th ed., text revision). Washington, DC: Author.

American Psychological Association (2002). *APA ethical principles of psychologists and code of conduct.* [Electronic version] Retrieved from http://www.apa.org/ethics/code2002.html

Ansbacher, H. L. (1947). Adler's place in the psychology of memory. Individual psychology of memory. *Individual Psychology Bulletin, 6,* 32–40.

Ansbacher, H. L. (1953). Purcell's "Memory and psychological security" and Adlerian theory. *Journal of Abnormal and Social Psychology, 48,* 596–597.

Ansbacher, H. L. (1978). An early recollection of Lyndon Johnson. *Individual Psychologist, 15*(2), 29–33.

Ansbacher, H. L., & Ansbacher, R. R. (1956). *The Individual Psychology of Alfred Adler.* New York: Basic Books.

Arth, M., Ashmore, H., & Floyd, E. (1997). *The newsletter editor's handbook: A quick-start guide to the Internet, news writing, interviewing, copyright law and desktop publishing.* St. Louis, MO: Newsletter Resources.

Ashby, J. S. (1996). Inferiority as a distinction between normal and neurotic perfectionism. *Individual Psychology, 52*(3), 237–245.

Attarian, P. J. (1978). Early recollections: Predictors of vocational choice. *Journal of Individual Psychology, 34*(1): 56–62.

Bach, G. R. (1952). Some diadic functions of childhood memories. *Journal of Psychology, 33,* 87–98.

Barker, S. B., & Bitter, J. R. (1992). Early recollections versus created memory: A comparison for projective qualities. *Individual Psychology: Journal of Adlerian Theory, Research and Practice, 48*(1), 86–95.

Bartlett, F. C. (1932). *Remembering: A study in experimental and social psychology.* New York: Macmillan.

Bauman, M. G. (2003, July 4). Textbook writing 101. *The Chronicle of Higher Education. The Chronicle Review,* Section 2, B5.

Berne, E. (1964). *Games people play.* New York: Grove Press.

Blanchard, K. H., & Johnson, S. (1983). *The one-minute manager.* New York: Berkley Books.

Blonsky, P. (1929). Das Problem der ersten Kindheitserinnerung und seine Bedeutung [The problem of the first childhood memory and its meaning]. *Archiv für die Gesamte Psychologie, 71,* 369–390.

Boldt, R. M., & Mosak, H. H. (1997). Characterological resistance in psychotherapy: The getter. *Individual Psychology, 53*(1), 67–80.

Brooks, J. L. (Producer), Claybourne, D. (Executive Producer), & DeVito, D. (Director). (1989). *The War of the Roses* [Film]. United States: 20th Century Fox & Gracie Films.

Bruhn, A. R. (1990) *Earliest childhood memories: Theory and application to clinical practice (Vol. 1).* New York: Praeger.

Bruhn, A. R., & Bellow, S. (1987a). Warrior, general, and president: Dwight David Eisenhower and his early memories. *Journal of Personality Assessment, 48,* 371–377.

Bruhn, A. R., & Bellow, S. (1987b). The Cognitive-Perceptual approach to the interpretation of early memories: The early memories of Golda Meir. In C. D. Spielberger & J. N. Butcher (Eds.), *Advances in personality assessment* (Vol. 6, pp. 69–87). Hillsdale, NJ: Lawrence Erlbaum.

Buber, M. (1958). *I and thou.* New York: Scribner.

Buchanan, L. P., Kern, R., & Bell-Dumas, J. (1991). Comparison of content in created versus actual early recollections. *Individual Psychology, 47*(3), 348–355.

Burgess, E. W., & Cottrell, L. S., Jr. (1939). *Predicting success or failure in marriage.* Oxford, England: Prentice-Hall.

Carson, A. D. (1994). Early memories of scientists: Loss of faith in God and Santa Claus. *Individual Psychology, 50*(2), 149–160.

Chren, M., & Landefeld, S. (1994). Physicians' behavior and their interactions with drug companies: A controlled study of physicians who requested additions to a hospital drug formulary. *JAMA, 271*(9), 684–689.

Colegrove, F. W. (1899). Individual memories. *American Journal of Psychology, 10,* 228–255.

Cooley, H. K. (1983). Alcoholism and drug dependency: Some mistakes we can avoid. *Individual Psychology, 39,* 145–155.

Coram, G. J., & Hafner, J. L. (1988). Early recollections and hypnosis. *Individual Psychology, 44*(4), 472–480.

Coram, G. J., & Shields, D. J. (1987). Early recollections of criminal justice majors and nonmajors. *Psychological Reports, 60*(3, Pt. 2), 1287–1290.

Corsini, R. J. (1964). *Methods of group psychotherapy.* Chicago: William James Press. (Original work published 1957).

Curlette, W. L., Wheeler, M. S., & Kern, R. M. (1993). *BASIS—A Inventory technical manual.* Highlands, NC: TRT.

Dailey, C. A. (1966). The experimental study of clinical guessing. *Journal of Individual Psychology, 22*(1), 65–79.

Di Pietro, R. (2003). *The relationship of subject variables to BASIS-A and SCL-90 scores for sex offenders court mandated for psychological treatment.* Unpublished doctoral dissertation, Adler School of Professional Psychology, Chicago.

Dreikurs, R. (1935). The choice of a mate. *International Journal of Individual Psychology, 1,* 99–112.

Dreikurs, R. (1946). *The challenge of marriage.* New York: Duell, Sloan and Pearce.

Dreikurs, R. (1947). The four goals of the maladjusted child. *Nervous Child, 6,* 321–328.

Dreikurs, R. (1948). *The challenge of parenthood.* Oxford, England: Duell, Sloan and Pearce.

Dreikurs, R. (1953). *Fundamentals of Adlerian psychology.* Chicago: Alfred Adler Institute. (Original work published 1935.)

Dreikurs, R. (1954). The psychological interview in medicine. *American Journal of Individual Psychology, 10,* 99–122.

Dreikurs, R. (1966b). The holistic approach: Two points on a line. In *Education, guidance and psychodynamics.* Proceedings of the Conference of the Individual Psychology Association of Chicago, St. Joseph's Hospital, November 13, 1965 (pp. 19–24). Chicago: Alfred Adler Institute.

Dreikurs, R. (1967). *Psychodynamics, psychotherapy, and counseling: Collected papers of Rudolf Dreikurs.* Chicago: Alfred Adler Institute.

Dreikurs, R. (1968). Determinants of changing attitudes of marital partners toward each other. In S. Rosenbaum and I. Alger (Eds.), *The marriage relationship: Psychoanalytic perspectives* (pp. 83–102). New York: Basic Books.

Dreikurs, R. (1970). *Solving conflicts: Four steps of conflict resolution.* Unpublished manuscript.

Dreikurs, R., & Mosak H. (1966). The tasks of life I: Adler's three tasks. *Individual Psychologist, 4,* 18–21.

Dreikurs, R., & Mosak H. (1967). The tasks of life II: The fourth life task. *Individual Psychologist, 4,* 18–22.

Dudycha, G. J., & Dudycha, M. M. (1933). Adolescents' memories of preschool experiences. *Journal of Genetic Psychology, 42,* 468–480.

Dudycha, G. J., & Dudycha, M. M. (1933). Some factors and characteristics of childhood memories. *Child Development, 4,* 265–278.

Dudycha, G. J., & Dudycha, M. M. (1941). Childhood memories: A review of the literature. *Psychological Bulletin, 38,* 668–683.

Eckstein, D. G. (1976). Early recollection changes after counseling: A case study. *Journal of Individual Psychology, 32*(1), 212–223.

Eckstein, D., Baruth, L. G., & Mahrer, D. (1975). *Life style: What it is and how to do it.* Chicago: Alfred Adler Institute.

Eisenstein, V. W., & Ryerson, R. (1951). Psychodynamic significance of the first conscious memory. *Bulletin of the Menninger Clinic, 15,* 213–220.

Eisenstein, V. W. (1956). Sexual Problems in Marriage. In Victor W. Eisenstein, (Ed.), *Neurotic interaction in marriage* (pp. 101–124). New York: Basic Books.

Elliott, D., Amerikaner, M., & Swank, P. (1987). Early recollections and the Vocational Preference Inventory as predictors of vocational choice. *Individual Psychology: Journal of Adlerian Theory, Research and Practice, 43*(3), 353–359.

Ellis, A. (1962). *Reason and emotion in psychotherapy.* New York: Lyle Stuart.

Evans, C. D. (1980). *Self written early recollections.* Published Doctoral dissertation, University of Arizona.

Fakouri, C. H., Fakouri, M. E., & Hafner, J. L. (1986). Early recollections of women preparing for nursing careers. *Perceptual and Motor Skills, 63*(1): 264–266.

Fakouri, M. E., & Hafner, J. L. (1984). Early recollections of first-borns. *Journal of Clinical Psychology, 40*(1), 209–213.

Farley, F. (1986, May). The big T in personality. *Psychology Today,* 45–52.

Ferguson, E. D. (1964). The use of early recollections for assessing life style and diagnosing psychopathology. *Journal of Projective Techniques and Personality Assessment, 28,* 403–412.

Festinger, L. (1957). *A theory of cognitive dissonance.* Stanford, CA: Stanford University Press.

Freud, S. (1897). Letter 70. In James Strachey, (Ed.), *The standard edition of the complete psychological works of Sigmund Freud* (pp. 261–263). London: Hogarth Press.

Freud, S. (1910). Leonardo da Vinci and a memory of his childhood. In James Strachey, (Ed.), *The standard edition of the complete psychological works of Sigmund Freud* (pp. 57–137). London: Hogarth Press.

Freud, S. (1946). *A childhood recollection from Dichtung und Wahrheit. Collected papers (Vol. 4)*, 357–367). (Original work published 1917.)

Freud, S. (1950a). *The interpretation of dreams*. New York: Basic Books. (Original work published 1900.)

Freud, S. (1950b). *The question of lay analysis: An introduction to psychoanalysis*. New York: Norton.

Freud, S. (1950c). Screen memories. In *Collected papers* (Vol. 5, pp. 47–69). London: Hogarth Press. (Original work published in 1899.)

Friedman, A. (1950). Early childhood memories of mental patients. *Journal of Child Psychiatry, 2*, 266–269.

Gordon, K. (1928). A study of early memories. *Journal of Delinquency, 12*, 129–132.

Gordon, W. C. (1989). *Learning and memory*. Pacific Grove, CA: Brooks/Cole.

Gregerson, D. L., & Nelson, M. D. (1998). Striving for righteousness: Perfection as completion. *Canadian Journal of Individual Psychology, 28*(2), 21–28.

Guinness World Records (n.d.). Retrieved September 28, 2003, from http://www.guinnessworld-records.com

Gushurst, R. S. (1972). *The reliability and concurrent validity of an approach to the interpretation of early recollections*. Unpublished doctoral dissertation, University of Chicago.

Hafner, J. L., & Fakouri, M. E. (1984a). Early recollections and vocational choice. *Individual Psychology: Journal of Adlerian Theory, Research and Practice, 40*(1), 54–60.

Hafner, J. L., & Fakouri M. E. (1984b). Early recollections of individuals preparing for careers in clinical psychology, dentistry, and law. *Journal of Vocational Behavior, 24*(2), 236–241.

Hafner, J. L., Fakouri, M. E., & Etzler, D. R. (1986). Early recollections of individuals preparing for careers in chemical, electrical, and mechanical engineering. *Individual Psychology: Journal of Adlerian Theory, Research and Practice, 42*(3), 360–366.

Harris, T. (1999). *I'm OK, you're OK: A practical guide to transactional analysis*. New York: BBS Publishing.

Hart, J. L. (1977). Perils of the pleaser. In J. P. Madden (Ed.), *Loneliness* (pp. 41–55). Whitinsville, MA: Affirmation Books.

Hedvig, E. B. (1963). Stability of early recollections and thematic apperception stories. *Journal of Individual Psychology, 19*(1), 49–54.

Hedvig, E. B. (1965). Children's early recollections as basis for diagnosis. *Journal of Individual Psychology, 21*(2), 187–188.

Heidbreder, E. (1933). *Seven psychologies*. New York: D. Appleton-Century.

Henri, V., & Henri, C. (1935). Earliest recollections. *International Journal of Individual Psychology, 1*, 88–101. (Original work published in 1898.)

Holmes, D. S. (1965). Security feelings and affective tone of early recollections: A re-evaluation. *Journal of Projective Techniques, 29*, 314–318.

Holmes, D. S., & Watson, R. (1965). Early recollections and vocational choice. *Journal of Consulting Psychology, 29*(5), 486–488.

Horney, K. (1950). *Neurosis and human growth: The struggle toward self-realization*. New York: Norton.

Jackson, M., & Sechrest, L. (1962). Early recollections in four neurotic diagnostic categories. *Journal of Individual Psychology, 18*(1), 52–56.

Kadis, A. L., Greene, J. S., & Freedman, N. (1952). Early childhood recollections—an integrative technique of personality test data. *American Journal of Individual Psychology, 10*, 31–42.

Kahana, R. J., Weiland, I. H., Snyder, B., & Rosenbaum, M. (1953). The value of early memories in psychotherapy. *Psychiatric Quarterly, 27*, 73–82.

Karliner, R., Westrich, E. K., Shedler, J., & Mayman, M. (1996). Bridging the gap between psychodynamic and scientific psychology: The Adelphi Early Memory Index. In J. M. Masling and R. F. Bornstein (Eds.), *Psychoanalytic perspectives on development psychology. Empirical studies of psychoanalytic theories*. (Vol. 6, pp. 43–67). Washington DC: American Psychological Association.

Kearns, D. (1976). *Lyndon Johnson and the American dream*. New York: Harper & Row.

Kefir, N. (1971). *Priorities*. Paper given at International Committee for Adlerian Summer Schools and Institutes (ICASSI), Tel Aviv, Israel.

Kefir, N., & Corsini, R. J. (1974). Dispositional sets: A contribution to typology. *Journal of Individual Psychology, 30*(2), 163–178.

Kearns Goodwin, D. (1976). *Lyndon Johnson and the American dream.* New York: Harper & Row.

Klopfer, B., & Davidson, H. (1962). *The Rorschach technique: An introductory manual.* New York: Harcourt, Brace & World.

Köhler, W. (1929). *Gestalt psychology.* New York: H. Liveright.

Kopp, R. R. (1986). Styles of striving for significance with and without social interest: An Adlerian typology. *Individual Psychology, 42,* 17–25.

Kopp, R. R. (1995). *Metaphor Therapy: Using client-generated metaphors in psychotherapy.* Bristol, PA: Brunner/Mazel.

Lamb, C. S. (1985). Hypnotically-induced deconditioning: Reconstruction of memories in the treatment of phobias. *American Journal of Clinical Hypnosis, 28,* 56–62.

Langs, R. J. (1965a). Earliest memories and personality. *Archives of General Psychiatry, 12*(4), 379–390.

Langs, R. J. (1965b). First memories and characterologic diagnosis. *Journal of Nervous and Mental Disease, 141*(3), 318–320.

Langs, R. J. (1967). Stability of earliest memories under LSD-25 and placebo. *Journal of Nervous and Mental Disease, 144*(3), 171–184.

Langs, R. J., Rothenberg, M. B., Fishman, J. R., & Reiser, M. F. (1960). A method for clinical and theoretical study of the earliest memory. *Archives of General Psychiatry, 3,* 523–534.

Lashever, L. R. (1983). *Early recollections among physicians: The incidence of death, accident, and illness.* Unpublished master's thesis, Adler School of Professional Psychology, Chicago.

Lashever, L. R. (1990). *Early recollections (Ers) of individuals who are mentally retarded and/or mentally impaired: An update of Adler's comments on feeblemindedness.* Unpublished doctoral dissertation, Adler School of Professional Psychology, Chicago.

Levy, J. (1965). Early memories: Theoretical aspects and application. *Journal of Projective Techniques, 29,* 281–291.

Levy, J., & Grigg, K. A. (1962). Early memories (Thematic-Configurational Analysis). *Archives of General Psychiatry, 7,* 83–95.

Lieberman, M. G. (1957). Childhood memories as a projective technique. *Journal of Projective Techniques, 21,* 32–36.

Lowe, R. N. (1977). An Adlerian view of Richard Nixon. In C. L. Morse (Ed.), *Proceedings of the symposium* (pp. 125–144). Eugene: University of Oregon Press.

Manaster, G. J., Berra, S., & Mays, M. (2001). Manaster-Perryman early recollections scoring manual: Findings and summary. *Journal of Individual Psychology, 57*(4), 413–418.

Manaster, G. J., & Perryman, T. P. (1974). Early recollections and occupational choice. *Journal of Individual Psychology, 30*(2), 232–237.

Maslow, A. H., Hirsh, E., Stein, M., & Honigmann, I. (1945). A clinically derived test for measuring psychological security-insecurity. *Journal of General Psychology, 33,* 21–41.

Mayman, M. (1963). Psychoanalytic study of the self-organization with psychological tests. In *Proceedings of the Academic Assembly on Clinical Psychology* (pp. 97–117). Montreal: McGill University Press.

Mayman, M. (1968). Early memories and character structure. *Journal of Projective Techniques, 32*(4), 303–316.

Mayman, M., & Faris, M. (1960). Early memories as expressions of relationship paradigms. *American Journal of Orthopsychiatry, 30,* 507–529.

McAbee, H. V., & McAbee, N. (1979). Draw an early recollection. In H. A. Olson (Ed.), *Early recollections: Their use in diagnosis and psychotherapy* (pp. 141–148). Springfield, IL: Charles C Thomas.

McCarter, R. E., Tompkins, S. S., & Schiffman, H. M. (1961). Early recollections as predictors of Tomkins-Horn Picture Arrangement Test performance. *Journal of Individual Psychology, 17*(2), 177–180.

McFarland, M. (1988). Early recollections discriminate persons in two occupations: Medical technology and nursing. *Individual Psychology: Journal of Adlerian Theory, Research and Practice, 44*(1), 77–84.

Meir, G. (1976). *My life.* New York: G. P. Putnam's Sons.

Menninger, K. (1973). *Whatever became of sin?* New York: Hawthorn Books.

Miles, C. (1893). A study of individual psychology. *American Journal of Psychology, 6,* 534–558.

Mittelmann, B. (1956). Analysis of reciprocal neurotic patterns in family relationships. In Victor W. Eisenstein (Ed.), *Neurotic interaction in marriage* (pp. 81–100). New York: Basic Books.

Mosak, B., & Mosak, H. H. (1985). *A bibliography for Adlerian Psychology (Vol. 2)*. New York: John Wiley.

Mosak, H. H. (1958). Early recollections as a projective technique. *Journal of Projective Techniques, 22*(3), 302–311.

Mosak, H. H. (1959). The getting type: A parsimonious, social interpretation of the oral character. *Journal of Individual Psychology, 15*, 193–196.

Mosak, H. H. (1965). Predicting the relationship to the psychotherapist from early recollections. *Journal of Individual Psychology, 21*, 77–81.

Mosak, H. H. (1968). The interrelatedness of the neuroses through central themes. *Journal of Individual Psychology, 24*, 67–70.

Mosak, H. H. (1970). Early recollections: Evaluation of some recent research. *Journal of Individual Psychology, 25* (1), 56–63.

Mosak, H. H. (1971). Lifestyle. In A.G. Nikelly (Ed.), *Techniques for behavior change* (pp. 77–81). Springfield, IL: Charles C Thomas.

Mosak, H. H. (1977a). The controller. A social interpretation of the anal character. In H. H. Mosak (Ed.), *On purpose* (pp. 216–277). Chicago: Adler School of Professional Psychology.

Mosak, H. H. (1977b). The interrelatedness of the neuroses through central themes. In H. H. Mosak (Ed.), *On purpose* (pp. 138–143). Chicago: Adler School of Professional Psychology.

Mosak, H. H. (1979a). *Adlerian psychotherapy*. In R. J. Corsini (Ed.), *Current psychotherapies* (3rd ed., pp. 44–94). Itasca, IL: F. E. Peacock.

Mosak, H. H. (1979b). Mosak's typology: An update. *Journal of Individual Psychology, 35*, 192–195.

Mosak, H. H. (1979c). Predicting the relationship to the psychotherapist from early recollections. In H. A. Olson (Ed.), *Early recollections: Their use in diagnosis and psychotherapy* (pp. 187–193). Springfield, IL: Charles C Thomas.

Mosak, H. H. (1987a). Guilt, guilt feelings, regret and repentance. *Individual Psychology, 43*(3), 288–295.

Mosak, H. H. (1987b). Ha ha and aha: The role of humor in psychotherapy. Muncie, IN: Accelerated Development.

Mosak, H. H. (1991). "I don't have social interest": Social interest as a construct. *Individual Psychology, 47*(3), 309–320.

Mosak, H. H. (1992). The "traffic cop" function of dreams and early recollections. *Individual Psychology: Journal of Adlerian Theory, Research and Practice, 48*(3), 319–323.

Mosak, H. H., & Kopp, R. R. (1973). The early recollections of Adler, Freud, and Jung. *Journal of Individual Psychology, 29*, 157–166.

Mosak, H. H., & Maniacci, M. (1998). *Tactics in counseling and psychotherapy*. Itasca, IL: F. E. Peacock.

Mosak, H. H., & Mosak, B. (1975). *A bibliography for Adlerian Psychology (Vol. 1)*. New York: John Wiley.

Mosak, H. H., & Schneider, S. (1979). *William O. Sessions 1–5*. (Cassette recording). Chicago: Adler School of Professional Psychology Library.

Mosak, H. H., Schneider, S., & Mosak, L. E. (1980). *Life style: A workbook*. Chicago: Alfred Adler Institute.

Mosak, H. H., & Shulman, B. H. (1961). Introductory Individual Psychology: A syllabus. Chicago: Alfred Adler Institute.

Mosak, H. H., & Shulman, B. H. (1988). *Life Style Inventory*. Bristol, PA: Taylor & Francis.

Mozdzierz, G. J., & Lottman, T. J. (1973). Games married people play: Adlerian view. *Journal of Individual Psychology, 29*(2), 182–194.

Mullis, F. Y., Kern, R. M., & Curlette, W. L. (1987). Life-style themes and social interest: A further factor analytic study. *Individual Psychology, 43*(3), 339–352.

Munroe, R. (1955). Schools of psychoanalytic thought. New York: Dryden Press.

Niederland, W. G. (1965). The role of the ego in the recovery of early memories. *Psychoanalytic Quarterly, 34*, 564–571.

Nikelly, A. G. (Ed.). (1971). *Techniques for behavior change*. Springfield, IL: Charles C Thomas.

Nixon, R. M. (1978a). *RN, the memoirs of Richard Nixon*. New York: Warner Books.

Nixon, R. M. (1978b). *Six crises*. Garden City, NY: Doubleday.

Oberndorf, C. P. (1938). Psychoanalysis of married couples. *Psychoanalytic Review, 25*, 453–475.

Olson, H. A. (1979). The hypnotic retrieval of early recollections. In H. A. Olson (Ed.), *Early recollections: Their use in diagnosis and psychotherapy* (pp. 223–229). Springfield, IL: Charles C Thomas.

Opedal, L. E. (1935). Analysis of the earliest memory of a delinquent. *International Journal of Individual Psychology, 1*(3), 52–58.

Orgler, H. (1952). Comparative study of two first recollections. *American Journal of Individual Psychology, 10,* 26–31.

Orgler, H. (1963). *Alfred Adler: The man and his work.* New York: Capricorn Books. (Original work published in 1939.)

Pattie, F. A., & Cornett, S. (1952). Unpleasantness of early memories and maladjustment of children. *Journal of Personality, 20,* 315–321.

Pearson, M. S., & Wilborn, B. (1997). Ann Richards: A psychobiography. *Individual Psychology, 51*(3), 266–281.

Peven, D. (1973). The victim. *Individual Psychologist, 10*(2), 18–21.

Peven, D., & Shulman, B. H. (1983). The psychodynamics of bipolar affective disorder: Some empirical findings and their application for cognitive theory. *Individual Psychologist, 39,* 2–16.

Pew, M. L., & Pew, W. L. (1972). Adlerian marriage counseling. *Journal of Individual Psychology, 28*(2), 192–202.

Pew, W. L. (1978). *The number one priority.* Minneapolis, MN: Pew and Associates.

Plewa, F. (1935). The meaning in childhood recollections. *International Journal of Individual Psychology, 1*(1), 88–101.

Potwin, E. B. (1901). Study of early memories. *Psychology Review, 8,* 596–601.

Purcell, K. (1952). Memory and psychological security. *Journal of Abnormal and Social Psychology, 47,* 433–440.

Ravich, R. A. (1966). Short term intensive psychotherapy of marital discord. *Voices, 2*(1), 42–48.

Rogers, C. R. (1942). *Counseling and psychotherapy: Newer concepts in practice.* New York: Houghton Mifflin.

Rogers, C. R. (1951). *Client-centered therapy, its current practice, implications, and theory.* Boston: Houghton Mifflin.

Rom, P. (1965). Goethe's earliest recollection. *Journal of Individual Psychology, 21*(2), 189–193.

Rosten, L. (1968). *The joys of Yiddish.* New York: McGraw-Hill.

Santayana, G. (1924). *The life of reason or the phases of human progress: Reason in common sense* (2nd ed.). New York: Charles Scriber's Sons. (Original work published in 1905.)

Saul, L. J., Snyder, T. R., Jr., & Sheppard, E. (1956). On earliest memories. *Psychoanalytic Quarterly, 25,* 228–237.

Shulman, B. H. (1973). An Adlerian theory of dreams. In B. H. Shulman (Ed.), *Contributions to Individual Psychology* (pp. 60–80). Chicago: Alfred Adler Institute.

Shulman, B. H., & Mosak, H. H. (1988). *Manual for life style assessment.* Bristol, PA: Accelerated Development.

Sicher, L. (1955). Education for freedom. *American Journal of Individual Psychology, 11*(22), 97–103.

Simpson, J. (1988). *Simpson's Contemporary Quotations.* [Electronic Edition] Boston: Houghton Mifflin. Retrieved September 29, 2003, from: http://www.bartleby.com/63/36/836.html

Socolar, D., & Sagar, A. (2001) Pharmaceutical marketing and research spending: The evidence does not support PhRMA's claims. American Public Health Association Meeting. Atlanta Georgia. Session 2018.0. Update on Medicare and Prescription Drug Issues for the New Millennium, Sunday, 21 October 2001. Retrieved from: http://dcc2.bumc.bu.edu/hs/sager/pdfs/020402/Pharmaceutical%20Marketing%20and%20Research%20Spending%20APHA%2021%20Oct%2001.pdf

Sullivan, H. S. (1953). *The interpersonal theory of psychiatry.* New York: Norton.

Sweeney, T. J., & Myers, J. E. (1986). Early recollections: An Adlerian technique with older people. *Clinical Gerontologist, 4,* 3–12.

Terner, J., & Pew, W. L. (1978). *The courage to be imperfect: The life and work of Rudolf Dreikurs.* New York: Hawthorn.

Tulving, E. (1972). Episodic and semantic memory. In E. Tulving & W. Donaldson (Eds.), *Organization and memory* (pp. 381–403). New York: Academic Press.

Tulving, E. (1983). *Elements of episodic memory.* Oxford: Clarendon.

Vettor, S. M., & Kosinski, Jr., F. A. (2000). Work-stress burnout in emergency medical technicians and the use of early recollections. *Journal of Employment Counseling, 37*(4), 216–228.

Wagenheim, L. (1960). First memories of "accidents" and reading difficulties. *American Journal of Orthopsychiatry, 60,* 191–195.

Waldfogel, S. (1948). The frequency and affective character of childhood memories. *Psychological Monographs, 62*(4), 39.

Watkins, C. E., Jr. (1982). The self-administered life-style analysis (SALSA). *Individual Psychology, 38*(4), 343–352.

Way, L. (1962). *Adler's place in psychology: An exposition of Individual Psychology.* New York: Collier Books.

Wheeler, M. S. (1989). A theoretical and empirical comparison of typologies. *Individual Psychology, 45,* 335–353.

Wheeler, M. S., Kern, R. M., & Curlette, W. L. (1986). Factor analytic scales designed to measure Adlerian life style themes. *Individual Psychology: Journal of Adlerian Theory, Research and Practice, 42*(1), 1–16.

Wheeler, M. S., Kern, R. M., & Curlette, W. L. (1993). *BASIS-A Inventory.* Highlands, NC: TRT Associates.

Willhite, R. G. (1979). "The Willhite": A creative extension of the early recollection process. In H. A. Olson (Ed.), *Early recollections: Their use in diagnosis and psychotherapy* (pp. 108–130). Springfield, IL: Charles C Thomas.

Winthrop, H. (1958). Written descriptions of earliest memories: Repeat reliability and other findings. *Psychological Reports, 4,* 320.

Yalom, I. (1989). *Love's executioner.* New York: Basic Books.

Index